HS
525
.V35
1983

Vaughn, William
Preston.

The Antimasonic
Party in the United
States, 1826-1843

# The Antimasonic Party

# The Antimasonic Party
## in the United States
### 1826-1843

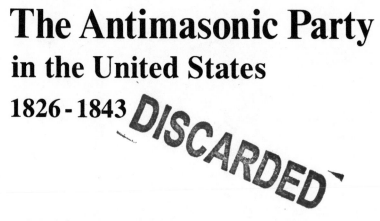

WILLIAM PRESTON VAUGHN

THE UNIVERSITY PRESS OF KENTUCKY

Copyright © 1983 by The University Press of Kentucky

Scholarly publisher for the Commonwealth,
serving Berea College, Centre College of Kentucky,
Eastern Kentucky University, The Filson Club,
Georgetown College, Kentucky Historical Society,
Kentucky State University, Morehead State University,
Murray State University, Northern Kentucky University,
Transylvania University, University of Kentucky,
University of Louisville, and Western Kentucky University.

*Editorial and Sales Offices:* Lexington, Kentucky 40506-0024

**Library of Congress Cataloging in Publication Data**

Vaughn, William Preston, 1933–
   The Antimasonic Party in the United States, 1826–1843.

   Bibliography: p.
   Includes index.
   1. Antimasonic Party.   I. Title.
HS525.V35   1983        324.2732        82–40180
ISBN 0–8131–1474–8

*For My Mother*

# Contents

# Preface

As the 1832 Antimasonic presidential campaign of William Wirt dragged to its dismal conclusion, the *Boston Daily Advocate* of May 9 exhorted the party faithful to remember that maintenance of principles was more important than electoral victory. Firebrand editor Benjamin F. Hallett declared that the remedy for the evils of Freemasonry was "in our political organization as an inflexible minority. Let this never be lost sight of. The character of Antimasonry is not understood. Perseverance insures to its principles respect, and will eventually triumph." On the basis of Hallett's editorial, it is possible to conclude that the Antimasonic party remained faithful to principles and ideology, making no bargains with any individuals or other political organizations. It is the purpose of this book to demonstrate, however, that although political Antimasonry during the period 1827-1843 did generally remain adamant and inflexible with respect to its bitter foe, Freemasonry, it became quite open to all sorts of coalitions, deals, and alliances with the two major parties, the Jacksonian Democrats and National Republicans (who later reorganized as Whigs). These alliances were made against the most bitter protests of the Antimasonic "purists," who opposed the crusade's becoming political in the first place, favored party existence and action only until Masonry was destroyed, or desired a continuation of political Antimasonry untainted by association with any other party.

The major paradox and triumph of Antimasonry is that although it declined rapidly as an independent political entity after 1833, it achieved its major success as a social or reform movement in the nearly total, albeit temporary, destruction of Masonry in those states where it was an active force. Politically, Antimasonry's greatest achievements were the introduction of the national nominating convention to American presidential politics and contributions to the formation and development of the Whig party.

I thank the research and reference staffs of some forty libraries and research facilities in the United States and Great Britain who were consulted in the preparation of this book. I am grateful to the faculty research committee of North Texas State University and to Graduate

Dean Robert B. Toulouse for research grants; to William Kamman, chairman, Department of History, North Texas State University, for his encouragement and cooperation, and to Ronald E. Marcello, who read and critiqued the entire manuscript. I also thank the membership of the Texas Lodge of Research, A.F. & A.M., for their support and encouragement, and the Advisory Conference of the Dallas Scottish Rite Bodies and its chairman, Robert L. Dillard, Jr., Thirty-third Degree, Past Grand Master, for special assistance in the publishing of the manuscript. As always, I must express heartfelt appreciation to my wife, Virginia Meyer Vaughn, for support and assistance during more than a decade of work on this project.

# 1. The Morgan Affair and Its Consequences

On the night of September 12, 1826, William Morgan, an obscure and derelict stonemason, disappeared outside the jail at Canandaigua, New York, after serving time for failing to repay a debt of $2.69. Morgan had just finished writing an exposé of the secret rituals of Freemasonry, of which he claimed to be a member, and his authorship was known to the increasingly alarmed Masons of this western New York area, a region known as the "infected," or "Burned-over," district because it was "burnt" by the flames of religious revivals. Morgan was never seen in public again, and the general public transformed the crime of abduction into one of alleged murder and implicated all Masons from the Finger Lakes westward to the Niagara frontier.

Morgan's fate, never officially determined, "invested the consequent horror with enchantment," and as law enforcement and investigative procedures lagged, non-Masons came to believe that a great Masonic conspiracy in the United States had produced a "cover-up" of the true events. No other crime of the period attracted as much attention in the northern press, and for so long a period, as did the Morgan affair. Morgan's kidnapping revived a dormant hostility to Freemasonry and to all secret societies, which now swept most of the northeastern and Middle Atlantic states, taking shape first as a moral crusade and then, after 1827, as the impetus for the nation's first significant third, or minor, party.[1]

Writing in 1902 as the first scholarly historian of political Antimasonry, Charles McCarthy barely noted Morgan's abduction, describing it as "merely incidental"—an event that had happened at the right time and place to provide the thrust for a "sturdy, young political party." Of the earlier professional historians who wrote in a general context about Antimasonry, only John Bach McMaster observed the full impact of Morgan's abduction and the public's reaction to it. During the late nineteenth and early twentieth centuries, Masonic authors, notably Rob Morris, premier Masonic man of letters, in emphasizing the "vile treachery" of Morgan and his confederates, made martyrs of the victims of the crusade. Later Masonic historians have generally been less argumentative, deemphasizing the importance of the affair and insinuating that Morgan was not abducted but went willingly, later living out his life in a foreign land.[2]

Two scholars of the late twentieth century, Ronald P. Formisano and Kathleen Smith Kutolowski, view the Morgan episode and its aftermath as a Masonic "Watergate." They declare that by early 1827 it was widely believed throughout western New York that Morgan had been murdered as well as abducted and that "reasonable" men outside the fraternity considered the Masons to have too much influence in the administration of the law. Many judges, prosecutors, and attorneys, and at least three sheriffs in the five counties holding Morgan-related trials, were Masons. Many discharged their duties impartially, but some ignored their obligations to the community. The general public came to believe that Masonic behavior had contradicted "republican virtue," an attitude that opened the way for a concerted attack on Masonry.[3]

The saga of William Morgan is fraught with confusing contradictions and details.[4] Morgan was born in Culpeper County, Virginia, in 1774. Originally a stonemason, he became a merchant in Richmond for a time and then suddenly departed for York (Toronto), Canada, where he worked in a brewery and later on a farm. He subsequently returned to the United States, clerking in Niagara County, New York. In 1823 he resumed his trade as a stonemason, working first in Rochester and then in Batavia, Genesee County. In 1819, at age forty-five, while still in Virginia, he had married Lucinda Pendleton, the sixteen-year-old daughter of a Methodist minister. Morgan is usually described as "lazy, intemperate, quarrelsome and dishonest," yet he obviously possessed some basic intelligence, although he had had little formal education, and evidently his manner charmed acquaintances at least initially, for otherwise he would not have been welcomed into several lodges as a visitor, nor would he have been asked to speak at several Masonic functions. His tendency toward alcoholism and his argumentative nature, however, soon wore out his welcome.[5]

The question of Morgan's Masonic membership has fascinated fraternal historians for generations, but exhaustive research into the existing records of lodges in the various areas where Morgan lived has failed to unearth any evidence of his ever having taken any of the three basic, or "Blue Lodge," Masonic degrees—Entered Apprentice, Fellow Craft, and Master Mason. Lodge record keeping in those days was casual by today's standards, and it is conceivable that in the hysteria that followed publication of Morgan's *Illustrations,* the minutes of meetings during which he received these degrees might have been destroyed by embarrassed lodge officers. Records do indicate that Morgan visited Wells Lodge No. 282, Rochester, and Olive Branch Lodge No. 215, then meeting at East Bethany, New York. There is evidence, however, that in May 1825 Morgan received a York Rite degree, being initiated as a Royal Arch Mason in Western Star Chapter No. 33, LeRoy, New York. It is, of course, of great interest to Masonic historians to determine how Morgan acquired his intimate knowledge of Blue Lodge Masonry. Perhaps he had read one of the numerous eighteenth-century exposés of Freemasonry published in England and, by the 1820s, readily available in the United States.[6] Morgan probably gained knowledge of Masonry sufficient for his examination and admission into a lodge by posing as a brother in the presence of Masons in some convivial tavern situation. Dues cards indicating membership in good standing were not in general use, although "traveling" certificates of membership, or patents, were common and could easily be forged. Once admitted to a lodge meeting, Morgan was evidently able to retain enough knowledge of the secret ritualistic work to enable him in the future easily to pass as a Master, or Third Degree, Mason.

The major reason for Morgan's frustration and anger with his Masonic "brethren" in Genesee County and his subsequent and successful effort to write and publish a detailed account of the three Blue Lodge degrees is less difficult to explain. After being "exalted" (initiated) into the Royal Arch chapter at LeRoy, Morgan signed a petition that called for the establishment of another chapter in Morgan's village of Batavia. Some Batavia Masons were unwilling to have Morgan as a member, and one of them drew lines through his name, thus eliminating him from the petition. Infuriated by this action, possibly denied a job in the construction of a new Masonic temple at LeRoy, and spurred on by visions of fame and especially fortune, Morgan began to compile his *Illustrations of Masonry.* Most historians agree that the desire for money was a primary motivation. Morgan was a man harassed by debts and was now cut off from Masonic charity because of indolence and alcoholism. He had a wife and two children to support, and he hoped to make a great deal of money from publication of his book.[7]

In March 1826 Morgan formed a partnership with David C. Miller, John Davids, and Russell Dyer. Miller, who had taken only the first Masonic degree, was a printer and publisher of the *Batavia Republican Advocate.* Like Morgan, Miller sought profit, but in addition he was infuriated by the establishment of a rival local newspaper, the *People's Press*, whose editors were Masons. Davids and Dyer were to furnish capital for the publication. News of this enterprise spread quickly among Masons of the towns and villages throughout the Burned-over District—Rochester, Buffalo, Lockport, Canandaigua, LeRoy, and Lewiston. These Masons, not realizing that published exposés were commonplace in England and France and were available in the United States, and knowing only that to write and publish such secrets was a heinous offense in light of Masonic tradition, determined to prevent the book's publication. Morgan and his partners received various threats and were constantly harassed, but the book appeared nevertheless. On August 4 Morgan's partners drew up a bond for $500,000, which the author was to receive in exchange for his manuscript. The bond evidently was worthless, for two days later he wrote his partners and charged them with evasion and dishonesty. Amid rumors, purported violence, and intrigue, Morgan's book received a copyright on August 14 under the title of *Illustrations of Masonry, By One of the Fraternity Who Has Devoted Thirty Years to the Subject.* It was a detailed and, by all accounts, accurate narrative of the three Blue Lodge degrees as then conferred in New York, giving all the secret signs, passwords, obligations, and grips, and was replete with woodcut illustrations. When Miller advertised the book for sale at one dollar a copy in the *Republican Advocate* on December 14 (after Morgan's abduction), its contents included an introduction by the printer that denounced Masonry in scathing terms.[8]

In mid-September 1826 local Masons began to take direct action against Morgan, hoping to stop the book's appearance. On September 10, an unsuccessful attempt was made to destroy Miller's print shop by fire. Prominent Masons in Batavia later offered a reward of $100 if it could be proved that any of the brethren were responsible. That same day, Nicholas Cheseboro, master (head) of Ontario Master's Lodge at Canandaigua, obtained a warrant for Morgan's arrest on a charge of theft, claiming that he had stolen a shirt and cravat from a local tavern keeper, from whom he had rented a room in May 1826. The following day, a constable (who was not a Mason) and five others who were lodge brothers journeyed to Batavia, arrested Morgan, and took him to Danold's Tavern. Morgan was then taken to Canandaigua on the theft charge, but the magistrate released him because of lack of evidence. He was rearrested immediately on the claim of $2.69 due an innkeeper. Morgan admitted the debt, and the authorities incarcerated him about 10:00 P.M.[9]

The next evening, September 12, 1826, the Canandaigua jailer was absent. Cheseboro, with two Masonic assistants, after some difficulty persuaded the jailer's wife to release Morgan upon payment of the debt. Morgan was then escorted from the jail. About 9:00 P.M., a shrill whistle sounded, and the jailer's wife rushed to the window, only to see Morgan struggling with two men and shouting "Murder!" A yellow carriage appeared, and four men threw Morgan into it. The carriage went "clattering" into the night, and Morgan was never seen in public again.

Morgan's exact fate has remained a mystery since that dark evening, for his corpse was never found. From the mass of confusing and contradictory testimony, some obtained in court, some given many years later in deathbed "confessions," it appears that the approximately sixty-nine Masons involved in Morgan's abduction had made an arrangement with Masonic brethren in Canada by which Morgan was to receive a sum of money (perhaps $500) and a farm on which he would live out his days incognito. The plan collapsed, however, and no satisfactorily documented explanation was ever offered by those involved. Morgan was apparently held a prisoner in the French powder magazine at abandoned Fort Niagara. On September 19, 1826, he was allegedly bound with weights and thrown into the Niagara River (below the falls), near the place where the river sluggishly flows into Lake Ontario. Of course, this account is conjecture, for authorities never located Morgan's body, and although his abduction was ultimately proved in court, his murder was not. For years it was rumored that Morgan had been seen in Canada and in more exotic places—in Smyrna in the Ottoman Empire and in British Honduras. It was also reported that Morgan had become an Indian chief and that he had "turned pirate" and had been hanged in Cuba for his crimes.[10]

This writer agrees with New York's third special counsel of 1831, Victory Birdseye, that Morgan was probably murdered by misguided Masons who, when the Canadian deal fell apart, panicked and decided that by getting rid of the author, they would somehow prevent publication of *The Illustrations.* To their chagrin, not only did the book appear, duly advertised, in mid-December, but within a year, Morgan's abduction and alleged murder had produced a violent moral crusade against Masonry and an incipient political party as well.

Initial reaction of the non-Masonic public was intense but not hysterical. As time passed and Morgan's fate remained a mystery, the original issue underwent a series of changes. The question of one man's fate was translated into public concern as to whether there existed a secret society powerful enough to establish its own system of justice and to prevent punishment of the Morgan collaborators.

Masonic response to the Morgan affair varied at first, with some New York lodges issuing disclaimers of any connection with Morgan while many others remained silent on the issue. The capacity of Masonry to obstruct the Morgan investigations and trials depended less on actual Masonic numerical strength than on "placement" of many of the brethren in key positions in society and government. By 1826-1827 probably a majority of public officeholders throughout New York were Masons. In Genesee County, where the abduction had occurred, sixteen of twenty-two townships had Masonic lodges, and Masonry was as much a part of rural life as it was of the village social structure. From 1821 to 1827, half of all Genesee County officials were Masons. After the early shock and surprise had passed, Masons began to battle the protestors of Morgan's "murder" with the zeal that historians have traditionally reserved for the Antimasons, and yet lodge members showed little interest in punishing the brethren who had been involved in Morgan's disappearance. After months of inquiries and trials, which produced reams of incriminating evidence, no New York lodge had expelled a member for involvement in the Morgan affair, but two Masonic jury foremen were expelled from Olive Branch Lodge at East Bethany in October 1827 for saying that Masonry was no longer a useful institution. That lodge expelled another former jury member in 1829.[11]

One Genesee County Mason who took a more objective view of the Morgan affair and its aftermath was Henry Brown, a forty-year-old attorney, Van Buren Democrat, and Episcopalian, who in 1829 published *A Narrative of the Anti-Masonic Excitement, in the Western Part . . . of New York. . . .* Brown, a loyal member of the fraternity, was extremely critical of the Antimasonic crusade, declaring that it had destroyed the "peace of families," had "armed" one portion of the community against the other, and had caused violations of the law. Yet Brown also described Morgan's abduction as "unjustifiable, impolitick and illegal." He realized that Masonic foot dragging and obstruction of justice simply made matters worse but concluded that organization of a political party to destroy the fraternity was "wholly unnecessary," for "public opinion is sufficient if Masonry is worthless."[12]

In September and October 1826, New York governor DeWitt Clinton, one of the highest ranking Masons in the United States, issued two proclamations. One urged apprehension of the offenders involved in Morgan's abduction and requested the cooperation of citizens with all civil authorities. The second offered rewards of $300 for the discovery of any offenders, with another $100 to be paid upon conviction.

In November a grand jury at Canandaigua indicted four men, including Cheseboro, who had handled the Batavia-Canandaigua end of the abduction. They were tried in the latter town in January 1827, and on the advice of their attorneys, three of the accused pleaded guilty to "conspiracy to kidnap," claiming no knowledge of Morgan's later whereabouts. Kidnapping was still classified as a misdemeanor in New York. The three were sentenced to two years, three months, and one month, respectively, in the Canandaigua jail. Their attorney, John C. Spencer, in 1829 was appointed as the (second) special counsel by Gov. Martin Van Buren, succeeding Daniel Mosely (appointed in 1828). The fourth defendant, sometimes described as a "notoriety seeker," received a three-month term.[13]

The light sentences and the abrupt end to the trial shocked the spectators, and 200 witnesses were released to trudge home through the snow. As Thurlow Weed later declared, the acquittals did not restore public confidence but instead implicated Freemasonry more deeply. In pronouncing sentence on the Morgan conspirators, circuit judge Enos T. Throop castigated the defendants, referring to the excitement caused by Morgan's abduction as a "blessed spirit, and we do hope that it will not subside." The term "blessed spirit" became a synonym for Antimasonry. Shortly after the Canandaigua trial had concluded, the first Antimasonic conventions, held at LeRoy and Lewiston, asked for a strengthening of the laws relating to kidnapping and requested appointment of a special counsel to conduct the Morgan trials.[14]

These trials dragged on for five years, 1826-1831, but produced few convictions. Some twenty grand juries were called, fifty-four Masons were indicted, thirty-nine were brought to trial, and ten received convictions and jail terms ranging from thirty days to twenty-eight months. Of those not tried, two died before their day in court, twelve left New York for other states, and one fled to Europe. Of the ten convicted, only six were involved with Morgan's abduction. Four were punished for illegally moving David C. Miller from Batavia. Five indictments remained on the judicial calendar when the term of the third and last special counsel, Birdseye, expired in 1831.[15]

In mid-March 1827, Clinton placed before the legislature all the information he had secured regarding the Morgan affair. A reward of $1,000 had been offered for the discovery of Morgan alive and $2,000 for identification of his murderers if a body were found. The following month, a special, or select, legislative committee, chaired by attorney Francis Granger of Canandaigua, at this time a supporter of President John Quincy Adams, resolved that the assembly authorize the governor to offer a reward of $5,000 for the discovery of Morgan if alive or $5,000 for apprehension of his alleged killers. Granger also requested that the governor appoint a joint house-senate committee to visit seven western counties and to investigate the "abduction, detention and disposition" of Morgan, as the courts of Genesee County were inadequate to handle such an emergency.[16]

The resolutions met defeat by a margin of three to one, an event that pleased the *Albany Argus,* journalistic voice of pro-Van Buren Bucktail Democrats and their ruling clique, the Albany Regency. The *Argus* declared that proposal of such a large reward and creation of a special committee would produce "unjust attempts to convict innocent persons, and possibly offer temptations to perjury." Five days after defeat of the Granger resolutions, Clinton signed two laws that obviously responded to the growing outcry against the light sentences given to the Morgan abductors. This legislation made kidnapping a felony punishable by imprisonment from three to fourteen years at hard labor, denied sheriffs the power to summon grand juries, and authorized town supervisors to prepare lists of prospective jurors.[17]

To many frustrated non-Masons, failure of the legislature to pass the Granger resolutions appeared to be the result of Masonic influence in that body and obstructed investigation. Rumors that juries and judges were under the influence of the fraternity and that the legislature would continue to do nothing to bring Morgan's abductors to justice gradually produced a belief that Masonry was incompatible with good citizenship and must be abolished. Morgan's abduction was pronounced not a trivial occurrence or a fantasy but an event that actually happened, one in a series of "outrages" committed by Masons, and the kidnapping preceded a cover-up that transformed public opinion. The "cry of 'Morgan' became symbolic of Masons holding themselves above the law, both before and long after the event." Even U.S. senator Martin Van Buren (not a Mason) worried about Masonic opposition to the Morgan investigation, urging a pro-Regency and pro-Masonic editor to let the Morgan affair alone and to cease attacking the inquiries and trials. Thus, within a year after Morgan's abduction, a crisis in confidence had caused many people to believe that Masons were violating the principle of equality before the law and the due process of the legal system. This belief, in turn, fostered a militant spirit among Antimasons.[18]

On October 7, 1828, a badly decomposed male corpse drifted ashore at the point where Oak Orchard Creek joins Lake Ontario, about forty miles east of Youngstown, New York. An immediate burial followed, but the news reached David C. Miller of Batavia and

Thurlow Weed, editor of the *Rochester Telegraph*. They assembled a group who had the body exhumed and moved to Carlton, New York. A coroner's inquest indicated the presence of heavy hair and whiskers on the body; Morgan had been clean shaven. A second inquest was held, and by this time the corpse was bald, devoid of facial hair but having heavy hair in the ears and nostrils, thus resembling Morgan. Weed and his friends declared that the original body had been stolen and another substituted for it. Others charged Weed with mutilating the corpse to make it resemble Morgan, while still others attributed to Weed the comment that it was a "good enough Morgan" until after the autumn elections, an accusation that followed Weed to his grave. Lucinda Morgan and twenty-three of the (second) coroner's jury declared the body to be that of Morgan. Local Antimasons buried it in Batavia cemetery with great (Antimasonic) pomp and ceremony.[19]

Mrs. Timothy Munroe, a resident of Canada who read of these events, decided that the corpse might be her lost and presumably drowned husband. She gave testimony in Orleans County, New York, that was read to a jury at Batavia on October 22. The body was again exhumed, a third coroner's jury was assembled, and it decided from Mrs. Munroe's detailed description of clothing that the corpse must be that of Munroe. The body was then reinterred under that name.[20]

Many years later, in September 1880, during a post-Civil War revival of Antimasonry, the National Christian Association erected an elaborate monument to the memory of William Morgan. It is located in the cemetery where the Morgan-Munroe corpse had been buried. Nothing more was known at the time about Morgan's fate. All that five years of investigation and at least thirty-nine trials had proved was that Morgan had been kidnapped at Canandaigua and eventually had been taken to the powder magazine at Fort Niagara. Beyond that point, all accounts were based on circumstantial evidence or on conflicting and confusing testimony.[21]

Morgan's abduction and probable murder occurred at a crucial time in New York state politics. The Adams-Clay party was in a rapid state of decline, and Clinton had affiliated with the Jacksonians, leaving many of his followers in a quandary, for most of them could hardly follow Clinton into a party controlled on the state level by Van Buren and the hated Regency. Conditions were ripe for creation of a new organization that would submerge factional differences and would unite voters behind a platform pledged to defend democracy and equality before the law. It was no accident that this party evolved in January 1827 from a series of local conventions that met while the first trial of Morgan's kidnappers was taking place.[22]

# 2. The Origins of Antimasonry

Definitions of Masonry are as numerous and diverse as the fraternity itself. Simply stated, Masonry is an oath-bound order of men with a secret ritual based upon the medieval guilds of stonemasons and cathedral builders. A more philosophical definition from the early nineteenth century describes Masonry as "a peculiar system of morality, veiled in allegory and illustrated by symbols," whereas a contemporary explanation declares the order to be an "esoteric system of ethical teachings which manifests itself in the conduct of its members, especially in their responsibilities and relationships to one another."[1]

Although many Masons attempt to trace the fraternity's origins to antiquity and the reign of King Solomon, a group of nineteenth-century British Masonic historians known as the "Realistic School," led by Robert Freke Gould (1836-1915) and sustained by twentieth-century researchers, concluded that modern Masonry developed from the lodges of the "operative" English and Scottish stonemasons working on the cathedrals, castles, and monasteries of the Middle Ages. Laboring in places where there were no trade guilds or organizations, Masons formed themselves into clubs, or lodges, imitating the guilds, so that they would have some type of on-the-job self-discipline while remaining removed from other forms of trade control. The transition from operative, or working, Mason to "speculative," or theoretical, Mason lasted some 200 years and began about 1600. In London, as late as 1720, Englishmen still distinguished between the operatives, who carved gargoyles, inscribed tombstones, or built walls, and the clubs of speculatives, who came from all trades and occupations. The idea of a club designed to inculcate the ancient moral truths associated with the history and ritual of the guilds was an ingenious way to elevate both the club and the guild to a higher purpose.[2]

Freemasonry appeared in Britain's North American colonies within a few years after organization of the (national) Grand Lodge of England in 1717. The first lodge in the colonies probably met in Philadelphia in 1730, but the first body to receive a legal charter from the Grand Lodge of England was St. John's Lodge in Boston, established in 1733 by Provincial Grand Master Henry Price, a member of Lodge No. 75, London. In 1733-1734 Price issued charters for lodges in Pennsylvania, New Hampshire, and South Carolina. By 1776 there were about 100 lodges in the thirteen colonies, with a membership estimated at somewhere between 1,500 and 5,000—of a total population of 2,500,000.[3]

The American Revolution had a temporarily negative effect on Masonry in America; lodges were cut off from their parent organizations in Great Britain, and splits occurred in the local bodies between patriots and Loyalists. After the Revolution ended in 1783, American Masonry developed at a rapid rate, accelerated by the acceptance of deism and religious freethinking during the previous decade, the weakening of formal church establishment, and the formation of military lodges during the recent war. The Masonic affiliation of prominent military and political figures, such as George Washington, undoubtedly encouraged other men to lodge membership. Of course, many Americans who had been prominent in the patriot cause were not members of the fraternity, including John Adams, Thomas Jefferson, and James Madison, and conversely, many colonial Masons had supported the king's cause. Several attempts in 1779 and 1780 to establish a national American grand lodge failed, and American Masons organized state grand lodges to administer the local bodies within their respective jurisdictions, embodying the idea of state sovereignty. By 1800 there were 11 grand lodges, some 347 subordinate lodges, and a total membership of about 16,000.[4]

Unfortunately, so few local and state studies are available that we cannot yet develop an accurate national profile of the typical Mason during the period between the American Revolution and the beginning of the Antimasonic crusade, 1826-1827. Dorothy Ann Lipson, in analyzing Masonry in Connecticut, indicates that prominent Masons were among the more mobile elements of the population and were often leaders of political and religious dissent who challenged the long-established hierarchy. Concentrating on the membership of Putnam Lodge No. 46 at Woodstock from 1810 to 1835, she compared the Masons and non-Masons of that community using an 1822 lodge census and a federal census of 1820 and discovered that the percentage of Masons in commerce and the professions was much higher than that of nonmembers (22.7 percent versus 1.5 percent). Masons were also active in other occupational categories, including agriculture and manufacturing. The brethren represented all income levels, but a higher proportion came from groups with more taxable wealth. Putnam Lodge's membership of that era was diverse in terms of occupations, financial status, and social position. It was a young membership:

of the 207 men initiated between 1801 and 1835, 80 percent were under age thirty when they took their first degree. Woodstock Masons also tended to be politically active, filling public office more often than was consistent with their proportion of the total population.[5]

A recent study of politics in Genesee County, New York, the site of Morgan's abduction, shows that as in Connecticut, the local political leadership had joined the Masonic lodge in much higher proportion than adult males who were not active in politics. Masons composed some 50 percent of the county central corresponding committees of each major party. In addition, nearly half of the committee members were "professionals," more than 70 percent were Episcopalians, and nearly two-thirds lived in the county's two major villages of Batavia and LeRoy. Although the above analyses provide insufficient data for an accurate national Masonic profile, they do indicate, at least with reference to Connecticut and western New York, that early nineteenth-century Masons tended to be prosperous and politically active, and they frequently assumed leadership roles for protracted periods of time. This fact in itself was enough to make the Antimasons, with their strong belief in social egalitarianism, constantly suspicious of the fraternity.[6]

Antimasonry is as old as Masonry itself and actually predates organization of the Grand Lodge of England in 1717. The earliest known attack on Freemasonry in print appeared in England in 1698. Probably the most important exposure in the eighteenth century was Samuel Prichard's *Masonry Dissected,* first published in 1730. It was the first publication to explain the three degrees in detail and created a sensation, selling three authorized printings and one pirated edition within eleven days. Ironically, like most of its successors over the years, it was purchased primarily by Masons as a memory aid, and *Masonry Dissected* remained in print for more than thirty years, forcing competitors off the market. Prichard explained that he was publishing his thirty-two-page pamphlet to "prevent so many credulous persons being drawn into so pernicious a society," but he never indicated why he considered Masonry "pernicious." Numerous similar publications followed *Masonry Dissected* in Great Britain and France. Of those, undoubtedly the most important in connection with William Morgan's later effort was *Jachin and Boaz,* first printed in London in 1762 and reprinted in thirty-four separate editions from that year until 1800. Between 1793 and 1818 twelve editions were printed in the United States, and all were readily available prior to 1826.[7]

Antimasonic attacks in Britain's North American colonies quickly followed the establishment of lodges. In 1737 the *New York Gazette* recognized Masonry in that colony and attacked its secrecy, which it assumed was a shield for immoral practices, and denounced the "brutal" oaths sworn by Masonic initiates. Within sixty years following the charges made by the *Gazette,* the first concerted attack on Masonry in the United States took place in Federalist-dominated New England, where the political hierarchy and its religious counterpart, the Congregational clergy, had begun to associate Masonry with the French Revolution, atheism, Jeffersonian Republicanism, and various assaults on authority, Christianity, and private property.[8]

By the late 1790s certain New England Federalists with Antimasonic tendencies had tried to establish a connection between the Masonic lodges in the United States and a notorious secret European organization known as the "Bavarian Illuminati," alleged to be part of Freemasonry. Masons were accused of fomenting political revolutions to promote anarchy and to destroy all forms of authority. John Robison, a professor at the University of Edinburgh, in 1797 published *Proofs of a Conspiracy Against All Religions and Governments of Europe Carried on in the Secret Meeting of the Free Masons, Illuminati and Reading Societies,* which declared that Illuminati-dominated lodges now flourished in the United States. This charge was taken up by the renowned geographer and clergyman the Reverend Jedidiah Morse of Charlestown, Massachusetts, who, in several well-publicized sermons of 1798-1799, declared that the Illuminati intended to subvert American political and religious institutions. Morse pointed to a lodge in Portsmouth, Virginia, composed of French exiles, as living proof of this conspiracy. Investigation proved the charge spurious, however, and this finding, along with increasing pressure from the Jeffersonian press, helped to stifle the conspiracy charges by the end of 1799.[9]

It is impossible to forge a direct link between the crisis of 1797-1799 and the events following Morgan's abduction to show that the anti-Illuminati hysteria was a precursor of post-1826 Antimasonry. Yet as Arthur B. Darling wrote in 1925, "there remained the tradition of Masonic intrigue and vague but repellent feeling, to hold some men aloof from Masonry." In addition, the Burned-over District of western New York, seedbed of nineteenth-century Antimasonry, was settled largely by transplanted New Englanders, many of whom must have brought with them a deep-seated distrust and suspicion of Freemasonry when they migrated westward.[10]

The rhetoric and ideology of nineteenth-century Antimasonry was an expansion of that found in the seventeenth- and eighteenth-century publications and the propaganda of 1797-1799. Antimasonry evolved from a centuries-old distrust of all secret organizations. The secret rites and oaths of Masonry made the lodge a natural object of envy and fear to those excluded from the order, and an allegedly egalitarian society readily associated Masons with "impermissible snobbery and exclusivism." Although to categorize the Antimasons of 1826-1843 merely as paranoid, conspiratorial-minded, right-wing bigots is extremely simplistic, there is no question that much of their extremist propaganda emphasized the existence of a great Masonic conspiracy against the entire nation, whereas the "Antis" of the 1790s had proclaimed a conspiracy primarily against the Federalist party and the Congregational church. Post-1826 Antimasonry claimed to be the defender, not only of Protestantism, but of democracy as well, as against the "forces of darkness and evil," thus appealing to a much larger audience than the earlier movement had. As the historian examines the hundreds of Antimasonic books, almanacs, pamphlets, newspapers, songs, poems, and acrostics—the "rhetoric of protest"—he cannot help but admit that in spite of all the Antimasons' legitimate grievances arising from the Morgan affair and from Masonic domination of politics and law enforcement, in one sense the crusade attacked the right of one group of citizens to exercise the constitutionally guaranteed freedom of assembly as well the rights of speech and press.[11]

Like other mass movements, the Antimasonic crusade attracted all types of followers with divergent motives, including those angry about Morgan's abduction and the subsequent Masonic cover-up; political opportunists; those whose religious beliefs turned them against secret societies; those who believed Freemasonry was a subversive force in a democratic nation; and those who were drawn into the movement by their "fantasies" about the wicked, sinful, and terrible events that transpired both during and after lodge meetings.[12]

Almost all Antimasonic literature dwelled upon the matter of secrecy to some extent. Masonry allegedly had to be an evil institution, for it restricted its rites and ceremonies to the membership, and those excluded could only guess at the horrible events taking place behind closed doors. Secrecy forced Masons to block the channels of public information and to conceal the most important facts relative to civil and political questions. Antimasons viewed secret organizations as a threat to democratic society and declared that in a republic there should be no secret orders. Masonic secrecy became synonymous with darkness, sin, immorality, intemperance, treason, and the work of Satan. In an age that paid much attention to egalitarianism, the mere fact that someone was barred from a Masonic function because he was not a brother infuriated many Americans.[13]

The Antimasons quickly developed a conspiracy theory with respect to Masonry, "suddenly" uncovering a group of unscrupulous leaders plotting to overthrow the American social order. According to Richard Rush of Pennsylvania, the United States had more to fear from secret societies than did any other nation, since popular sovereignty, the basis of this country's liberties, required perfect freedom of public inquiry and judgment. Many Antimasons believed that Masonic secrecy concealed the members' "unconditional loyalty" to an autonomous state, and this allegiance far exceeded any loyalty to the nation. Because Masons had so greatly penetrated the bureaucracy in the state and national governments, only drastic action could restore the country to democratic purity. Antis declared that Masonry exercised absolute jurisdiction over the lives of its members and that Masons had erected for themselves a separate and distinct government within the United States, concealing an odious aristocracy. Lebbeus Armstrong, a New York minister and prominent (and early) seceding Mason, suggested in his 1830 pamphlet, *Masonry Proved to be a Work of Darkness,* that if the lodge went unchecked, the United States would have a Masonic monarchy for its government, a Masonic church, a "Masonic way to a Masonic heaven, and blood and massacre and destruction to all who subscribe not to the support of the Monarch."[14]

The use of high-sounding titles such as "master," "high priest," "king," and others by Masonic bodies, and the wearing of elaborate regalia for public ceremonies, including processions, funerals, and the laying of cornerstones, angered Antimasons. Solomon Southwick, Antimasonic candidate for governor of New York in 1828, declared that Masonry could never be a republican institution, for "its Knights, Kings, High Priests, and other dignitaries more extravagantly ridiculous, in this age and time, are at war with the simplicity of manners and equality of rights, which distinguish a republican government; and are not safely to be tolerated among a free people." Masonic claims to ancient origins also infuriated other opponents, who declared that the fraternity was not the product of the ancient world and hence not an institution to be venerated. Instead it was a recent development, having been shaped by "Jews, Jesuits and French atheists" to promote infidelity; it was also said to have been a tool used by aristocrats and monarchs to subvert republican institutions.[15]

By the late 1820s the frustration of many clergy with the decline of their political power and influence with their congregations and communities, the ending of church "establishment" in Connecticut and Massachusetts, and the failure of Protestant evangelicals to stop Sunday mail service had caused many religious leaders to do battle with an organization claiming religious origins and appearing to serve as a church substitute. Antimasons viewed Masonry as attempting to fill important functions traditionally associated with religious organizations, without any reference to church doctrine or membership, especially the inculcation of universal moral standards. Masonry, in the eyes of its opponents, could be used as a surrogate religion, for the lodge, like religious bodies, transmitted esoteric knowledge through rituals, myths, and symbolism, and Masons of the early nineteenth century frequently alluded to the similarity between baptism in a church and initiation in the lodge. Antimasonry found much support in a growing conviction that the fraternity was "irreligious," an attack that could be advanced by any sect or denomination with some degree of credence.[16]

Antimasonic religious leaders called for the defeat of Masonry in a plethora of well-circulated books and tracts that described the fraternity as a "counterfeit religion." Unless it was destroyed, Masonry as a tool of Satan would overthrow the church and its moral code along with the American system of justice and other republican institutions. Antimasons, using the religious argument, therefore condemned Masonry as an evil and dealt with it as they would with any other form of "flagrant sin." They refused to admit that although some brethren regarded Masonry as a religious substitute, others held denominational membership and took an active church role. Armstrong declared that Masonry was the work of Satan because it grossly perverted the Holy Scriptures, for many Masonic passwords, signs, and degree histories had been "taken from the sacred writings, and hence the doctrine is palmed upon the world that Masonry is founded on the word of God." He added that the fraternity provided for the concealment of capital crimes, and he urged all Masonic ministers and Masonic members of Christian churches to renounce the lodge at once. He became so concerned about the need for Masonic clergy to denounce the lodge and to sever their fraternal ties that he compiled a pamphlet, *An Appeal to Christian Ministers in Connection with Speculative Free Masonry.* Its first question demanded whether , as "Ambassadors of Christ," Masonic clergy found a warrant authorizing them "to strike hands with the wicked, and enter a secret combination and league with unbelievers, who, by their wicked words, prove themselves to be enemies of the Cross of Christ?"[17]

Another key statement that Antimasons reiterated in many of their writings concerned the "barbarity" of Masonic oaths (which Masons usually call "obligations") and penalties, which were, of course, immediately connected with William Morgan's demise. In the modern Masonic context these sanctions are entirely moral and ethical, "and if the offender suffers from his transgressions, it is in the knowledge of the disapprobation of his brethren." Modern Masonic scholars insist that the penalties, based upon savage punishments inflicted in the Middle Ages, were intended, at least since the advent of speculative Masonry, to be interpreted never literally but only allegorically. The oaths or obligations together form the nucleus of the Masonic structure and set forth in "pragmatic terms the duties, responsibilities and limitations of the fraternal relationship which they establish." Each oath contains a vow of silence concerning the secrets of Masonry and is combined with a penal clause "said to be applicable" in case of violation. Unfortunately, at least for Morgan, the allegorical nature of the penalties was not universally comprehended by the brethren of western New York in 1826.[18]

The mere taking or swearing of oaths in the degree work offended certain nonjuring sects and denominations, including the Quakers and Moravians. Moses Thatcher, addressing Antimasonic meetings in Massachusetts in 1829-1830, observed that no lodge member could reflect on Masonic oaths and penalties as "literally expressed . . . and yet be at a loss to account for the sacrifice of William Morgan." He declared that these oaths could not be legally, religiously, or morally binding because they were illegal, irreligious and immoral. John G. Stearns, a leading "seceder" and Baptist minister in New York, as early as 1827 expressed an objection upon which Antimasons in several state legislatures would later seize, namely, that any oaths administered by Masons during the course of degree work were extrajudicial and therefore illegal, for Masons had no authority to impose such oaths.[19]

Antimasons also frequently charged that lodge meetings camouflaged wild, drunken revels. Part of the basis for this accusation was that the rapid growth of Masonry after 1800 coincided with rising concern about the high consumption of liquor everywhere and the beginnings of the temperance movement, which would later attract many reformers who had been active in Antimasonry. Liquor was not consumed in any of the Blue Lodge meetings, but wine was used for ceremonial purposes in some of the appendant York and Scottish Rite degrees. Many early lodges in America, like their English counterparts, met in the private rooms of taverns, probably the only building in town large enough to accommodate the fraternity. When the drinking of alcoholic beverages occurred, it was after the meeting at the "Festive Board," where consumption by Masons was likely to approximate that by the rest of the community. To zealous Antimasons, however, Masonry and debauchery went hand in hand. The drunkard, the "tavern haunter," the idler, and the dissipated were allegedly among Masonry's strongest supporters, and lodges were "cages of uncleanliness." Antimasons also liked to emphasize that Masonry could ruin a man financially, not only through the expense of initiation fees and annual dues, but by forcing him to be more attentive to the fraternity than to his business or profession. Charles P. Sumner, sheriff of Suffolk County (Boston), Massachusetts (and father of the abolitionist-Republican U.S. senator), a seceding Mason, declared that the influence of Masonry was not "favorable to domestic happiness." He recounted his visit to a poverty-stricken home, where he had seen the starving wife and two tiny children huddled before a small fire while the husband was enjoying himself at a lodge meeting.[20]

One aspect of Antimasonic ideology almost ignored by historians until the late 1970s was the quiet but strong dislike that many women felt for an organization that completely excluded them from membership. In addition to its inherent elitism as a male secret society, Masonry invited the antagonism of those women who considered themselves the primary custodians of moral standards and social values, whereas the fraternity bestowed charity on its own terms. Few documents describing aspects of female Antimasonry are extant, and general characteristics are therefore difficult to confirm. It is evident, however, that there was a silent, unorganized Antimasonic sentiment among many women, who frequently exerted a powerful influence on their voting husbands and, if their spouses were Masons, caused them to abandon their membership. Shortly after Morgan's abduction, a group of women assembled in Wheatland Township, New York, and passed various Antimasonic resolutions, but this is the only verifiable example of a women's Antimasonic meeting. The time had not yet arrived for men and women to assemble together for such purposes (it would within a few years, during the antislavery agitation). Nevertheless, in 1830 the Antimasonic *Ravenna* (Ohio) *Star* did feature an editorial on "Women and Masonry," lamenting the exclusion of females from the lodge and the plight of the Masonic wife, "left in solitude, left in the shades of night, ignorant of the employment in which her husband is engaged.[21]

Seceding Masons played a vital role in the dissemination of Antimasonic ideology and propaganda. Antimasonry at times seemed to be "the creation of ex-Masons; it certainly attached the highest significance and gave the most unqualified credulity to their revelations." Like other aspects of nineteenth-century Antimasonry, Masonic renunciations were not new, the first recorded instance having taken place in Scotland in 1739. Antimasons viewed the conversion of Masons as a twofold gain, for as the Reverend Henry Dana Ward wrote in his *Anti-Masonic Review,* the transition of a seceding Mason to the Antimasonic cause meant a loss to the enemy and an increase in the crusaders' ranks. "None are truer to our cause, none are more dangerous to Freemasonry, none are so hated and dreaded by the Adversary as renouncing Masons." So highly regarded were the seceders that frequently, when an Antimason could not claim prior Masonic membership, he would resort to declaring that he had once admired the order or had applied for initiation. There were generally two types of seceders—those who defected under pressure and those who had renounced Masonry of their own volition, usually vilifying the lodge to an extreme, exaggerating the dangers they faced in doing so and the harm these revelations would inflict upon the fraternity.[22]

Unquestionably the two most vital Masonic recruits to the Antimasonic crusade were Stearns and Elder David Bernard, both ministers of the Baptist church, a denomination whose membership was greatly angered by the interposition of Masonic ties among their clergy and laymen in seeming violation of the closed communion principle. Bernard, who for thirty years pastored some fifteen small rural churches, had purchased the first copy of Morgan's *Illustrations* after renouncing his membership in Oneida Lodge No. 123, Utica, in October 1826. He thus became the first Mason to desert the fraternity following Morgan's disappearance. He served as secretary of the first LeRoy convention and was appointed to the committee charged with publishing the advanced degrees of Masonry. The result of his efforts was *Light on Masonry,* first printed in Utica in 1829, which offered a detailed account of some fifty degrees, together with a narrative of Morgan's abduction and reports of various Antimasonic conventions. It was still in print by 1860. *Light on Masonry* was probably the single most important Antimasonic publication because of its detailed description of the degrees (obtained from interviews with seceders), its inclusion of reports and depositions concerning Morgan, and its historical narrative of the Antimasonic movement in New York until

1829. It became the leading Antimasonic source book on the nature and working of Masonry and was known as the "Bible of Antimasonry." John Quincy Adams would write that the world was indebted to Bernard for revealing the "execrable mysteries" of the order.[23]

Less well known than Bernard, but as important to the Antimasonic crusade in the late 1820s, was Elder John G. Stearns, also a Baptist clergyman. Considered to be the "most quoted and least commemorated" of the religious Antis in New York, Stearns actually renounced Masonry in July 1826 (prior to Morgan's disappearance) because of what he considered to be the theological and eccelesiastical deficiencies of the fraternity. In September of that year, he published his views in *An Inquiry Into the Nature and Tendency of Speculative Masonry.* Antimasons regarded *An Inquiry* as a sequel to Morgan's *Illustrations,* and it went through five printings between 1826 and 1830. Taking an almost purely theological approach, Stearns tried to prove that Masonry was a fraudulent "substitute religion" that attempted to compete with Christianity. He led the way in expounding the theory that Masonry was a state within a state and that one day Masons would overthrow the democratic government of the United States and would crown one of their "grand kings" as ruler of this nation. He also tried to forge a connection between the principles of certain Masonic degrees with the Illuminati and the French Revolution.[24]

Through the efforts of seceding Masons such as Bernard and Stearns, as well as those of church members who had never affiliated with Masonry, Antimasonry began as a church-oriented crusade, but it soon entered the volatile world of politics to do battle with the fraternity described by Southwick on various occasions as: "the steps that lead down to the gates of hell; the paths of perdition; conclaves of corruption, atheism and infidelity . . . ; the modern whore of Babylon . . . ; a monster . . . ; mystery and moonshine . . . ; school of Old Nick; [and the] dark altars of infidelity."[25]

# 3. Beginnings in New York, 1827-1829

Before Antimasonry became a political party, it existed in New York as a moral crusade with strong religious overtones, being led both by clergy and by concerned laymen. Religious Antimasonry found a forum in Protestant churches as an independent, altruistic, moral crusade characterized by enormous enthusiasm and a deep sense of immediacy. Eventually the independent crusade eclipsed the congregational and denominational efforts. Both endeavors, of course, embodied the evangelical desire to convert the entire American population to Christianity and to create a "moral, homogeneous commonwealth."[1]

The frontier of western New York, site of Morgan's abduction, had been settled largely by New Englanders, who possessed strong Yankee characteristics, especially in their political and religious attitudes. These "Yorkers" were extremely receptive to Antimasonic propaganda, not only because of the proximity of the Morgan affair, but also as a result of their heritage and concern for behavior that would be acceptable to God. The Antimasonic fervor that swept the Burned-over District was enthusiastically evangelical, its advocates "preaching" with profound conviction, its written materials almost identical to missionary tracts, and its literary style reminiscent of revivalistic sermons. Early Antimasons, like the evangelists of former years, relied heavily upon a biblical rationale to achieve their goal and hoped their converts would respond to this new challenge with the destruction of Freemasonry. Most of the evangelical Antimasons appear to have been orthodox fundamentalists in religious orientation, possessing a strong dislike for the more "liberal" denominations such as Universalism and Unitarianism and worrying about the rise of deism and rationalism in the United States.[2]

In the fourteen western New York counties most affected by religious Antimasonry, the Baptists led in terms of membership by 1830, having approximately 14,000 members, followed by the Presbyterians, with 13,000, and the Methodists, with 9,000. Approximately one-fourth of all Protestant clergy in the District were Masons, although not more than one-twentieth of the laymen were lodge members. Most of the pastors who became active Antimasons were Baptists and Presbyterians; few Episcopalian, Unitarian, or Universalist clergy became involved in the crusade.[3]

In Rochester, early Antimasons tended to be Presbyterians, but with the withdrawal from politics of the Rochester family and their Episcopal allies, leadership of the Masonic faction in the city fell to those Presbyterians who were also Masons. The correlation between political factionalism and denominationalism broke down, and leaders of both sides were present in almost every church, with heated disputes taking place within these congregations. As far as the entire Burned-over District was concerned, the Presbyterians usually took a definite position in favor of Antimasonry. In 1828 the Presbyteries of Genesee and Buffalo concluded that Masonry was evil, and church members should sever all ties with the fraternity. The Genesee Synod took more direct action in 1830, declaring that all Masons must cease lodge affiliation, and failure to comply meant dismissal from membership in the case of laymen and the loss of ministerial status as well for the clergy. Ironically, Masons had to swear an "oath" renouncing all connections with the fraternity.[4]

In contrast to the generally uninvolved Methodists, Baptists of the region became so preoccupied with the Blessed Spirit that by 1830 they were almost suffering a major schism. Traditionally zealous on any given issue, lacking the central ecclesiastical control of the Methodists and Presbyterians, conducting all affairs with the consent of the church membership, and motivated by Masonic seceders such as Stearns and Bernard, Baptists achieved the "fullest expression" of Antimasonry among all denominations of the "Genesee country." Regarding Masonry as contrary to Baptist methodology and as interfering with their doctrine of closed communion, congregations split over the Antimasonic issue. Associations passed proscriptive resolutions, and the more radical crusaders formed new conferences and conventions. Typical was the Livonia, New York, convention of August 1828, representing three Baptist associations, including that of Genesee. It met and passed resolutions that violently denounced any association with Masonry, one calling upon all associations of the New York (state) Baptist Convention to adopt an article in their constitution excluding any congregations or clergy sympathetic to Masonry. The state convention, however, took no action on this proposal or others against Masonry. Because of this equivocal stand and other compromises, an extremely radical Antimasonic group, the

Chatauque Baptist Conference was formed in 1828-1829 under the direction of Elder Charles La Hatt by twelve congregations seceding from the Chatauque Association. The secessionist group, favoring a no-compromise stand against Masonry, then took over the regular Baptist Association and assumed complete control by 1832.[5]

Religious Antimasonry met with limited success in the churches because it had to compete with other crusades, such as evangelism, temperance, and Sabbath observance. Antimasons quickly turned to independent conventions as a means of propagating their ideology, holding a series of meetings at Lewiston, LeRoy, Utica, and Albany from 1827 to 1830. The religious emphasis of these conventions was short lived, and the Antimasonry of Stearns, Bernard, and Solomon Southwick gave way to the rhetoric of politicians led by Thurlow Weed, who himself had little use for religious crusades or even for church membership. Religious Antimasons thus quickly abdicated their leadership role to the politicians because the churches did not control the political or social machinery necessary to destroy Masonry. Weed's refusal to give full support to the gubernatorial candidacy of the evangelically inclined Southwick ended whatever influence religious leaders still retained in the movement. Afterward the politicians rarely evidenced genuine concern about Masonry's alleged competition with Christianity or about Masonic blasphemy. The influence of Bernard and Stearns waned, while the careers of Francis Granger, Weed, and William H. Seward blossomed. As Benjamin Cowell, a "moral Antimason" of Rhode Island, declared a few years later, at first he had believed it improper to combine moral opposition to Freemasonry with political principles, but after studying accounts of the Morgan affair, he concluded "that the only way we have left to put down masonry is the BALLOT BOX. We must make it a political question and put it down by political means."[6]

The transition of New York Antimasonry from religious crusade to political party was a rapid one, generally complete within a year. Initially, political Antimasons seem to have thought more in terms of ousting Masons from judicial and political positions than about taking over courts, executive offices, and state legislatures. As the Antis knew only too well, Masonry was a powerful institution in the Empire State by 1826, with some 500 lodges and a total membership of about 20,000. In Genesee County during the years 1821-1827, some 50 percent of the leaders in the faction favoring DeWitt Clinton were Masons, while 58 percent of the pro-Van Buren leadership were members of the fraternity. In that county alone, Masons had formed ten new lodges and two new Royal Arch chapters in the early 1820s, making a total of seventeen lodges and three chapters by 1826. Although 90 percent of Genesee's residents were small farmers, some 90 percent of Genesee Masons engaged in nonfarm occupations such as merchandising, manufacturing, law, and medicine, pursuits that distinguished them from their non-Masonic neighbors in both social and economic status.[7]

In nearby Rochester, seat of Monroe County and a burgeoning mercantile and industrial center, Masonic influence was even more visible, and much of the general public found believable the idea that Masons were plotting to take over the government. Founders of the Rochester lodge included Abelard Reynolds, a business associate of Col. Nathaniel Rochester, and four of the colonel's sons. At the time of Morgan's abduction, Reynolds was Rochester's representative in the General Assembly. The sheriff of Monroe County, James Seymour, was a Mason, as was the local judge, John Bowman, who would have presided over cases relating to the Morgan affair had there been any indictments. Masonic political power became more obvious in 1827 when a write-in candidate and Mason, John E. Elwood, suddenly defeated Dr. Frederick F. Backus, a Clintonian turned Antimason, who was seeking his eleventh term as Rochester's treasurer.[8]

With the demise of the Federalist party in New York after the War of 1812, the Jeffersonian Republicans split into two factions, the followers of DeWitt Clinton, including many former Federalists, and the anti-Clinton Bucktails, who received their name from the deers' tails that adorned the hats of Tammany Society members at patriotic rallies. The ruling clique of the Bucktails was the powerful Albany Regency, which exercised near-absolute control over party patronage and policy. In the late 1820s, Governor Clinton, a great admirer of Andrew Jackson, switched his allegiance to the pro-Jackson Regency and Bucktails, taking a number of supporters, including some fellow-Masons, with him. Clinton, however, died suddenly in February 1828, leaving the undisputed leadership of the Bucktails to Van Buren. With the Clintonians now reduced in power and numbers, a place existed for a new anti-Bucktail party, a role that the Antimasons quickly assumed.[9]

Until the late 1970s historians have characterized New York Antimasonry as an agrarian small-town movement and party with a strong New England heritage, demonstrating "an early evidence of rural jealousy toward urban superiority, or at least toward the controlling middle class of the larger villages and country towns." It is true that until 1830 the party's major strength lay in western and central New York, with little support from New York City or the

Hudson River counties, and Empire State Antimasons wished to promote this rural image. Their state convention in 1830 declared that Antimasonry included principally farmers and "mechanics" who had derived too much independence from their ancestors to "submit under the thralldom of a privileged order." The convention delegates also asserted that their political opponents consisted primarily of "office holders and office seekers in the cities, towns and villages." Scholars such as Michael Holt who stress the rural image of Antimasonry, sometimes also view the party as having exerted a type of "Populist appeal," for Antimasonry promised a solution by which the average man could regain control of his government and could simultaneously attack monopoly and special privilege. Holt describes early Antimasonry in most areas as a movement of "poor farmers against the rich," whom the Antis identified as Masons; he also sees Antimasonry as the "major voice" of poor rural districts, raised in protest against the wealth and privilege of the cities.[10]

Kutolowski notes, however, that in Genesee County, "the poorest, most isolated farmers were less able to respond to Antimasonry." Contrary to prior opinion, which pictured Antimasons as rural "have-nots," it was the wealthier, more developed townships that returned the highest Antimasonic tallies from 1828 to 1832. LeRoy Township, the country's most prosperous jurisdiction, produced a 78 percent Antimasonic vote during the elections of 1828, 1830, and 1832. The least developed townships, with one exception, returned the lowest Antimasonic vote. In two townships, Antimasonic voting did not cut across socioeconomic lines, but in Genesee County generally the greatest Antimasonic margins usually occurred in the wealthiest townships, a trend that accelerated with the 1832-1833 elections, when the poorer voters, who had earlier embraced Antimasonry, began to abandon it. In Monroe County (Rochester), as in Genesee, Antimasonry traversed socioeconomic lines, and the more thriving townships returned the highest percentage of Antimasonic ballots. Attorneys and businessmen residing in the county seats, not poor farmers, dominated Antimasonic country committees and slates of candidates. In the poorer townships, a combination of factors— wretched transportation, bad communications, a lack of time to spend at political gatherings—meant that subsistence farmers saw and heard less of Antimasonry and therefore did not support it as actively as the more affluent citizens, who had more time for politics.[11]

Political Antimasonry created its state organizations, and later its national framework, through the convention system. Although Antimasons would hold the first national presidential nominating convention (1831), they were by no means innovators of that political technique on the local level, for there is evidence of a Bucktail nominating convention in Genesee County as early as 1821, and both Bucktail and Clintonian conventions seem to have met in that jurisdiction the following year. The pro-Clinton "People's party" used local conventions to nominate delegates to the state meeting in 1824. Conventions proved vital to the Antimasons as a means of selecting candidates, as a forum for party propaganda, and as a method of enlarging the young party's skeletal organization. Later, on the national level, the nominating convention would serve as a practical tool for the Antis, because they did not have enough delegates in Congress or most of the state legislatures to make a valid presidential nomination through the congressional caucus or by legislative methods.[12]

The convention system had a strong advocate in Thurlow Weed, who had considerable experience with such gatherings prior to his association with Antimasonry, having organized town meetings and county conventions for the People's party in 1823-1834. No man exerted as great and continuous an influence on Antimasonry and did more to make it a working political instrument than Weed, the "Wizard of Lobby." Born in 1797 of a poor family in Greene County, New York, and a printer and journalist by trade, Weed became an editorial writer for the *Rochester Telegraph,* rising to the position of editor in 1824 and part owner by 1825. A semiweekly until 1827, the *Telegraph* was pro-Clinton and pro-canal. A 500-vote majority sent Weed to the forty-eighth session of the New York General Assembly on the People's ticket in 1824, and he was elected again in 1829 as an Antimason, each time serving the prescribed one-year term. The two brief sojourns in the New York assembly seemed to satisfy whatever desire Weed might have had for public office. Thereafter he preferred to assume the role of power broker and behind-the-scenes manipulator, first in the Antimasonic party and later in the Whig and Republican organizations. In the autumn of 1826, Weed initially paid little attention to the Morgan abduction, using it merely as an occasion to make some sarcastic remarks about Masonry's exclusion of women—his reason, he said, for avoiding the "mystic tie." He evidently was offered an opportunity to publish Morgan's *Illustrations* but declined because his partner, Robert Martin, was a Mason. This indifference to the "excitement" was reflected in the editorial pages of the *Telegraph,* which expanded to a daily edition in 1827. Practical considerations were involved in Weed's decisions, of course, for when he did become an active participant in Antimasonry, the *Telegraph*'s subscription list decreased noticeably.[13]

Weed became interested in Antimasonry early in 1827, when he joined a committee to raise funds for the Morgan investigation. Traveling with a group to Lewiston, he became convinced that Morgan had been murdered and that the Masonic order must disavow the crime and help bring the guilty parties to justice. In addition he realized that the time was propitious for the creation of a new anti-Van Buren, anti-Jackson party. Forced by a boycott of local Masonic subscribers and advertisers to sell his interest in the *Telegraph,* Weed, after unsuccessfully attempting to find work in Utica and Troy, returned to Rochester and established the *Anti-Masonic Enquirer,* which commenced publication on February 2, 1828.[14]

New York Antimasonry transformed itself from a moral crusade to a political party during 1827 through a series of town meetings and conventions. At a gathering in Seneca in late January, those attending resolved not to vote for any Mason on the town, county, or state level. A number of committees elected on the local level between September 1826 and January 1827 to investigate the Morgan affair assembled in February at Lewiston, site of a Masonic gathering that allegedly had plotted Morgan's death. Many future Antimasonic leaders were present, including Backus and Frederick Whittlesey. Members of seven committees met for four days, and their principal accomplishment was the appointment of a central correspondence committee to coordinate all future Morgan investigations. The central committee, afterward known as the "Lewiston Committee" or "Rochester Morgan Committee," consisted of Weed, Whittlesey, Backus, and Samuel Works, all Rochester business and professional men, and it quickly became the driving force of Antimasonry in western New York. This body then memorialized the New York legislature, giving the facts about Morgan's abduction, explaining the difficulties of apprehending the guilty parties, asking that the kidnapping laws be strengthened, and requesting appointment of a special agent, unsympathetic to Masonic interests, to conduct the prosecutions and trials. The committee also organized the Monroe County convention at Rochester and meetings in all of the counties of the Eighth Senatorial District.[15]

In September and October 1827, nominating conventions met throughout western New York to select candidates for the legislature. The desire to "root out a privileged class" and to win elections was rapidly displacing concern for punishment of the Morgan abductors among New York Antis. By autumn, Antimasonry had clearly attracted an uneasy coalition of political pragmatists and moralistic idealists. For the next fifteen years, disagreements about its purpose would plague the Antimasonic movement everywhere and would ultimately play a major role in its disintegration. The idealists wished to use Antimasonry as a means of remaking society by protecting equal rights and opportunities. Some also favored limited political action, hoping to see the Antimasonic party disbanded after it had obliterated Masonry. In contrast were the pragmatic politicians like Weed and Granger, interested primarily in establishing a permanent political organization to elect candidates and to distribute the spoils of office. This latter group had no qualms about forming alliances with other parties (which, of course, contained many Masons) in order to achieve a victory, whether it consisted in the destruction of secret societies or in the more attractive alternative of electing public officials.[16]

As the 1827 elections approached, it became evident that in the Burned-over District the Adams-Clay party was abandoning the anti-Regency field to the Antimasons. In Monroe County, Weed and his friends promoted a "Republican Anti-Masonic" ticket for the legislature, also called the "People's" ticket. In the midst of the controversy surrounding the "Morgan-Monroe corpse," the Antis did reasonably well, electing fifteen men to the assembly, as compared with ninety-four Regency delegates, twelve Adams men, and four "friends of Jackson." Not a single Anti state senatorial candidate achieved victory, however, even in the Eighth District, hotbed of the crusade. The Antimasons, of course, carried Genesee County, soon to be known as the "citadel of political Antimasonry," where between 1827 and 1832 they polled an average of 69 percent of the vote. Anti leaders had reason to be encouraged about the future of their party.[17]

The year 1828 witnessed a series of Antimasonic conventions, mostly political in nature, that gave the embryonic party substance and structure. The first, however, was the aforementioned and relatively nonpolitical gathering of seceding Masons held at LeRoy on February 19-20, where twelve western counties were represented. The delegates made no nominations, agreed to hold a genuine statewide meeting at Utica in August, declared Morgan's *Illustrations* to be an accurate account of the first three Masonic degrees, drafted plans to publish information about the higher degrees of Masonry, and prepared a memorial to Congress requesting an investigation into the use that Masons had made of abandoned Fort Niagara during the Morgan abduction. Antimasonic Congressman Albert H. Tracy of New York's Twenty-Ninth Congressional District presented this memorial to the House of Representatives in May 1828. After it had been read for purposes of "information," members of the House argued about the proper course of action. The House finally adopted the proposal, 143 to 70, of Democrat and future President James Buchanan of

Pennsylvania, who moved to refer the petition to President John Quincy Adams for consideration. It was so referred and was quickly forgotten. This is the only recorded instance of discussion by the federal Congress of any subject dealing with Antimasonry during the years 1826-1843.[18]

Another convention, held at LeRoy on July 4-5, marked the zenith of evangelical, religious Antimasonry, for within a month the politicians had assumed almost complete control of the crusade. Southwick became chairman of this convention, which made its most notable contribution in the form of a "Declaration of Independence from the Masonic Institution," which was signed by 103 seceding Masons and indicated the number and type of Masonic degrees each had taken. The declaration asserted that Freemasonry was "opposed to the genius and design of this government, the spirit and precepts of our holy religion, and the welfare of society generally." The delegates, evidently dissatisfied with Weed's leadership and friendship with the Adams hierarchy, resolved that any campaigning by Antimasons for the presidency was "entirely disconnected with Antimasonry." The *Albany Argus,* a hostile pro-Regency mouthpiece, declared that failure of this convention to name a gubernatorial candidate had been the object of one of Weed's schemes, that he had intended to give the Adams forces an opportunity to nominate someone suitable to both parties who would later be endorsed by another Antimasonic gathering.[19]

The Adams forces refused to coalesce with the Antis and pushed back the time of their meeting, holding their state convention at Utica two weeks before the Antis and nominating Judge Smith Thompson (not a Mason) for governor and Francis Granger, now in part associated with Antimasonry, for lieutenant governor. Weed was present for this meeting, but not, of course, as a delegate. To Antimasonic purists this slate of pro-Adams candidates was a ruse intended to forestall their own separate nominations. The pro-Regency Democrats selected U.S. Senator Van Buren for governor and for lieutenant governor named Judge Enos T. Throop, who had recently sentenced the Morgan abductors but mildly disapproved of Antimasonry.[20]

New York Antimasons next met in convention at the Baptist church in Utica on August 4, 1828, and adopted a course of action that established Antimasonry as a separate anti-Jackson political entity on the state level for some five years. Meeting in the same town as the recent Adams convention, this gathering was characterized by an atmosphere "distinctly unreligious and decidedly socio-political." The Utica representatives, refusing to compromise and to accept the

Adams party ticket, nominated Granger, a thirty-six-year-old state
assemblyman from Canandaigua, Ontario County, for governor and
John Crary, a state senator from Washington County, for lieutenant
governor. The choice of Granger for governor was intended to show
that the former Clintonian's principal loyalty was to Antimasonry
and not to the Adams party, which had given him only second place
on its ticket. Granger, the son of Gideon Granger of Connecticut,
postmaster general under Presidents Thomas Jefferson and James
Madison, had become an advocate of Antimasonry while serving in
the General Assembly, but he nevertheless retained intimate ties with
the friends of Adams. A perplexed Francis Granger took more than
three weeks to make up his mind but finally rejected the Antimasonic
offer and accepted the Adams party's nomination. His decision was
not widely known until the second week in September. Among Antimasons, Granger was quickly, albeit temporarily, transformed from
a favorite into a traitor.[21]

Bereft of a gubernatorial candidate, New York Antimasons quickly
held another convention at LeRoy on September 7, nominating
Southwick and reaffirming Crary's selection for lieutenant governor.
Southwick, a recent convert (1827) to both Christianity and Antimasonry, had achieved some notoriety, if not fame, as an eccentric
journalist, politician, orator, author, and seceding Mason. Leader of
the Antimasonic religious enthusiasts, he represented the transition to
political methodology. In his younger days he had joined the Masonic
lodge, primarily for material gain, but he broke with his brethren in
Albany in 1813 over their refusal to aid him during a time of financial
exigency. By 1828 Southwick was busy editing the *Albany National
Observer,* then the premier state journal of Antimasonry. For a short
time the *Observer* became the major publisher of Antimasonic
events.[22]

As Antimasonry's first gubernatorial candidate in any state, Southwick proved to be an embarrassment and a disaster, especially to
political realists like Weed. Whittlesey later described Southwick as
being "at all times, vain and egotistical in his claims to personal
consequences, visionary and unsound in his political views, and unsta-
ble and wavering in his political course." The basis of Southwick's
1828 campaign was a proposal to amend the state constitution to
prohibit any member of a secret society from holding public office or
serving on a jury. Hampered by a lack of funds, he spent most of his
time in the Burned-over District, where he ultimately carried six
counties. He was also hurt by the open hostility and opposition of
Weed and his friends, who seemed willing to endorse anyone but

Southwick. Weed studiously avoided any reference to Southwick's candidacy in his *Anti-Masonic Enquirer* until September 30, when he declared that if, "under these multiplied difficulties," Antimasons still wished to vote for Southwick, "though our convictions of duty will compel us to withhold our own from him, we shall by no means impugn their motives." Finally, on October 7, Weed grudgingly placed Southwick's name in the *Enquirer* at the head of the Antimasonic ticket, convinced that a majority of Monroe County Antis were going to vote for him anyway. Southwick's purist supporters now condemned Weed for his traitorous course and for espousing the cause of Adamsite Smith Thompson, but to no avail. By November, Weed was wagering $500 that Thompson would lose to Van Buren because of the independent Antimasonic ticket.[23]

In the gubernatorial contest, division of the anti-Regency forces into the Adams and Antimasonic parties and the subsequent splitting of the anti-Regency vote produced success for Van Buren, who achieved election as a minority governor with only a plurality of the vote. In this contest Van Buren received approximately 136,795 votes; Thompson, 106,415; and Southwick, 33,335 (12 percent). The "Little Magician" thus achieved victory with about 3,000 popular votes fewer than the combined totals of Thompson and Southwick. The Antimasons did better in the legislative races, electing four state senators and seventeen assemblymen and emerging as a force in the legislature.[24]

Weed was successful in getting two of his "henchmen" elected to the assembly, men who would play a substantial political role in years to come on both the state and national levels. One was Philo C. Fuller, a twenty-three-year-old law clerk when he first met Weed. Fuller would serve in the assembly (1829-1830), the New York Senate (1831-1832), and later as a Whig in the federal House of Representatives (1833-1836). Another friend of Weed who gained election as an Antimason (representing Erie County) was Millard Fillmore, whom Weed had first met in 1828 at an Adams convention in Buffalo. During his three years in the assembly, Fillmore was responsible for helping abolish the law that provided for imprisonment of debtors. Elected as an Antimason to the U.S. House of Representatives in 1832 and subsequently serving in that body for eight years, he became associated with the Whigs in 1834.[25]

New York Antimasons took little part in the presidential election of 1828 apart from generally maintaining the fragile alliance forged by Weed, who acted as Adam's unofficial campaign manager in western New York. Antimasons generally supported the president because he was not a Mason and because they agreed with his economic policies; conversely, they opposed Andrew Jackson for his fraternal affiliation. "Old Hickory" was an active Mason, having served as grand master of the Grand Lodge of Tennessee, 1822-1824, and Antimasonic leaders attempted to make the voters aware of this fact. In Cayuga County, William H. Seward, still an Adams man but soon to make the transition to Antimasonry, assisted eager but inept local Antis with drafts of resolutions, addresses, and speeches. Seward later remarked that the coalition, "as all coalitions must be, was covered during the preparatory stage with the veil of secrecy."[26]

The presidential race, which resulted in a heavy Jackson majority in the national tally of electoral votes, was closer in New York, where the voting was now done by congressional district, with two electors being chosen at large. Jackson received twenty of the Empire State's thirty-six votes (including the two at-large); Adams had the remaining sixteen. The popular tabulation found the two contenders only some 8,000 votes apart, Jackson having received 139,412 and Adams 131,-563. Jackson's victory brought hopeless defeat to the Adams forces but increased confidence and vigor to the Antimasons. The future, nevertheless, was questionable, even for the Antimasons, for as pleased as Weed might be about welding a coalition of Antimasons and the followers of Adams and Clinton, the alliance had existed for the presidential race only and even then was a disaster. It had proven impossible for the Wizard to persuade the two parties to agree to a single gubernatorial ticket, largely because of the opposition of pro-Adams Masons, strong in the eastern and southern counties of New York, but also because of the opposition of the pro-Southwick Antimasonic purists. Had the two parties been able to unite in this contest, Van Buren might have lost, and the Regency's ten-year domination of the governor's office would have been prevented or delayed. Seward, now seeing no future for the Adams forces and about ready to "jump," found Antimasonry "spirited and vigorous;" nevertheless, he had grave doubts about the prospects for a party that had arisen from a single issue, possessed a character more social than political, and still had as its major goal the vindication of the laws. The little red-headed attorney from Auburn wondered if Antimasonry "could succeed to the position of one of the two great contending parties."[27]

1829 saw New York Antimasons basking in the relative success of the 1828 election and achieving the official status of a truly separate political party, while the Adams organization continued to decline. Weed, as one of the five members of the central committee, took a leading part in summoning and directing the Antimasonic state convention that met at the capitol in Albany on February 19, with forty-two county delegations in attendance. To outsiders there appeared to have been a reconciliation between the purists and the pragmatists; Southwick gave the keynote address, but the most active participants were Weed and his friends Whittlesey, Tracy, Seward, Myron Holley, and Henry Dana Ward. Weed gave the principal speech, presenting a "highly selective history of the Antimasonic movement," paying special attention to political victories, and declaring that the one way in which public opinion could be fully applied to Freemasonry was through the ballot box. Directed by the central committee, this convention passed two vital resolutions, one disavowing all connections with existing political parties, the other calling for a national Antimasonic convention, the exact purpose of which was not revealed at this time. Although Timothy Fitch of Batavia proposed the national convention resolution, it is uncertain who first entertained the idea, and Weed never claimed the honor. The delegates appointed a five-man committee, chaired by Granger, to select the time and place for the meeting. Before this Albany convention adjourned, the Granger committee had chosen Philadelphia as the site and September 11, 1830, as the date. The committee also determined that the number of delegates a state could send to Philadelphia would be equivalent to its number of senators and representatives in Congress.[28]

A few days after the convention adjourned, the *Argus* attacked it in an editorial that accused the "profligate Weed" of having transformed Antimasonry into a political movement composed of neo-Federalists, who had as their aim the overthrow of the Jackson party. Editor Edwin Croswell declared that this true goal of the political Antis had nothing to do with the abduction of Morgan, with the principles and practices of Masonry, "nor with the real intentions of antimasonry." In addition to the expected diatribe from the *Argus*, Weed began to receive protests from the Antimasonic purists, who objected to the prostitution and transformation of the Blessed Spirit into a party dedicated more to the ruination of Van Buren and Jackson than to the destruction of Masonry. Even Fuller reminded Weed that Antimasons should stress increasing their representation in the New York General Assembly before attempting a venture in presidential politics. "Like other people, we are a little prone to whoop before we are out of the woods."[29]

New York Antis spent the remainder of 1829 cooperating with Adams's supporters in the assembly on almost every issue and preparing for the legislative contests in the autumn. In this election, Weed again won a term to the assembly by a narrow margin. This was merely part of his general plan of establishing a new Antimasonic

journal at Albany. The Antis also elected the devious Tracy as senator
from the Eighth District by a majority of 8,000 votes, carried fifteen
western counties, and polled a record total of 67,000 votes. Although
the election had generally favored the Jacksonians, Antimasonry had
done well. In Rochester, the *Anti-Masonic Enquirer* trumpeted that
"the fairest, most fertile, enterprising, enlightened and patriotic portion of our state has been redeemed from the thralldom of Freemasonry. . . . The whole section of the state in which Freemasonry
trampled upon the laws, invaded personal liberty, and sacrificed human life, has wiped out the foul stain. Henceforth Free Masonry had
no hiding place west of Cayuga Lake." As would soon be realized, it
was not only Masonry that lacked a hiding place in the Burned-over
District but Jacksonianism as well.[30]

# 4. New York, 1830-1835

William Henry Seward finally left the Adams party and became an active Antimason in 1830 because he agreed with Antimasonic principles and had nowhere else to go politically. The Auburn attorney attended his first Antimasonic state convention at Albany in 1829 and in January 1830 addressed a convention in his native Cayuga County, where he denounced Masonry as a "secret government" that made its own laws and then enforced them, even invoking the death penalty.

Later that year, Seward represented New York as a delegate to the first national Antimasonic convention at Philadelphia. On his way he stopped at Albany and visited with Thurlow Weed, who indicated that there was support for Seward as a senatorial candidate for the six-county Seventh District. Upon returning from the convention, Seward learned he had been nominated for that senate seat, long held by the Regency, and he ultimately achieved election by a 2,000-vote margin. Seward's strength among the workingmen of his district ultimately influenced the direction of Antimasonry on the state level. His terms in the senate, 1831–1835, reflected his interest in the "mechanics" with strong support of bills to reform the state militia system and to abolish imprisonment for debt. Interestingly, few of his published legislative speeches that have survived touch on Antimasonry or Masonry.[1]

New York Antimasons held their first convention of 1830 at Albany on February 25. In addition to preparing a memorial charging the Grand Lodge of New York with furnishing funds to help the Morgan conspirators, the delegates selected thirty-six representatives to attend the Philadelphia convention, including Tracy, Whittlesey, Granger, Seward, and Maynard, and they sounded the death knell for Southwick's *Observer* by authorizing establishment of a new journal at Albany.[2]

During most of 1829, Weed had found himself under constant pressure to leave Rochester and to come to the state capital and edit a paper that would be the official spokesman of New York's Antimasonic party. Aided by Whittlesey, Seward, and others, he overcame early doubts and managed to raise $2,500, mainly in small amounts.

With this meager financial support, he moved to Albany and commenced publication of the *Albany Evening Journal* in the spring of 1830. Weed's premier editorial contained a pledge of his devotion to constitutional liberty and "Republican principles," a portent of events to come, which preceded a rather mild attack on the "barren and bald" institution of Freemasonry.[3]

The *Journal* became Weed's principal means of broadening the appeal and constituency of the Antimasonic party, an action that he considered vital in terms of political survival and success. His pragmatic friends in the party agreed with this approach. As Whittlesey commented, "We cannot conceal from ourselves that Antimasony is not alone powerful enough to triumph, but appreciate, with all the other materials of opposition to the present administration, it will succeed—and Antimasonry will receive . . . the credit of the victory." He also warned Weed to be moderate in his *Journal* editorials, reminding the editor that a large number of his readers were not yet "thoroughly Anti-Masonic," cleverly adding that they must be inducted into Antimasonry "by degrees." Weed was quite willing to follow this advice, and through his service in the assembly as well as in his editorials, he, like Seward, courted the labor vote, advocating reform of the militia system, abolishing imprisonment for debt, and preventing the seizure of worker's tools for nonpayment of debt. He also favored an extension of New York's canal system, especially in the Chanango Valley but opposed the Regency's efforts to increase canal tolls.[4]

The state convention at Utica in August 1830 represented the Antimasonic party's final break with the religious crusade of the past three years. Seward made this point extremely clear: "We are impelled in the undertaking to abolish Freemasonry not by fiery excitement, or fanatical zeal, but by a deep sense of our responsibilities to perpetuate this government." The delegates, indicating the party's ever-increasing rapprochement with the Adamsites, now known as National Republicans, adopted a platform fully in accord with "National" principles and with the "American system" of Henry Clay. The Antimasonic platform attacked the Regency for its extravagance, canal policy, and attempts to reduce the tax rate of state chartered banks, but the Antis expressed support for a protective tariff and for federally financed internal improvements.[5]

The efforts of Seward, Weed, and others to woo the workingmen's vote, particularly in New York City, received recognition in the Utica convention's choice for lieutenant governor. Although Granger was once again the party's gubernatorial nominee, far more interest centered upon the selection of Samuel Stevens for the second position on the ticket. Stevens was a young, talented attorney and alderman from the "City" previously associated with the Clay faction of the Workingmen's party, but he had no previous identification with Antimasonry. The Southwick purists attempted to make a separate nomination but failed. It was Seward's task to persuade the delegates to support Stevens over John Crary, Anti candidate for lieutenant governor in 1829, whom the zealots wished to nominate as "an act of justice and . . . loyalty to the cause." This rout of the Southwick forces produced a bitter postconvention letter from Crary, who asserted that Stevens was not an Antimason and urged that the party purge itself by breaking ties with individuals who had affiliated with Antimasonry from unworthy motives. Weed refuted Crary's charges in the *Journal,* urging support of the Granger-Stevens slate, made "by men who had the cause, the whole cause, and nothing but the cause, in view." The casual observer of this squabble, nevertheless, cynically might have wondered, "Which cause?"[6]

The nomination of Stevens for lieutenant governor represented the climax of negotiations between the Antimasons and one faction of the Workingmen's party in New York City—negotiations that began in 1829 and produced a coalition that lasted into 1831. Reflections of this alliance were seen in Antimasonic support in 1830–1831 of worker-oriented bills in the legislature to abolish imprisonment for debt for all but fraudulent debtors and to reform the state's militia system. The Workingmen's party itself was of recent origin, having organized in April 1829, to nominate candidates for the assembly and the senate —all to represent New York City. One of the "Workie" assembly nominees, Dr. Cornelius Blatchley, had recently served as secretary of the (state) Antimasonic general committee. Obviously, pragmatic Antimasonic leaders like Weed were interested in attracting a core of 6,000 voters into their camp, especially since the Workies were concentrated in the area of New York Antimasonry's greatest weakness —the city, where the Antis had polled only 2 percent of the vote in 1829.[7]

Oddly enough, the new Workingmen's party had attracted a number of former Adams supporters, some drawn by Workie programs such as the ten-hour day; others, however, clearly hoped to use this new party as an "effective counterpoise" to the pro-Jackson Tammany organization. Among the latter group was Noah Cook, a commission merchant and former delegate to the 1828 Adams state convention. In 1830 the Cook faction of the Workies gave positive endorsement to the Antimasonic Granger-Stevens ticket. Stevens himself was pleased with the nomination, although he privately admitted to Weed that not all members of the Workingmen's organization favored his nomination by the Antimasons.[8]

Serious attacks on the coalition came from the faction of the Workingmen's party that was led by George Henry Evans and Thomas Skidmore and were presented by the *Working Man's Advocate*. This group eventually nominated Ezekial Williams, a leather manufacturer from Auburn, for governor and eight candidates for Congress. The *Advocate* used its pages to attack the Workie faction led by Cook and his paper, the *Reformer,* in addition to venting rage against Antimasonry as being a "CHURCH AND STATE party." This accusation stemmed from efforts by certain Antis to promote a legal observance of the Sabbath, the closing of post offices on Sunday, and stopping movement of the mails on that day. Asserting that Antimasonry was merely a "cover" for this church-state faction, the *Advocate* declared that those "very men" who had joined the Antimasonic party and had decried all secret societies were *"themselves members of the most dangerous Secret Society that ever existed in this Republic."*[9]

In January 1830 Whittlesey wrote to Weed that the entire future of the Antimasonic party, throughout the nation as well as in New York, depended on the results of that year's gubernatorial election. It was an unusual race in the sense that Antimasonry was the only official anti-Regency party, the National Republicans having decided not to name candidates for governor and lieutenant governor, instead giving their tacit support to the Granger-Stevens ticket. The Jackson party, now gradually assuming the name of "Democrats," had nominated Acting Governor Enos Throop. Although Granger seemed confident about his election, Weed became concerned about mounting Masonic opposition to the Antimasonic ticket and apathy among the party faithful. The editor was also quite angry with Granger for having accepted the presidency of the national Antimasonic convention at Philadelphia in September, because Granger would be "appearing in too bold an Antimasonic role" and might alienate some 2,000–3,000 voters. Granger's prominent position in the convention also interfered with Weed's calculated efforts to appeal to all voters; Weed was attempting to convince voters outside the Anti fold that a vote for Granger was a ballot not just for Antimasonry but also for equal rights. On October 30 the *Journal* published a paraphrase of the Declaration of Independence, advocating not only freedom from the oppression of Masonry but from "all allegiance to the ALBANY REGENCY."[10]

The gubernatorial contest ended with a disappointing defeat for Granger, who lost to Throop, 120,667 to 128,947. The election was decided in the heavily pro-Clay counties of eastern New York, where many National Republicans, especially those belonging to the Masonic lodge, crossed party lines and voted for Throop. Ten eastern counties that Thompson and Granger had carried in 1828 (Rensselaer, Columbia, Albany, Saratoga, Washington, Montgomery, Oneida, St. Lawrence, Franklin, and Essex) went for Throop in 1830. In the eastern part of the state, Granger carried only Queens County on Long Island. Most Antimasonic leaders blamed defecting "Clay Masons" for the party's defeat. On the eve of the election, the *Albany Advertiser,* organ of the National Republicans, suddenly switched its support from Granger to Throop, an action taken with the approval of party leaders in the Albany area. Weed accused the *"Royal Arch Daily Advertiser"* of selling out to the Jacksonians. He asserted that although Antimasons were friendly to Clay's American system, especially to protective tariff, "Mr. Clay's *Masonic friends* voted the Jackson ticket, and by so doing, *have politically cut his throat.*"[11]

Amid gloom over their defeat in the gubernatorial race, Antimasons could take some comfort in the realization that they had carried three of the nine senate seats elected in 1830 and, together with the National Republicans, had elected 33 of 128 members of the assembly, the Antimasons claiming all but 6. Antimasonic newspapers, nevertheless, carefully ignored the news that Rochester, one of the citadels of the Blessed Spirit in the Genesee country and center of Weed's organization, had voted Democratic, showing how rapidly the Antimasonic fever could subside, especially in an urban environment. The election showed the inherent weakness of the Antimasonic party in New York, that is, the difficulty of uniting divergent elements under the banner of Antimasonry.[12]

In 1831 Antimasonic zealots won a temporary victory over the Weed clique at the party's state convention at Albany. Meeting in mid-February, the purists, through Poughkeepsie delegate and editor John Vethatke, immediately urged adoption of a resolution that stated: "We renew our league and covenant ... [and] we will not support any Mason for office, under any circumstances whatsoever who adheres to Masonic obligations." Vethatke also accused the Weed leadership of openly supporting Masons for office. Although they never openly said so at this convention, the purists were undoubtedly looking ahead to the next national convention, to be held at Baltimore, where a presidential nomination would be made. It was no secret among Antimasons that Weed was supporting Henry Clay, a major contender for the National Republican nomination and notable foe of Jackson but, like his arch-enemy, a Mason and past grand master (of Kentucky). The Vethatke resolution received strenuous opposition from some of Clay's Antimasonic followers at the Albany convention and was ultimately referred to a committee, from which it emerged as modified by Philo C. Fuller. It asserted "that inasmuch as very erroneous sentiments respecting the views of the Antimasonic party have been industriously circulated by its enemies, we do not support any man for office under the state or General Government who at the time of his nomination is an adhering Mason." The resolution, as passed, did not technically apply to Clay, who had demitted (resigned) from his Kentucky lodge some years before.[13]

The influence of the Albany convention upon Antimasons in the legislature was evident in the "Address to the People," written by Seward. In addition to giving his party full credit for passage of a statute outlawing imprisonment for nonpayment of debt and blaming the Regency for trying to block it, Seward used this opportunity to restate the opposition of the Antimasons "to all privileged orders, aristocracies and secret societies." Objecting to recent legislative action allowing the prosecution of Morgan's "murderers and kidnappers" to expire, he reminded his followers that almost all of the "high votaries" of the Masonic institution belonged to the Jackson party and remained ardent opponents of Antimasonry. He declared that Antimasons were called "intolerant" for "seeking to destroy an institution which will not tolerate any inquiry into its objects, its means or its obligations." For refusing to vote for Masons, Antis were called "proscriptive," and for insistence upon equal rights and privileges, "we are charged with denying to our fellow-citizens equal rights." Regardless of these strong words, Antimasons in the legislature lacked sufficient strength to secure the passage of laws outlawing the administration of Masonic oaths or requiring lodges to report names of members and officers, as was done later in Vermont, Massachusetts, and Rhode Island.[14]

By mid-October 1831, Seward was exulting that in the Eighth Senatorial District of western New York, there were no opposition candidates to Antimasonic nominees for any office. This halcyon situation, however, did not hold true for the remainder of the state, and Weed more accurately predicted the outcome of the legislative contests when he observed, "Nothing can be done this year in New York. The Tammany ticket will have a large majority." Although accounts vary, it appears that the Antis elected about thirty men to the assembly, the National Republicans, six, and the Jacksonians, ninety-five. The Antis carried only one senatorial race, with Seward winning again in the Seventh District, giving them seven votes in the upper chamber. This election was a disaster, particularly to optimists like Seward. He asked Weed why this "unexpected check in the advance of the 'blessed spirit' " had occurred and then, rhetorically, attributed the result to the "Clay Masons," who had voted the Jackson ticket, and to the non-Masons within that party, who had stayed home on election day. The senator concluded that the entire election was part of a National Republican plot to destroy Antimasonry.[15]

In retrospect it does seem clear that this poor showing of the New York Antis was more the result of the National's anger at the Antimasons for failing to nominate Clay for president at the 1830 Philadelphia convention or at least for failing to give the Kentuckian an endorsement, which would have unified the anti-Jackson opposition. Myron Holley admitted that the Jacksonians were more ambitious and better organized than the Antis, who had delayed in making nominations and had counted on the support of the "few Clay men among us . . . [who] were all against us in effect." In addition, votes were lost from the Antimasonic purists, who believed "that Mr. Wirt is not an antimason but a candidate selected from motives too conciliatory." In reevaluating the situation with reference to New York and to the forthcoming presidential election in 1832, Seward reluctantly predicted that "under the circumstances there can be no doubt of the success of General Jackson." Although few Antimasons would openly admit it, by the end of 1831, Morgan's abduction and Masonry's continued existence had ceased to be crucial, volatile issues in the Empire State, and consequently the Antimasonic party was rapidly losing its crusading image and was becoming, instead, primarily an anti-Jackson, anti-Regency organization. Unfortunately that role was already being performed, albeit poorly, by the National Republicans.[16]

In 1832 Weed continued his efforts to widen the appeal of Antimasonry, attempting to transform it from a crusade against secret societies into a broadly based anti-Van Buren, anti-Jackson party. He refused to publish resolutions in the *Journal* of a Pennsylvania Antimasonic convention, gave only limited encouragement to the rural Antimasonic press in New York, and worked out an arrangement with National Republican leaders in which their support for the Antimasonic gubernatorial candidate would be exchanged for assistance to Clay in the presidential contest. Several anonymous Anti leaders, one of them probably Weed, now warned Seward to "downplay"

Antimasonry in composing his 1832 address of the Antimasonic legislators and to deal only with the "conduct and doings" of the General
Assembly. Another told him to confine himself solely to Antimasonic
matters. Seward decided to compromise, using most of the address to
castigate the Democrats for their extravagance and for their indifference to progress and reform; only at the end did he make the requisite
charges against Masonry. These continuous efforts to broaden Antimasonry brought both Weed and Seward hostile retorts. Purist
George Boughton told Weed to pay a little more attention to the cause
of Antimasonry, for to stress any other principle was both hopeless
and useless. Amos Phelps Granger of Syracuse urged the editor to
organize a legislative investigation against Masonry: "Charge it with
almost any thing and it can be proved. There are few things it is not
guilty of."[17]

Weed's two-year program of broadening the Antimasonic party in
New York achieved fruition at the party's state convention at Utica
in June, when the delegates approved an unpledged presidential electoral ticket, evenly divided between Antimasons and National Republicans, in return for National support of a Granger-Stevens
gubernatorial slate. The electors, if victorious, would supposedly vote
unanimously for either Wirt or Clay, whichever stood the best chance
of being elected president. Rumors concerning such a coalition had
circulated for months prior to the convention, producing the expected
statements of approval from Weed's partisans and screams of anguish
from the purists. Tracy and Spencer feared that this joint ticket would
mean abandonment of Wirt, and they insisted that an understanding
or pledge to this effect must be secured from the Nationals. Timothy
Childs, however, believed that such pledges, although possibly helpful
in Western New York, would be "hurtfull [sic]" in New York City
and the eastern counties, where the Antis anticipated heavy support
from the Nationals. By the end of May 1832, Weed could report to
Seward that matters were progressing with "entire harmony. The
path of duty and wisdom, for the Nationals is so plain, that I do not
see how they can miss it."[18]

The convention that assembled at Utica on June 21 was Antimasonic only in name, with the delegates, as orchestrated by Weed,
deciding to shift the emphasis from Masonic intrigues to the "mon-
strous pretensions" of Jacksonianism. After they had selected Tracy
as convention president, the delegates dutifully renominated Granger
and Stevens for governor and lieutenant governor. Their next task was
concurrence in the national convention's nominations of William
Wirt and Amos Ellmaker for president and vice president and selec-

tion of a prearranged electoral ticket of forty-two names evenly divided between Antimasons and National Republicans. Spencer headed the Anti segment, and James Kent the National slate. Kent was chancellor emeritus of the court of chancery and one of his party's most illustrious personages. In addition to Spencer and Kent, there were five nominees from each of the state's eight senatorial districts. Although the Antimasonic inner circle, headed by Weed, knew that in reality the electoral ticket was pledged to Clay, as Wirt had little chance of winning the presidency, nevertheless the Wizard of the Lobby could assert in the *Journal* that there were "spontaneous" demonstrations of public sentiment for the joint slate throughout New York. Years later Weed blandly observed, "We aimed, in the selection of candidates, to secure the vote of all who were opposed to the reelection of General Jackson." When, during the next month, the National Republicans ratified the Granger-Stevens nomination and the "unpledged" joint electoral ticket, the Jacksonians began referring to the resulting amalgam as the "Siamese Twin" party.[19]

The joint ticket and unofficial coalition with the Nationals in the gubernatorial race produced screams of anguish from Antimasonic zealots. One wrote to Weed, "It is said you have made dreadful havoc with our once popular cause—How is this?" Negative comments from out-of-state Antimasons also reached Weed, one of the nastiest coming from Vermont radical Edward D. Barber, who asked whether Antimasonry in New York was "a *humbug.*" Barber declared that the course of Antimasonry in the Empire State and in the pages of the *Journal* had done much to undermine the "complete triumph" of the party in Vermont. The culmination of this anti-coalition sentiment came in September with the "Appeal of the Antimasons of Columbia County," in which seven Antimasons denounced the coalition and asked the unpledged electoral nominees to reveal for whom they would vote. They declared that the principles of Antimasonry had been "grossly and shamelessly abandoned." Croswell sarcastically observed in mid-October that it had been some three months since Weed had attacked Masonry in the *Journal.* "Has Whiskercando formed a league with the old hag?" he inquired. This accusation and others prompted Weed to retort that if the editor of the *Argus* had such a horror of all coalitions, what must he think of the alliance between Van Buren and Morgan's publisher, David C. Miller, "by which it was expected to blow old Genesee high."[20]

In presenting a united front on issues other than Masonry, the Antimasons had no problem in coordinating policy statements with the Nationals, at least on the county level. These platforms, after the

usual resolutions attacking Masonry, condemned the doctrine of nullification and attacked Jackson for failing to execute decisions of the
Supreme Court and for removing federal deposits from the Bank of
the United States. They then advocated a protective tariff, federally
funded internal improvements, and continuation of a sound national
currency through rechartering of the Bank. Seward naively believed
that Antimasonic agitation of Jackson's veto of the Bank rechartering
bill would aid the party's cause in the election. Throughout the summer and early autumn, he remained enthusiastic about the coalition's
prospects, as did gubernatorial candidate Granger, who was now
describing Clay's supporters as "sincere, candid and reasonable," for
the two believed that the only way to save the nation was by preventing the Democrats from carrying New York.[21]

Unfortunately, both Antis and Nationals found it difficult to "ar-
range" compatible nominations on the local level. To assist in this
effort, Weed, representing the Antimasons, and Matthew L. Davis (a
great friend of the aging Aaron Burr), representing the National
Republicans, attended numerous district and county conventions.
One example of the resulting cooperation occurred in the Fourth
Senatorial District, where, after much wrangling, both parties were
pressured into nominating, "unknowingly," Louis Hasbrouck of St.
Lawrence, a National Republican but not a Mason. Hasbrouck received the support of both parties and was elected senator. After
attending several conventions, Davis exulted to Weed that he had
found nothing but the "best feelings and a spirit of compromise." He
predicted the result would be *"victory."* As election day approached
Weed asserted that the Antimasonic cause was "that of the Laws and
the Constitution. It unites, in its support, the INTELLIGENT and
the PATRIOTIC, and is opposed by the PROFLIGATE and the
MERCENARY." Amid such positive statements and numerous public assurances of victory, Granger nervously observed to Weed some
two weeks before the election, "I fear the old Jackson feeling of '28
when the electors get to the polls."[22]

Granger's worst fears were realized when he ran some 10,000 votes
behind the Democratic candidate, U.S. senator William L. Marcy, in
an election spread over three days. It was even a more decisive rout
than that of 1830. As a small consolation, Granger did carry three
counties, Washington, Essex, and Franklin, which he had lost in 1830
but had won in 1828 as the Adams party candidate for lieutenant
governor. He also gained two counties that had never before voted for
him, Madison and Cortland, but lost six that he had won in 1830—
Chenango, Cayuga, Seneca, Tompkins, Steuben, and Wayne. The

popular totals were: Granger, 156,672; Marcy, 166,410. Marcy was therefore elected to the first of what became three consecutive terms. The presidential phase of this election, in which 84 percent of the voters participated, was even more discouraging for the Antimasons. Their coalition ticket lost to the Jackson-Van Buren slate by a margin of some 13,000 votes, 154,896 to 168,497. The anti-Jackson slate carried eighteen counties, with its greatest majorities in Erie, Genesee, and Washington. As the Democratic victory in both the gubernatorial and presidential races became increasingly apparent, the *Argus* trumpeted: "The fraud, which represented an electoral ticket in one part of the state as for Wirt and *Anti-masonry,* and in another for Clay and Masonry, stands exposed by the honest suffrages of an intelligent Democracy, and the remembrance of it is wormwood and disgrace to its projectors and abettors."[23]

As more time elapsed from news of the disaster, opinions of New York's Antimasonic pragmatists tended to harden concerning the party's future, for most blamed the defeat, as in the gubernatorial race of 1830, on defections of the Clay Masons. George W. Patterson, assemblyman from Livingston County, countered that the election was lost by those Antimasonic voters who stayed home. He declared that Antimasons must look to the future and must prevent Van Buren's election as president in 1836, either "by continuing under the name of antimasonry or by sailing under a different flag." Seward was in a state of despair but recovered sufficiently to write a "manifesto" for the party, which was published in the *Journal* on November 21, 1832. In this document, he attributed defeat to insufficient organization, infighting among coalition politicians, and an underestimation of the strength of Jacksonianism and the "Hero's" military prestige throughout the nation and especially in New York. He insisted that formation of the coalition ticket and support of Wirt for president had not resulted in the yielding of an inch of Antimasonic ground, although a few Anti malcontents might have voted for Jackson from fear that the coalition electors would ultimately support Clay. Although Antimasonic strength in the legislature had diminished, the party elected eight men to the U.S. House of Representatives. Seward urged Antimasons not to give up but to continue the fight. "And when we consider the whirlwind of popular commotion, in which our small bark was put to sea, we have no reason to be grieved for the slight damage she has sustained." He exhorted Antimasons to remember that they must inculcate principles and extend their organization until all secret societies had been suppressed.[24]

As 1832 came to a close, it was increasingly clear to political savants that Weed and Seward had decided to abandon Antimasonry as a separate political movement and to forge a new organization. Weed was not only tired of Antimasonry as a distinct entity but weary with the "Nationals" as well, especially with their "intolerable burden" of support for the Bank of the United States. Weed, Granger, and Seward had realized that Antimasonry might serve some purpose beyond "discrediting a ritual." Seward admitted that by December 1832 he had come to believe that Antimasonry could not be called upon again to challenge the political opposition in either the state or nation. Even Childs agreed that Antimasonry must be dropped until Freemasonry should attempt a revival. Holley, an opponent of the recent coalition ticket, predicted that the National Republicans would soon expire and that Antimasonry would become one of the two major parties, attracting many recruits from the Nationals. Urging a return to true Antimasonic principles and concentration on the total destruction of Masonry, he concluded, "I am not, in the slightest degree, for giving up the ship."[25]

Not only the National Republicans but the Antimasons as well fell apart in New York after the 1832 election. Leaders of both parties now regarded the coalition as "a union the more firmly cemented by a common defeat." Horace Clark of Sardinia, defeated for reelection to the assembly, declared that Antimasonry "has wilted like a cabbage leaf in a warm summer day—but I don't believe in giving up the ship yet. I entered it at a late hour and I mean to stick to it until the last plank sinks." One stalwart, when asked by Seward to revive Antimasonry in Cayuga County, refused, asserting that every hope for an Antimasonic victory was dead and that the general public had lost sight of the real aims of the party "in contemplating the ambitious and selfish views of its leaders." The defection of long-time politician Tracy to the Democrats in 1833, however, showed the true state of confusion within Antimasonic ranks. Tracy, who had served his Buffalo district in the U.S. House of Representatives from 1819 to 1825, had taken a seat in the New York Senate in 1829 as an Antimason, remaining until 1837. Later described by Weed, an authority on the subject, as being unsurpassed in his capacity for intrigue, Tracy as late as May 1833 urged Seward not to desert Antimasonry. During some point within the next six months, however, convinced of the futility of further Antimasonic success at the polls, Tracy transferred his allegiance to the Democrats—the result, his enemies declared, of several interviews with Vice President Martin Van Buren.[26]

During most of 1833, Weed continued to display a public front for Antimasonry while privately laying the groundwork for the new Whig party. In late May he wrote to Patterson, "Let us give a long, a strong pull for Anti-Masonry this fall." As late as August 10 he was still taunting Freemasonry on the editorial page of the *Journal,* and by November 1 he was promoting four "Antimasonic" candidates for the state senate (including Tracy) and three for the assembly. Evidently Weed considered the party too weak to hold a state convention in 1833 for the purpose of making formal nominations, even though Childs urged him to do so. Childs declared that such a convention should be assembled, either to declare Freemasonry to be "practically abandoned, and we are willing to let the institution alone; or to say that the people have refused longer to sustain political Antimasonry."[27]

Unmoved by Childs's plea, Weed did nothing, and the Democrats scored a "one-sided" victory over both the Antimasons and National Republicans in the 1833 legislative races. Of 128 members elected to the assembly, 104 were Democrats; of the remaining 24, only 8 or 9 were Antimasons. The Antis claimed one state senator, but that was Tracy, who had won reelection by a mere 165 votes. His Eighth Senatorial District, which had returned an Antimasonic (coalition) majority of 12,000 votes in 1832, returned a Jacksonian surplus of 1,000 votes in 1833. The *Argus* gloated: "This fierce spirit had run its inglorious and mad career. Good enough Morgans, and the wretched expedients of the Antimasonic leaders are no longer to the taste of the people [of the Eighth District]. . . . The Coalition of the last year was the expiring effort of a desperate party." In a more sober vein, Patterson examined the overwhelming defeat, and suggested retaining the principles of the Antimasonic party while changing the name, for a presidential election was looming in 1836, and Antimasons must join with other anti-Jackson men to defeat Van Buren. Weed replied that although many of the party faithful wished to preserve the present organization, some alteration before the next election was necessary, so that "we may change our front without changing our principles."[28]

New York Antimasons could sense the winds of political change by the spring of 1834, when Seward, in his "Address of the Minority of the Members of the Legislature of 1834," made not one reference or allusion to either Masonry or Antimasonry. Although most Antimasons seemed to accept the ongoing merger of their party into the Whig organization with "good grace," the purists were furious and continued to accuse Seward and Weed of betrayal. One of the fiercest denunciations came from Massachusetts. In his *Boston Daily Advocate,* Hallett commented on the absence of Antimasonic content in Seward's message and then accused New York Antis of accomplishing nothing. "Not a charter repealed, no laws against extra legal oaths; no investigations of an election of Masonic officers of the Grand Chapter." The editor declared that leaders in the Empire State had betrayed the cause to the enemy, while he and others in New England had given up "everything" to follow the cause.[29]

By March 1834 one zealot had complained, "Masonry still exists —why then should we spike our artillery? My voice is still for war against freemasons and their allies." Nevertheless, Antimasonry was rapidly being transformed into the new Whig party. Antimasonry in the Empire State absorbed the National Republicans to form the Whig coalition, not the opposite, as occurred in most other northeastern states. Weed, Seward, and their pragmatic allies justified such a merger on the following grounds: Masonry was virtually extinct in the state except in New York City and the Hudson River counties; the election of 1832 had demonstrated that Antimasonry was rapidly losing its hold on the public interest; and aside from the Masonic question, Antimasons and National Republicans were in general agreement on leading national issues such as the Bank and internal improvements and expressed an almost-universal hatred of Jacksonianism. During the winter of 1834, the state Antimasonic leadership met at Albany and decided to dissolve the party. When, on the local level, the Whig party formed at Rochester in the spring, among the seven Whig "founders" present were four Antimasons, including Whittlesey and Childs, two Bucktail Democrats, both Masons, and Alvah Strong, co-owner of the *Enquirer,* who acted as a peacemaker between the factions. In Rochester, as elsewhere, it was the Antimasons who dominated the new Whig organization. By the second week of April 1834, Weed was using the term "Whig" in the *Journal* with reference to the fledgling party's triumph in the New York City Common Council election. In Buffalo, as in Rochester, Antimasons controlled the new party, for "decided Antimasons" filled every committee. To outsiders, transformation of Antimasonry and National Republicanism into Whiggery seemed almost instantaneous, but Patterson justified this metamorphosis when, writing Weed in late May, he referred to a neighbor, an "early and steadfast anti-mason, [who] said to me a few days since, that he considered Jacksonianism so much more dangerous to our liberties at this time, than masonry, that he was prepared to vote for any honorable man, whether he be mason or anti-mason, for the purpose of putting down the present order of things—."[30]

Not all Antimasons had yet reconciled themselves to the new order of things. Clark declared that the Antis of his county were not prepared to become Whigs and were not ashamed of "the old name, 'ANTIMASONS.' " When the Whig party did hold its first state convention at Utica in September, the prominence of certain Antimasons, especially Weed, revealed itself in the nomination of Seward for governor. This choice was part of Weed's continuing effort to placate angry Antis, who believed that they had been sold out to Whiggery. In addition, the Auburn attorney was friendly, ambitious, and regarded as a "comer" by those who had worked with him in Antimasonic politics, including the influential Whittlesey. The Democrats renominated Gov. William L. Marcy and then tried to divide the Whigs with the charge that the "democratic Anti-Masons" had been sold out by Weed and Granger to the "Clay aristocrats." Whether this tactic was successful is uncertain, but Jacksonianism was still extremely popular with the mass of voters in the United States, including New York, and Seward lost to Marcy by more than 12,000 votes, 181,900 to 169,008. In addition, seven of the eight senatorial districts chose Democrats. Seward ran again, unsuccessfully in 1836, and then in 1838, being elected on that third attempt, with Weed's never-failing support, by approximately 10,000 votes. As expected, Hallett exulted in Seward's first (1834) loss to Marcy, asserting, "The notable project of merging Antimasonry in Whiggism has met with the fate it richly merited." Nevertheless, the Antimasonic faction within the New York Whig party could be counted on to vote faithfully and with regularity, and their continued strong showing in the western counties provided the basis of Whig victories for many years to come. In addition, the Weed-Seward wing of Whiggism remained the most progressive faction in an essentially conservative party, becoming the "Conscience Whigs" during the days of political antislavery after 1840 and emerging as the "radical core of the 'Black' Republican Party in 1856."[31]

Those historians who studied Antimasonry in New York have usually concluded that "Weed and Company" were extremely self-serving. In truth, Seward's speeches and letters prior to 1833 indicate that he was a genuine Antimason and adhered to a cause that he believed was based on the principles of democratic freedom. Weed likewise seems to have been reasonably sincere in the early years, although not as much as Seward was. In March 1835 the editor wrote to Seward concerning a young friend: "He has all the zeal we once had for Anti-Masonry. Will we ever again have our better and higher sympathies so warmly excited and so nobly directed. I fear not." Many years later, Weed declared that during the Antimasonic "excitement," he had been governed by a genuine desire to vindicate the "violated laws" of the United States and to "arrest the great power and dangerous influence of 'secret societies.' "[32]

From a practical viewpoint, and in partial defense of the motives of Weed, Seward, and Granger, it must be noted that by 1833–1834 Freemasonry had virtually ceased to exist in New York except in New York City and in the Hudson River counties. Without the passage of legislation circumscribing or outlawing the fraternity, the desired result had been achieved largely through propaganda, peer pressure, moral suasion, and the politicizing of issues. Years later a number of "horror stories" related by Masons who had lived through the Antimasonic crusade, or who knew someone who had, saw print. It is difficult for a scholar in the late twentieth century to separate fact from fantasy, for each story probably improved with every telling, particularly as those Masons who had lived through this difficult period came to enjoy the status of martyrs after Masonry's revival in the 1850s.

Masons at times were undoubtedly hooted or jeered as they walked the streets. Persuasion as well as force was used to pressure brethren to secede from the fraternity. Physicians were forced to resign in order to retain their patients, tradesmen did so to hold onto their customers, and preachers, to keep their pulpits. According to one "eyewitness," the mothers of a community in Caledonia County met and decided they would not permit their daughters to meet or to marry a Mason or a "Jack Mason" (a Masonic sympathizer). Their daughters retaliated by assembling and declaring that they would only "keep company with or marry a Mason or a Jack Mason." In the early days of the crusade, Antimasons conducted mock lodge meetings and initiations in public view, sometimes in theaters or lecture halls, sometimes on the street corners, frequently using Bernard's *Light on Masonry* as their script. In 1873, Frederick Follett, a member of the lodge and of the commandery of Knights Templar at Batavia, recalled that Antimasonry "interfered somewhat, and in some instances wholly broke up the social relations of life." Churches whose congregations became involved in controversy witnessed the excommunication of lodge members. Masons found themselves excluded from social gatherings as well as from jury boxes, were pressured not to run for public office, and often found it impossible to achieve election if they attempted to campaign.[33]

During the first years of the crusade, the policy of the Grand Lodge of New York was to ignore the excitement of Morgan's abduction and its aftermath altogether. During this period of "blissful unawareness," Masons dedicated in 1828 an imposing new Masonic temple on

Broadway in New York City. At the grand lodge convocation in June, only routine business was conducted, and those attending reelected Stephen Van Rensselaer III as grand master. What was needed was a statement by the grand lodge that addressed the Morgan situation, offered an additional reward for the capture of Morgan's abductors, or promoted the discovery of his remains, but the delegates, believing themselves to be innocent, did nothing. The 1829 convocation was similar, although subordinate lodges were dying by the score, and the grand secretary received notice of new desertions or secessions every day. James Herring was one of two men who most helped keep Masonry alive in the Empire State during the Antimasonic period, serving as grand secretary from 1829 to 1845. In 1837, on the occasion of a memorial service for two past grand masters, Herring gave the first public Masonic address since 1826. He insisted that Masonry should not be burdened with the collective guilt of the Morgan affair, reminding his audience that no Masonic obligation interfered with the duty of a man to his country. He added, however, "The abductors of Morgan were as much without excuse as though they had not been Masons, and their crime was never palliated nor defended by the Fraternity in general, nor by the Grand Lodge in particular, nor was there even a dollar of the funds appropriated, knowingly, to aid or shield the guilty." In light of all that transpired, it is unfortunate that Herring had not uttered these words some nine years earlier.[34]

The other New York Mason largely responsible for saving the fraternity from total extinction was Morgan Lewis, a former governor and chief justice who served as grand master from 1830 to 1843. In his installation address before the grand lodge, Lewis asked why the many should be blamed for the sins of the few. Such attacks on the lodge "must meet the reprobation of the virtuous and disinterested." Under the leadership of Lewis and Herring, the grand lodge attempted to prevent further defections and to ascertain the extent of the current damage. This effort is apparent in the action taken in 1830, when delegates passed a resolution declaring that all lodges more than eighteen months in arrears for dues (that is, grand lodge assessments) were to be discharged from the total debt if they paid the amount of the first year's delinquency. A lodge that failed to do so would be in default and would be required to surrender its charter. Then, in 1831, the grand lodge finally adopted a resolution concerning the Morgan affair, asking Herring to examine the records and to prepare a statement concerning those Masons indicted and convicted of abducting Morgan. The grand secretary collected the necessary material and submitted it to a committee of five in 1832. The committee demanded "extra time" to examine the information, but by the time the members were ready to report, the Antimasonic excitement had waned, and the committee never gave its evaluation.[35]

Between 1832 and 1834 Herring pressured the grand lodge to clear out the "dead wood." This task was accomplished by seizing the charters of subordinate lodges in default under terms of the resolution of 1830 or those of lodges that had not met for over a year. More than 300 charters were canceled under this program of attrition. When the charters were withdrawn, however, some lodges refused to deliver their "property" to the grand lodge, including regalia, officers "jewels" (badges), books, and money. Such a situation occurred in St. Andrews Lodge No. 7, New York City, when the remaining funds were distributed among impoverished brethren, the jewels were given to an institution for the blind, and the books and records were destroyed. Then in March 1835 St. Andrews Lodge surrendered its charter, the officers declaring that it no longer possessed any property, jewels, or money. Although the grand lodge officers knew what had happened, they took no action, such as expulsion of those involved, realizing that New York Masons had endured sufficient trials and tribulations at the hands of Antimasons without suffering further through the action of their own brethren. Probably the greatest humiliation for the grand lodge also took place in 1835, when the twelve remaining members of Watertown Lodge No. 289 publicly renounced Masonry. This time the grand lodge expelled the twelve at its 1836 convocation.[36] Statistics kept by the Grand Lodge of New York indicate the devastation wrought by Antimasonry on the fraternity. In 1825, the grand lodge had included 480 subordinate lodges, with a total membership of about 20,000. By 1832, only eighty-two lodges remained, with some 3,000 members. By 1836, only sixty-nine lodges retained their charters; of these, only fifty were active. Twenty-four active lodges were in New York City, two were in Brooklyn, and most of the others were scattered through the eastern portion of the state. West of the Genesee River only two lodges survived, one at Lockport, the other at East Bethany (Olive Branch Lodge). Olive Branch was the only one of sixteen lodges in Genesee County to outlive the crusade. Not only did it retain its charter, publishing the intention of doing so in the local press, but it also initiated two candidates in 1830. Although Olive Branch Lodge met regularly, the usual number attending was only seven. Lockport Lodge met irregularly from July 1827 to December 1838, assembling in attics and other secluded places. The losses that Freemasonry suffered in New York at this time are also apparent from the decrease in revenue paid to the grand lodge by the subordinate lodges through the annual assessment on members of good standing. This amount dropped from $5,301 in 1827 to a low of $1,400 in 1833, increasing to $1,631 by 1835. Of course, Antimasonry was not solely responsible for the weakening of Masonry in New York and other northeastern states; other factors notably included the cholera epidemic of 1830–1832 and the financial depression of 1837–1842. During the "panic," some members could not pay local lodge dues, and hence some lodges could not meet their obligations to the grand lodges. The panic of 1837, however, occurred at the end of the Antimasonic crisis and probably only extended, but did not accelerate, the membership decline, which had begun in the late 1820s.[37]

By 1836 the nadir of Masonic strength of New York was reached, and after that a period of rebuilding occurred. In that year, three lodges in New York City revived, and in 1839, Masons chartered the first new lodge since 1828. By 1840, the number of New York lodges had increased to seventy-nine, with an estimated membership of 5,000; a decade later there were 171 lodges with a membership of about 12,000. The greatest growth took place after 1850, and by 1860 New York had 432 lodges, almost as many as in 1825. It is obvious, therefore, that although Masonry did survive in New York, it took some thirty years to recoup the losses of the Antimasonic era.[38]

Although political Antimasonry had a relatively brief period of active existence in the Empire State, "missionaries" from New York helped establish the party elsewhere in the Northeast. Party leaders, especially Seward, Granger, and Weed, were extremely influential in determining the direction of the organization's national efforts in the conventions of 1830 and 1831 and in Wirt's ill-fated presidential campaign of 1832. The Seward-Granger-Weed triumvirate, in fact, was largely responsible for the enigma of Wirt's candidacy.

# 5. Wirt's Presidential Candidacy of 1832

The first national Antimasonic convention, held at Philadelphia on September 11, 1830, resulted from action taken by New York's state convention in February 1829. Not only did the Albany delegates, reflecting the wishes of the state central committee, disavow all connections with existing parties and resolve to hold a national meeting, but they also arranged for the site, date, and composition of the Philadelphia gathering. Each state was to send the number of delegates equivalent to its electoral vote.

Selection of the date for the national convention was no random matter, for September 11, 1830, was the fourth anniversary of Morgan's abduction. Ninety-six delegates attended, representing ten states—Massachusetts, Connecticut, Rhode Island, Vermont, New York, Pennsylvania, New Jersey, Maryland, Delaware, and Ohio. One territory—Michigan—was also represented. The necessity of selecting delegates to the Philadelphia conclave forced Antimasons in Massachusetts, Rhode Island, New Jersey, and Ohio to hold their first state conventions. Virtually all of the proceedings at Philadelphia were controlled by the large contingents from New York (twenty-six delegates), Pennsylvania (twenty-five), and Massachusetts (fifteen), which accounted for some 70 percent of the total. Convention planners had originally requested the use of Independence Hall, but local authorities denied them permission, the result of Masonic influence, the Antimasons believed. The delegates first gathered in a downtown district courtroom, but this space proved too small, and the meeting adjourned to the larger Music Fund Society Hall. Delegates chose Granger as president and then selected four vice presidents: Joseph Ritner, Pennsylvania; Abner Phelps, Massachusetts; Robert Hanna, Ohio; and Samuel W. Dexter, Michigan Territory. Weed, always preferring to work in an unofficial capacity, was not a member of the New York delegation, but Seward was, and he served on several important committees.[1]

New Yorkers dominated the entire proceedings. Even the "Address to the People," considered by one contemporary to be Antimasonry's "most effective manifesto," was written by Myron Holley of the Empire State. The real work of the convention, which lasted six days, was accomplished by some twenty committees, the most important being the committee to consider nominations. On this vital question, the delegates divided into three classifications: some, especially the Pennsylvanians, wanted an immediate nomination; others opposed national nominations at any time as being irrelevant to the party's purposes; still others, especially the New York leaders, wanted action postponed for at least a year. The last view inevitably prevailed, for the Empire State hierarchy did not want anything to mar the success of Granger's gubernatorial candidacy, which was being supported by the National Republicans as well as by Antimasons. Many delegates also believed that postponement of the nomination would permit the party to grow and would allow some type of consensus to develop concerning a presidential candidate. After a bitter fight between the purists and pragmatists as to whether to make any nominations at all, delegates adopted a resolution proposed by John L. Curtenius of New York calling for appointment of a committee to report on the most expedient time, place, and manner for selecting a presidential ticket. Such a committee was subsequently appointed, chaired by Amos Ellmaker of Pennsylvania.[2]

On September 17, William Slade of Vermont, representing the committee on nominations, made a report in which he recommended that a second national convention meet at Baltimore on September 26, 1831, to nominate candidates for president and vice president of the United States. When the report was debated on the following day, delegate William W. Irwin of Pittsburgh related how, to his surprise, another delegate had expressed astonishment at learning that the Philadelphia convention had assembled for political purposes. Irwin wryly declared that it "had met for no other than political purposes." After some haggling over wording, delegates eventually adopted a resolution containing the essence of the committee report. As a last item of business, the convention created a national correspondence committee to maintain communications with similar committees in the states.[3]

During the year that elapsed between the two conventions, the purists and pragmatists more intensely disputed the criteria to be used for selection of a presidential candidate. The zealots, of course, wanted a genuine Antimason who was firmly dedicated to party principles. This group included Ellmaker (Pennsylvania) and Holley and Ward (New York), the latter two definitely no part of Weed's inner circle. Weed's group represented by the wily editor together with Granger, Maynard, Whittlesey, and Seward, wanted to nominate someone capable of attracting votes from National Republicans and perhaps even from Democrats. The major task for the New Yorkers was to find a candidate who would be acceptable to a majority of the anti-Jackson voters, preferably a charismatic figure under whom they could unite. The leaders considered seven men but ultimately selected none of them, instead turning to an eleventh-hour choice whose name had never been mentioned prior to the convention.[4]

To the pragmatists, the obvious choice was Sen. Henry Clay of Kentucky, leader of the National Republicans and certain to be nominated by them for the presidency at their December 1831 convention. Clay presented several major problems, however, for he was not only a Mason but a past grand master (1820-1821) of the Grand Lodge of Kentucky. Antimasons were pleased to learn, nevertheless, that he had demitted from his lodge at Lexington in 1824 because of a lack of interest and now claimed that he had been inactive for many years. In fact, during the years 1830-1831, Clay actually conducted a bit of political intrigue with certain Antis, hoping for their presidential endorsement but never daring to condemn Masonry sufficiently from their viewpoint. Had Clay satisfied the Antimasons on this point, he would, of course, have alienated numerous Masons within his own party.[5]

Many Antimasons, including Weed, put great pressure on Clay to denounce Masonry throughly, but to no avail. In June 1831 the Kentuckian wrote that he had been "urged, entreated, [and] importuned" to make a declaration against Masonry that would satisfy the Antimasons, but he had "hitherto declined all interference on that subject. While I do not, and never did care about Masonry, I shall abstain from making myself any party to that strife." Clay believed, he said, that neither Masonry nor Antimasonry should have anything to do with politics. He seemed to regard Antimasonry as a phenomenon outside the political realm, with the great body of its followers honestly trying to redress what they considered to be a great evil. He did assert, however, that Antimasonic leaders were clearly "in the pursuit of power." Clay refused to admit that Antimasonry was a serious challenge to his forthcoming presidential candidacy and thought that, agreeing as they did with the Nationals on everything but Masonry, the Antimasons would eventually support him in 1832, even if it meant abandoning a hopeless candidate of their own.[6]

Clay's intransigence in refusing to denounce Masonry and to make Antimasonry a political issue forced the Antimasonic leadership to continue their search for a nominee. For a brief time, Richard Rush of Pennsylvania appeared to be the most likely candidate, for he had excellent credentials. The son of the prominent physician Benjamin Rush, he had served as comptroller of the treasury and attorney general under James Madison, minister to Great Britain during James Monroe's presidency, and secretary of the treasury under John Quincy Adams. He had also been Adams's vice presidential running mate in 1828. Rush attracted the attention of Antimasons when, after being questioned by party committees in Pennsylvania and Massachusetts, he responded favorably with two long "public" letters in May and June 1831. In these letters the Pennsylvanian pointed out that he had abandoned Masonry in 1826 prior to Morgan's murder and now regarded the fraternity as a subversive force and the greatest contemporary danger to American liberties. Ellmaker began to promote Rush for the presidency, much to the horror of Seward, Maynard, and Tracy, all of whom questioned Rush's "political responsibility." Tracy declared that "Ellmaker must be a blind old dotard to think for a moment of making a rallying point of him." In late July 1831 Rush, seeing his chances were nil, withdrew as a possibility on the Antimasonic ticket. He then lived up to his reputation for political unreliability by trying to prevent a National Republican-Antimasonic coalition in Pennsylvania. He changed to the Jackson party shortly before the presidential election, allegedly attracted by Jackson's stand against the Bank of the United States, a position that made Rush extremely unpopular in Pennsylvania and cost him a seat in the U.S. Senate and his membership in the American Philosophical Society.[7]

Probably the person most eager for the Antimasonic nomination was the one least willing to admit it—former president John Quincy Adams of Massachusetts. Although Adams always disliked the idea of party labels, he was beginning to think of himself as an Antimason by 1831. Strongly supported by Massachusetts Antimasons including Abner Phelps and George Odiorne, the former president, now a U.S. congressman, was encouraged to seek the nomination. This effort was opposed by the New York leadership, who could not tolerate the nomination of a candidate who bore the stigma of defeat. On September 14, 1831, Seward visited Adams at his home in Quincy, hoping to secure an endorsement for John McLean of Ohio. Three hours of tortuous conversation made Seward aware that Adams disliked McLean, whom he considered a protégé of Calhoun, and that the former president really desired the nomination for himself. Adams, of course, would do nothing to promote his own candidacy but admitted

that he would accept a convention draft. Seward wrote to Weed
following his encounter that New York Antimasons must unite in
blocking Adams's selection by the forthcoming convention, for such
a nomination would have a "disastrous" effect on the party's chances
in the Empire State.[8]

Vice President John C. Calhoun of South Carolina, now completely
alienated from President Andrew Jackson, made a few perfunctory
Antimasonic statements in letters to certain friends, hoping that he
might have an "outside chance" at the nomination, an effort being
promoted by his journalist friend Duff Green. Calhoun's involvement
with the doctrine of nullification and his recent "Fort Hill Address"
had displeased many Antimasons, most of whom were Northerners
with little sympathy for state's rights or slavery. The nomination of
Calhoun would undoubtedly have alienated voters in those states that
the Antimasons had to carry.[9] Another politician who was barely
considered was Sen. Daniel Webster of Massachusetts, occasionally
mentioned as one who might attract some Clay supporters because of
his strong protariff position. Webster, however, never received visible
support from the influential Antimasonic leadership prior to the Baltimore convention.[10]

As it became increasingly apparent that Clay was not a sufficiently
ardent Antimason to warrant the party's nomination, the attention of
Weed and his circle increasingly focused on John McLean of Ohio,
an associate justice of the Supreme Court who possessed an inordinate
desire to become president of the United States. McLean had been
born in New Jersey but had lived in Ohio since the age of fourteen.
He possessed the advantage of having a national reputation, being
popular in the West and also a friend of Calhoun, which might
produce some southern support but could also prove a distinct disad-
vantage in the Northeast. He had support in both the Adams and
Jackson parties, as is indicated by his service in the Adams cabinet
as postmaster general and by his subsequent appointment to the federal Supreme Court by Jackson in 1829. In May 1830, the Pennsylvania Central Antimasonic Committee asked McLean, as did Ohio
Antimasons later that year, to express his views on Masonry. His
response was consistently tepid: he had never had any connections
with the lodge, "but as I am not acquainted with the principles of
Masonry I can neither approve nor condone them."[11]

Antimasons from Ohio and New York continued to pressure
McLean in 1831 to produce a suitable condemnation of Masonry.
Weed hoped the Ohioan would accept the Antimasonic nomination,
having learned secondhand from Tracy that McLean would agree to

it if it was proffered by the convention. What Weed did not relate was his discovery that although McLean had said he would not turn down the nomination, he had also indicated to Tracy that he did not believe the Antimasons could elect him president. Much of McLean's preconvention support came from Thaddeus Stevens in Pennsylvania and from New Yorkers Boughton, Maynard, and Seward, the latter viewing the Ohioan as the most viable candidate and the perfect foil to an Adams nomination. Strenuous opposition to McLean's candidacy came from New York zealot Seth Hunt, who questioned the Ohioan's sincerity concerning political Antimasonry, and from Webster, who feared that a McLean nomination would siphon strength from the National Republican campaign. Webster also believed that it was improper for a Supreme Court justice to seek the presidency, for "it inflames proper prejudice against the Court . . . and . . . it more or less weakens confidence in the Tribunal."[12]

Although McLean was extremely eager to receive a presidential nomination, he did not desire one from a party that had little chance of electing him, especially if Clay became the National Republican candidate. Warned by friends about the extremism of certain Antimasons, the "violence and mendacity" of their publications, and the efforts of certain party leaders to ruin Clay's presidential ambitions, McLean declined that prospective nomination in a letter written on September 7 from Nashville, Tennessee, to the national committee. He explained that as there were already three candidates for the presidency, Jackson, Clay, and Calhoun (briefly an unofficial contender), a fourth name would be likely to "distract still more the public mind." Echoing Webster's sentiments, McLean declared that as a member of the Supreme Court, he was reluctant to accept any nomination unless it would "tranquilize the public mind."[13]

As news of McLean's declination spread among the Antimasonic delegates at Baltimore, party leaders faced a major dilemma. In desperation they turned to the ailing old chief justice of the Supreme Court, John Marshall, who was now seventy-six. Marshall had been a Mason since the Revolution and had served three terms as grand master of Virginia, from 1793 to 1795. Although he evidently retained his lodge membership and continued to serve the Grand Lodge of Virginia in various capacities, a letter written to Edward Everett of Massachusetts in July 1833 but not published until after Marshall's death indicates that Marshall turned against Masonry sometime after 1826. Until the Morgan affair, he had believed that Masonry was a "harmless plaything," but afterward he became convinced "that the institution ought to be abandoned, as one capable of producing much evil, and incapable of producing any good." In September 1831 Weed, Tracy, Spencer, and Phelps approached Marshall, who agreed to visit the Baltimore convention as a spectator on its second day. He did attend but refused to allow his name to be placed in nomination. The mere presence of the venerable judge, however, greatly impressed another spectator, former attorney general William Wirt of Maryland, who at this point had been mentioned only as a possible running mate for McLean.[14]

The 111 delegates who assembled at Baltimore on September 26, 1831, arrived with the tacit understanding that McLean would be the presidential nominee. Seward later described the Ohioan's letter of refusal as "a wet blanket upon our warm expectations." It forced the convention to make a genuine selection, and the meeting became a "nominating convention" in the present-day sense of that term. The delegates, meeting at the Athenaeum, represented twelve states, with more than half coming from New York (thirty-eight) and Pennsylvania (twenty-eight). Massachusetts sent fourteen delegates and Ohio nine. The New York, Pennsylvania, and Massachusetts delegations were the only ones meeting the criteria established in 1830, that is, a state's delegation should equal the number of its senators and representatives in Congress. Although Michigan Territory did not send a delegate as in 1830, Maine, Delaware, and New Hampshire did—states not represented at the 1830 session at Philadelphia. The accredited delegate from Maryland, John S. Shriver, was actually a spectator, which indicates how desperate the Antimasonic leadership was to present the facade of a national party. Innovations at this convention included the examination of delegate credentials by convention officers, assignment of special seats to representatives of the press, and adoption of a three-fourths rule for nomination.[15]

Weed was prominent at the convention, although he was not technically a delegate. He preferred to maneuver behind the scenes, free to skip official sessions, to lead the search for a candidate. In addition to meeting with Marshall, Weed and Spencer met with Wirt and Charles Carroll, surviving signer of the Declaration of Independence. Wirt, like Marshall, had been persuaded to visit the convention, and since he was a resident of Baltimore, the arrangements presented no problem. In fact, had the convention assembled anywhere but Baltimore, Wirt would never have been nominated. He did attend and was suitably impressed by the presence of the venerable Marshall, whom he revered, and by the convention itself, which he described as "one of the most respectable assemblies" containing "the display of more talent, and dignity" than he had ever witnessed. Wirt also received an

Antimasonic visitor at his Baltimore home (probably Phelps), who gave him the proceedings of the 1830 convention to read. The Marylander declared, after two days of study, that he had now become aware of the "crime and horror" of the Morgan affair and regretted his previous negative opinions of Antimasonry. He then sent the visitor a note saying that if the description of Masonry in the *Proceedings* was correct, then "it ought to be extinguished." He quickly qualified his assertion, however, with the observation that this was not the Masonry he had known years ago in the South.[16]

At the Athenaeum, Seward and Weed frantically tried to convince their fellow delegates that Wirt was the best if not the only choice for president. News that the former attorney general had been a Mason, had never publicly denounced Masonry, was a known admirer of Clay, and had already been selected as a delegate to the forthcoming National Republican convention displeased many delegates. Seward and Weed proceeded to gather support for Wirt among the New York contingent and the New England delegations. Seward spent an entire afternoon and evening pressuring Stevens, who still supported McLean, to change his mind. The Pennsylvanian's reluctant agreement removed the final barrier. The convention next moved into a committee of the whole for the nominating process on the evening of September 27. It was a completely routine affair, with no nominating or seconding speeches, announcements, or demonstrations permitted. Nominations were made by a roll call vote. As the roll was announced, each delegate walked to a table and placed his ballot in a designated box. Those nominated included Wirt, McLean, Granger, Webster, and Rush. On the first ballot, Wirt had 38 votes, McLean, 41, and the others had 5 or fewer. On the fourth ballot, taken at 2:00 A.M. on September 28, the delegates, realizing the futility of supporting McLean, gave Wirt 94 votes; McLean now had only 9. On the fifth ballot, Wirt had 108 votes, Rush, 1. The delegates then resolved to make the nomination unanimous. Although many were unhappy about this action, the alternatives were either nominating someone who would decline or adjourning without having selected a candidate.[17]

Nomination of Wirt's running mate was not the pro forma matter traditionally pictured. Prior to the convention, Seward had campaigned to have some New Yorker—Maynard, Tracy, or Whittlesey—nominated. He did not, however, want the convention president, Spencer, whom he distrusted. The decision to nominate Ellmaker of Lancaster County, Pennsylvania, was made immediately prior to the second roll call vote. Ellmaker, promoted by Rush and Stevens, pos-

sessed several advantages: he came from the vital state of Pennsylvania, which he had served as attorney general; his ardent enthusiasm
for Antimasonry offset Wirt's bare acceptance of the cause; and his
selection would calm the irate Keystone State delegation, still unhappy over Wirt's nomination. Ellmaker was chosen, receiving 108 of
110 votes cast. In a letter of acceptance, written later that day (September 28), Ellmaker declared that he had never sought "high office,"
but "a zealous and firm attachment to the cause of Anti-Masonry, will
not permit a refusal of the nomination."[18]

At the time he received the Antimasonic presidential nomination,
Wirt enjoyed a substantial reputation in both legal and literary circles,
although he was barely known to most politicians. Born in 1772 at
Bladensburg, Maryland, five miles from the future national capital,
and orphaned at eight, he eventually became an attorney and practiced in several areas of Virginia, settling in Richmond in 1797 after
the death of his first wife. In the early 1800s, Wirt achieved national
standing as a lawyer, serving as an attorney for the federal government in Aaron Burr's treason trial (1807). A two-year term in the
Virginia House of Delegates convinced Wirt that he was unsuited for
a political career, and he declined President Thomas Jefferson's suggestion in 1808 that he run for Congress.[19]

Appointed U.S. attorney general by Monroe, Wirt served longer in
that cabinet post (1818-1829) than any individual had to date. He
proved an excellent administrator, devising official records and opin-
ions-keeping systems. During this period he developed a great reverence for Chief Justice Marshall and his doctrine of judicial
nationalism. To supplement his annual salary of $3,000, Wirt ap-
peared in a private legal capacity in many cases before the district and
Supreme courts. He also enjoyed some renown as an author, primarily
for his 1816 biography, *Sketches of the Life and Character of Patrick
Henry.*[20]

Although Wirt obviously admired Henry's voluble, mercurial nature, similar qualities in Jackson repelled him. He considered Old
Hickory to be a rash, uneducated, ill-bred tyrant. By 1829 Wirt was
obsessed by the idea that with Jackson's rise to power, demagoguery
was overtaking the United States. He naively hoped, nevertheless, that
Old Hickory would retain him as attorney general and even called
upon the new president to inquire about this possibility, only to learn
that Jackson had just appointed John M. Berrien of Georgia. Wirt
continued an extensive legal practice, and his animosity against Jackson increased because of the president's attitudes toward the Cherokee Nation and its legal struggle with Georgia. The Marylander

represented the Indians in the celebrated 1831 case *Cherokee Nation v. Georgia.*[21]

After the Baltimore convention had selected Wirt, a committee consisting of Spencer, Tracy, Seward, and Phelps offered him the nomination. When he demurred, they told him that McLean had declined, and the Antimasons would support neither Clay nor Calhoun, the latter because of his nullification doctrines. As Wirt observed later, the alternatives were either "yielding without resistance" to Jackson's reelection or presenting the nation with an opportunity to rid itself of this "obnoxious administration." The committee assured Wirt that there was nothing in Antimasonry that would make his acceptance "disreputable," and afterward he asserted that the committee had sought no pledge of him, "expressed or implied." Immediately following the committee's departure, Wirt, assisted by his daughter, Catherine, composed a unique acceptance letter.[22]

Wirt's letter contained numerous assertions that the convention delegates, having no viable alternative, chose to ignore. He began by declaring that he had never sought the presidency, being "fully aware of its fearful responsibilities," and was completely surprised by the nomination. He had never imagined that the Antimasons would nominate a former Mason who refused to wage a war of "indiscriminate extermination" against the fraternity or to use the presidency "to direct its powers to the vindictive purpose of party proscription and persecution." Wirt's most vehement remarks against Masonry concerned the Morgan affair and the subsequent investigation, which he said proved that Masonry had become a tremendous political force in the nation, "with the power and the disposition to set the laws of the land at defiance." He lauded Antimasonry for its "determination to root out this noxious institution" but warned that this goal must be accomplished by legal and constitutional means, declaring that the prime objective must be to assert the "supremacy of the laws."[23]

In referring to the controversial issue of his Masonic affiliation, Wirt admitted that in his early life he had been initiated into a Richmond lodge, but he had never taken the Master's degree because of a lack of interest. He had not attended a lodge for more than thirty years but noted that this disinterest "proceeded from no suspicion on my part that there was anything criminal in the institution, or anything that placed its members in the slightest degree, in collision with their allegiance to their country and its laws." Wirt had seen nothing in Masonry that would violate a person's obligations as a patriot, a Christian, and a man, and he subsequently regarded the lodge primarily as a social club, designed to promote fellowship and to provide

financial relief for indigent brethren. He remarked that he was grieved
by the excesses of certain Antimasons against "so harmless an institution as freemasonry"; he also noted, however, that the newer Masonry
of the Morgan trials was not that of George Washington's day but a
"wicked conspiracy against the laws of God and man, which ought
to be put down." Wirt warned the Baltimore convention that "justice
and prudence" demanded that the presidential powers should not be
used for a "blind and unjust proscription, involving innocence and
honor with guilt and treason."[24]

Wirt concluded his letter by telling the delegates that if they disagreed with his views and wished to nominate someone else, he would
"retire from it with far more pleasure than I should accept it." If they
preferred to abide by his opinions, he was duty bound to remain the
Antimasonic candidate. Although many delegates were apparently
appalled by Wirt's statements, the party leadership forced through a
unanimous resolution of acceptance.[25]

On the same day that Wirt replied to the Antimasonic convention,
he wrote to the chairman of the National Republican central committee, withdrawing as a delegate to that party's December meeting.
Referring to his own recent nomination, Wirt declared that no one
could be more surprised than himself. A few days later, writing to his
close friend (and Jefferson's nephew), Dabney Carr, the former attorney general gave the first indication of his real reason for accepting
the Antimasonic nomination—the faint hope that he might also receive the call of the National Republicans and thus might unite the
anti-Jackson forces. Wirt admitted, nevertheless, "Such a union I do
not expect, for I am too obscure and I hope too honest to awaken any
such enthusiasm in this corrupt and factious age." Whether such an
alliance transpired or not, Wirt expected to become a martyr during
the campaign, especially from attacks by the Jacksonian press.
Throughout 1831 and 1832 he continued to insist to close friends that
he had accepted the nomination as a patriotic duty in order to defeat
that "despot" Jackson; and he asserted that vanity and political ambi-
tion had absolutely no effect on his decision. He also told Carr in
November 1831 that his acquiescence had nothing to do with further-
ing the Antimasonic cause but related to a higher goal, the nation's
welfare.[26]

The Jacksonian and National Republican parties reacted to Wirt's
nomination through their newspapers with surprise and disdain.
Francis P. Blair's pro-Jackson *Globe* pictured Wirt as a politician who
had taken up "a creed at a moment's warning," and it accused Joseph
Gales, editor of the National Republican *Intelligencer,* of having

engineered Wirt's nomination "as a means of ultimately *selling and transferring* the whole Antimasonic party to Mr. Clay." These opinions were ignored by the *Intelligencer,* which expressed astonishment at Wirt's nomination, declaring the Marylander to be no enemy of Masonry in the past and seeing no change of views in his acceptance letter. Gales observed that Wirt was an excellent candidate, although an eleventh-hour one; he could not, however, win without National Republican support. Since such backing seemed unlikely, Gales suggested that Antimasons support Clay for president, and Wirt could serve as the Kentuckian's vice presidential running mate.[27]

Many Antimasons expressed pleasure over Wirt's nomination and promised their support. Seward exulted that Wirt's selection produced more rejoicing in Cayuga County, New York, than any other nomination the Antimasons could have made. Hunt told Seward that Wirt was preferable to McLean on almost every account, and he predicted that the Marylander would win even Virginia. Whittlesey confided to Seward that the choice of Wirt, although obviously "the result of an accident," was the best alternative under the circumstances. He believed most Antimasons would vote for the former attorney general except some of the "bitter" ones, "who are very few." Tracy, however, believed Wirt's candidacy would ruin the party, for "the moment antimasonry becomes only another term for Anti Jacksonianism, that moment our fate is sealed."[28]

Wirt was possibly the most reluctant and most unwilling presidential candidate ever nominated by an American party. Painfully aware of his lack of charisma, almost from the day he accepted the nomination Wirt realized that he had made a grave mistake, for he could not win without National Republican support, which never developed. A few days after the nomination he wrote that "he had been drawn into a political scrape which has taken me as much by surprise as if a thunderbolt had dropped at my feet in a clear day." Wirt repeated his forlorn hope that by supporting him the Nationals could unite all anti-Jackson voters—wondering, nevertheless, if the American people would ever accept him as a "proper person" for the presidency, for "they do not know me—and will not be apt to feel much interest for so entire a stranger."[29]

Between October 1831 and February 1832, Wirt attempted unsuccessfully to withdraw from the election. If withdrawal occurred, it had to be the result of amicable negotiations, for the Antimasons had "honored me, and I cannot dishonor or offend them. It would be most ungrateful and unjust." In April he sent word to Maynard through a friend that he had no intention of leaving the race unless he had the concurrence of the New York hierarchy. After the election he admitted having had another reason for remaining a candidate—the fear of Clay and his friends that if Wirt withdrew, the Antis would "immediately supply my place with some more zealous partisan of their own, and feel increased hostility to Mr. Clay whom they would blame for my desertion of them." Wirt's confidence continued to fluctuate; by May 1832 he complained of being "weary and sick" of public life. As the period for selection of the presidential electors approached, the Marylander wrote that recent state elections in Ohio and Pennsylvania proved the futility of the Antimasonic cause, and he hoped the presidential contest would not have to be decided by the House of Representatives. He still maintained faint hopes for Clay's success, but none for himself, remarking, "As for me, I have never considered myself as playing for it [the presidency] or being in the game at all."[30]

As befitted a candidate who regretted his nomination and desired to be released from it, Wirt took no part in the presidential contest whatsoever, leaving it to the Democrats and National Republicans to fight over such issues as Jackson's recent veto of the Bank rechartering bill, the protective tariff, federal aid to internal improvements, and nullification. The party's campaign likewise reflected the candidate's inertia and consisted almost entirely of editorials in local newspapers and speeches at state conventions. Wirt later admitted, "In the canvass I took no part, not even by writing private letters, which, on the contrary, I refused to answer whenever such answers could be interpreted into canvassing for office." Disregarding the advice of the *Telegraph*'s editor, Duff Green, who had told the Marylander that he and his friends should conduct a "vigorous effort," Wirt was content to have letters written on his behalf, to see his candidacy extolled by the Antimasonic press, and to denounce Masonry and Jackson in correspondence never intended for publication. Wirt believed Jackson to be, intellectually, "among the weakest of men." He was also obsessed with what he considered to be the Jackson administration's corrupt attempts to control the election through bribery and patronage. He compared the president with Caesar, a Borgia, and Cataline and predicted that nothing less than civil war would purify the "moral atmosphere" by "fire and tempest."[31]

During the campaign, Wirt did attack Masonry with vigor, but to the dismay of his Antimasonic friends, none of these sentiments was publicized. To Rush, the Marylander commented that Masonry was doomed if the Antimasons remained "cool & judicious." He believed that Masons had pledged themselves to the overthrow of good government in the United States, and hearkening back to the Illuminati conspiracy of 1798, Wirt declared that the avowed purpose of Masonry was the creation of an international order ruled from Europe. He further believed that Masons also contemplated establishing "black lodges" in the South, which they would use to terrorize their white enemies. Masonic lodges were "mere nonsense, unnecessary & revelry—a rendezvous for low and vulgar dissipation which every decent & respectable man has long since retired—for who can bear to find himself continually elbowed by blackguards & hailed by the masonic signs in the streets by drunken, dirty, staggering & stinking vagabonds who are a disgrace to society." In addition to Wirt's private attacks on Masonry, there were, of course, the public barbs in the Antimasonic press aimed at Jackson, who was still an active Mason and a past grand master (1822-1824) of the Grand Lodge of Tennessee, and also at the four Masonic members of his cabinet: Secretary of State Edward Livingston, Secretary of War Lewis Cass, Secretary of the Navy Levi Woodbury, and Postmaster General William T. Barry. Jackson himself never publicly commented on the Masonic-Antimasonic controversy, although in 1828, through private correspondence, he insinuated that the Adams administration was attempting to make political capital out of the Morgan affair. The president's only known reference to the Masonic issue during the 1832 campaign came in a letter to Van Buren, when he wrote, "Everything is going well at present. Nullification and antimasonry, are both declining fast, and will ere long be *buried in oblivion,* doing no harm, but carrying with it they [*sic*] promoters, exciters, and supporters."[32]

As the campaign progressed, Wirt's despondency deepened. Suffering no illusions as to any hope of election by his supporters, to whom he had referred as a "motley crew," aging, ill, and angered by an accusation that his most recent sickness was the result of having accepted the Antimasonic nomination, Wirt came to terms with the inevitable. Resigned to his and Clay's defeat, which he blamed on those Antis "who have done their best to prevent the union" of the Antimasonic and National Republican parties, he wrote on the eve of the election: "What the use . . . it neither breaks my leg nor picks my pocket."[33]

In the presidential election of 1832, Antimasons presented separate electoral tickets in Vermont, Massachusetts, Connecticut, Rhode Island, New Jersey, and New Hampshire, although in the heavily Democratic Granite State, the Antimasonic electors wisely withdrew before the election day. Unable to unite on the national level, Antimasons and National Republicans sponsored joint electoral tickets in New York, Pennsylvania, and Ohio, allegedly reasoning that if the ticket won a majority of popular votes within a particular state, its electoral votes would go to either Clay or Wirt, whichever stood the best chance of defeating Jackson. One young New York Anti foolishly predicted the joint ticket would win that state by 10,000 votes. Others believed that if either Wirt or Clay did achieve the presidency, it would be through the House of Representatives, because none of the three candidates had received a majority in the electoral college. The joint tickets produced enormous distrust in New York, Ohio, and Pennsylvania between Antimasonic and National voters. Ellmaker believed that the coalition in Pennsylvania drove hundreds of former pro-Jackson men who had recently become Antimasons back to Old Hickory because they were so infuriated about union with the Clay forces. The divisive issue of whether the joint ticket would ultimately support Clay or Wirt proved to be an academic matter, however, as Jackson carried New York and Pennsylvania by comfortable margins and won a narrow but decisive victory in Ohio.[34]

The presidential contest of 1832 extended between October 31, when voters in Ohio and Pennsylvania cast their ballots, and November 19, when Rhode Islanders went to the polls. Of the twenty-four states in the Union, only South Carolina still selected electors through the state legislature. That body, in the midst of a nullification crisis, cast eleven electoral votes for states' rights governor John B. Floyd of Virginia, a close friend of Calhoun. By November 5, Elizabeth Wirt reported to her husband that the election news was "bad." This contest, in which 55 percent of the eligible male voters participated, became a triumph for Jackson and a disaster for Clay and Wirt. Jackson amassed 219 electoral votes, Clay 49, and Wirt 7. Wirt carried only Vermont, where he had a plurality (40.5 percent), 13,112 votes to Clay's 11,161 and Jackson's 7,865. Unfortunately for the Antimasons, Vermont, the citadel of political Antimasonry, was of minor importance in the great political struggles of that day. Clay won Massachusetts, Rhode Island, Connecticut, Delaware, Kentucky, and five of Maryland's votes, and Jackson carried the remaining sixteen states. The popular vote was not tallied in an exact manner. Except in Vermont, Wirt's popular votes were usually combined with Clay's, and it is difficult, if not impossible, to separate them. The estimated popular vote is: Jackson, 701,780; Clay, 484,205; and Wirt, about 100,715. The last figure, however, includes the 66,706 votes that the fusion ticket won in Pennsylvania, many of which were really for Clay.[35]

Wirt had proved to be a pitiful candidate for the Antimasons, demonstrating a complete lack of aptitude for office seeking: his letters following the nomination were defensive and apologetic in tone; he despaired of victory before the campaign had begun; and although his greatest task was to convince the National Republicans to support him, instead he had to defend himself concerning charges of duplicity against Clay and the Nationals. Following the election, Wirt appeared to be in a depressed but philosophical state of mind, blaming his defeat and Jackson's triumph in part on the rotting moral fiber of the nation and the tyranny of the majority, describing the electorate, as "that herd of swine into which devils were cast." He called the Antimasonic purists "fanatical fools" for refusing to join the Nationals and to support Clay in order to defeat Jackson. The Marylander repeated secondhand rumors that many Antimasons in New York and Pennsylvania had deserted his ticket, fearing a "sell-out" to Clay. Wirt described such an attitude as "fanatical, narrow and un-patriotic." Insisting that the basic weakness of political Antimasonry was its overemphasis of one issue while ignoring other problems such as Jackson's veto of the Bank rechartering bill, he observed, "Who with such a frightful array of evils before their eyes can say that masonry was the only thing or the principal thing to be considered in the election?" Wirt believed, nevertheless, that Antimasonry had dealt the fraternity in the United States a mortal blow from which it would never recover, and "there is no power of her restoration." He suggested that Antimasonry "sheath the sword" and permit Masonry to "faint and expire."[36]

Hardly had the final ballots been tallied when the (Providence) *Rhode Island American* suggested Wirt for the presidency in 1836. He quickly declined, noting that it was "premature to think of the future at this time" and stating that he had accepted the result of the recent contest as the decision of the people. He remained busy with his private law practice and numerous business ventures as well. In mid-February 1834 Wirt, in fragile health, caught a cold that was followed by complications, and he died suddenly on February 18, 1834, in Washington. President Jackson, members of the cabinet, Supreme Court justices, and other dignitaries attended his last rites. The following day, John Quincy Adams delivered a brief but stirring eulogy in the House of Representatives.[37]

Although the presidential candidate was dead, the party continued to flourish in certain states after 1832, especially in Pennsylvania and Vermont. The Green Mountain State, although unimportant in national politics, became a bastion of Antimasonry, in terms of success both in winning political office and in the near-destruction of Masonry through legislative means.

# 6. Vermont, 1829-1836

Vermont, described by 1830 as the only "exclusively frontier state east of the Appalachians," had entered the Union in 1791 as the fourteenth state, after settling with New York a complex and long-standing dispute over land claims. Local settlers had adopted a constitution in 1777 when the area, organized by Ethan Allen, actually possessed the status of an independent republic. Copied from the constitution of Pennsylvania, this plan created a unicameral legislature (General Assembly), a governor, and a council of twelve members. All officials had to seek election annually. The council acted with the governor in suggesting revisions of bills and could exercise a "suspensory veto" over legislation. The General Assembly possessed substantial powers through its prerogative to make all civil, military, and judicial appointments.[1]

Following the evolution of political parties in the 1790s, Vermonters remained loyal to Federalism until after the War of 1812. In the early and mid-1820s, they joined the rest of the nation in supporting Monroe, but in the presidential elections of 1824 and 1828, voters preferred John Quincy Adams to Andrew Jackson. The state temporarily became a citadel of National Republicanism and a strong source of support for Clay's American system. Then, from 1829 until after the Civil War, politics became characterized primarily by a three-party system rather than the two-party pattern of most other states. Another aspect of life in Vermont was the preoccupation of the press with religious or other moral-ethical issues. It was a press that after 1828 adopted the Antimasonic creed with great enthusiasm.[2]

Masonry, first organized in Vermont in 1781, was well-established by 1828, with some seventy-three lodges. Local Masons organized a grand lodge in 1794, and by the late 1820s it was common for the governor, Speaker of the Assembly, and a majority of the state supreme court judges to be Masons. Masonic affiliation, or the lack of it, had become a factor in state politics. In the eyes of nonmembers, Masonry had prospered "too well." Masons in Vermont *seemed* to be drawn mainly from the wealthy and prominent men of the town, and this discrimination rankled with poor farmers and villagers. A careful examination of Antimasonry in the Green Mountain State shows that the movement and party became the strongest in the poorest villages —those with the lowest tax assessments and property valuations per lot and dwelling. Antimasonry also appealed to those farmers with depleted soil, exhausted timber reserves, transportation problems, and few markets for their crops, a situation that motivated a massive population exodus in the 1820s and 1830s. Because most of the prominent legislators and lawyers were Masons, and these men dominated both the National Republican and Democratic parties, the disadvantaged flocked to the banner of Antimasonry.[3]

Antimasonry in Vermont had a strong religious impetus, and as in the Empire State, Baptists were in the forefront. Baptist antagonism to Masonry had appeared in the Shaftsbury Association as early as 1798, during the Bavarian Illuminati crisis. Following the Morgan affair of 1826, the first Baptist condemnation of Masonry in Vermont occurred in 1828 at Randolph among Free Will Baptists and quickly spread to other congregations. In Addison County, as had happened in New York, the Antimasonic issue hopelessly divided the regular Vermont Association and led to formation in 1833 of a new association opposed to Masonry. To a lesser extent, Vermont Congregationalists were exacerbated by the Antimasonic controversy, primarily as a result of the furor caused by the Reverend Henry Jones of Cabot, who became a vocal seceding Mason in 1828 as a result of reading the *Danville North Star,* the state's most radical Antimasonic newspaper. Of all the denominations and sects in Vermont, however, none was more Antimasonic than the "Christians," a fundamentalist but anti-Calvinist sect established in 1802. Although few in number, the Christians enjoyed considerable influence among the people living on the eastern slopes of the Green Mountains, expecially after a church elder, Edward Rollins, established the *Vermont Luminary* in 1829 for the purpose of attacking Masonry.[4]

Political Antimasonry in Vermont took a step forward in September 1827, when the *Danville North Star,* published in Caledonia County by the fiery Ebeneezer Eaton, carried an account of the Morgan affair with a sympathetic commentary. With its transition to Antimasonry, the *North Star* became for a time the most prominent Antimasonic journal in the state, each issue bearing the motto "Where Liberty Dwells, There Is My Country." The location of this newspaper in Danville, along with the presence of a three-man information bureau in Randolph (Orange County), helped make eastern Vermont an Antimasonic stronghold. "General" Martin Flint was the most important member of the bureau, or "Randolph Triumvirate," as it was generally called. He had served as a volunteer lieutenant at the battle of Plattsburg during the War of 1812 and was reputed to be the first Vermont Mason to secede from the fraternity (September 1827) following the Morgan affair. Flint then visited New York, where he met with prominent and zealous Antimasons. Anti-Calvinist in religion, opposed to the status quo in politics, he became infuriated in the spring of 1828 when his name was omitted from a list of nominees for town offices in Randolph and he found himself replaced by a Mason. This incident precipitated creation of the state's first Antimasonic ticket, which routed Flint's Masonic opponent. After the party became organized throughout the state, the Randolph Triumvirate, consisting of Flint, Lebbeus Egerton, and Calvin Blodgett, served as a type of propaganda office, collecting any available negative information on Masonry and sending it to Antimasonic newspapers for publication in order to keep the voters agitated.[5]

The Antimasons' success at Randolph inspired others to hold meetings throughout the state during the autumn of 1828. One result was the nomination of Gen. William Cahoon of Lyndon for Congress to represent the northeastern Fifth District. Because of a three-way split between Democrats, Antimasons, and National Republicans, the election continued for sixteen months, but Cahoon finally achieved victory on the eighth attempt in 1829 and became the first Antimason outside western New York to be elected to the U.S. House of Representatives. His election marked the entrance of the Antimasonic party as a serious contender in Vermont politics and also indicated that the Antimasons' most dedicated opponents would be the National Republicans, not the hapless Jacksonians.[6]

A series of county conventions in the winter and spring of 1829 produced the beginnings of a statewide party. Delegates at the Orange County convention called for a state meeting, and one assembled at Montpelier on August 5, 1829. The convention developed a highly centralized organization consisting of a "state central committee" and county "committees of vigilance," the latter having the power to appoint subcommittees in the towns and school districts. This type of organization characterized the Antimasonic party in Vermont for the next seven years, and together with unusually strong leadership, it helped make Antimasonry preeminent. Egerton presided over this convention of eighty-one delegates representing eleven of the state's thirteen counties, which met at the capitol building, that in itself an indication of the Antis' growing influence. The Reverend Henry Dana Ward of New York, Antimasonry's most famous "missionary," attended and witnessed the nomination for governor of Heman Allen

of Burlington, a National Republican and former U.S. minister to
Chile. The delegates then voted to nominate all incumbent Nationals
for state offices except those with a Masonic affiliation (Gov. Samuel
C. Crafts was a Mason). Although only a month separated the convention from the election, and Allen quickly declined the nomination,
the Antimasons supported him anyway. In spite of this action, Allen
came in second. More significant was the realization that the Antimasons had elected 33 representatives to the Assembly, in comparison
with the Nationals' 136 and the Jacksonians' 45.[7]

Montpelier was once again the site of a state Antimasonic convention in June 1830. Delegates reappointed a committee of vigilance and
correspondence for each county, designated the Randolph Triumvirate as a general correspondence committee, and resolved to petition
the assembly for repeal of the civil charters of incorporation for the
grand lodge and grand Royal Arch chapter. For a second time Allen
was nominated for governor; Egerton received the party's designation
for lieutenant governor; and Augustine Clarke, a Danville banker,
was nominated for state treasurer. One month after the Montpelier
meeting, Allen once again declined the gubernatorial nomination,
tersely asserting he had never been consulted about this offer or about
that of 1829 and declaring that he was neither a Mason nor an
Antimason. Answering an attack by the *Anti-Masonic Republican*
that his declination had "finished" him with the Antimasons, Allen
replied that they seemed to have "finished with me long before I ever
thought of beginning with them." The general committee acted
quickly and selected William Adam Palmer of Danville, recently
affiliated with the Nationals in the assembly, for governor.[8]

Palmer's nomination and the resulting three-way contest (Governor Crafts ran on the National ticket, and party boss Ezra Meech
represented the Democrats) produced a dilemma that would plague
Vermont during the next five years: no candidate received a majority
of popular votes, and the contest had to be decided by the legislature.
The tally in the general election was: Crafts, 13,476; Palmer, 10,923;
Meech, 6,285. Palmer's best showing came in Caledonia and Addison
counties, located on opposite sides of the state. The assembly, containing 121 Nationals, 76 Antimasons, and 28 Democrats, now had to
resolve the election. Thirty-two ballots were needed before the Nationals could recruit ten representatives from the other parties to join
them and reelect Crafts. The vote on the final ballot was: Crafts, 115;
Palmer, 72; and Bradley, 37. Following the gubernatorial debacle,
Eaton of the *North Star* rallied the party faithful to the cause and
implored them not to lose heart but to confirm to the world the

declaration that "'once an Antimason, always an Antimason . . .'
[and that ] the annihilation of an oath-bound, blood-stained aristocracy [is] our object, whose sinister and secret cooperation, in every
department of our government, contaminates the body politic and
threatens ruin to this highly favored Republic."[9]

A preview of the evil days that would eventually overtake Vermont
Masonry occurred in late October 1830, when William Slade and
Edward D. Barber, two radical Antimasons appointed by the state
convention in June, memorialized the General Assembly to repeal the
civil (legislative) charters of the grand lodge (1823) and the grand
Royal Arch chapter (1826). They requested repeal because of the
allegedly subversive, undemocratic, and political nature of Masonic
oaths, because the rules and regulations of these bodies were "repugnant" to the constitution and laws of Vermont, for Masonry "assumes
legislative power, upon grounds independent of, and irresponsible to,
all other human power and extending to the most precious of human
rights—to liberty and life." Two days after its introduction, the memorial passed on a third reading without opposition, both National
Republican and Democratic legislators evidently believing it unwise
politically to incur the Antis' wrath by fighting the measure. They also
undoubtedly realized that repeal of these legislative charters would
have little or no effect upon the grand lodge or grand chapter, which
existed, in a Masonically legal sense, on the basis of their Masonic
charters alone. On October 28, 1830, the governor and council concurred with the bill, and it became law.[10]

By 1831 it was becoming evident that the Antimasons were now the
dominant political party in Vermont, but they usually had to divide
votes with the National Republicans and Democrats, and only in 1833
did they briefly become the majority party. In terms of economic
issues, Vermont Antis, like their associates in other states, had much
in common with the Nationals, especially favoring the construction
of roads and canals financed at least in part by the federal government.
Although the eastern portion of the state was blessed by good water
transportation on Lake Champlain, most citizens had to overcome the
obstacles of poor roads and rugged terrain to take their products to
market, and the question of internal improvements remained important throughout this period.[11]

A new leader emerged among Antimasonic newspapers in 1831
with the *State Journal,* which the state committee established at
Montpelier with Chauncey L. Knapp as editor. Gradually the *Journal,* oriented to politics, candidates, and elections rather than merely
to the extermination of Freemasonry, replaced the *North Star* as the

voice of Vermont Antimasonry. Also in 1831, the party faithful, represented by 154 delegates from twelve counties, again met at Montpelier in June and nominated Palmer and Egerton for governor and lieutenant governor, Clarke for treasurer, twelve candidates for councillor, and seven delegates and alternates to September's national convention at Baltimore. The convention expressed its astonishment and regret "that no man is duly qualified to be a President of the United States unless he is a high Mason, murderer and duelist," declared Masonic membership a disqualification for holding any responsible state or national office, and vowed that Antimasonry would never cease its efforts until Masonry's "idol temples shall be demolished and every worshipper be fled from the uprooted and prostrate altars of its mysterious and unhallowed sanctuary." The National Republicans attempted to renominate Allen, but he proved no more eager to accept his own party's nomination than that of the Antimasons in 1829 and 1830, and party leaders substituted William A. Griswold of Chittenden County (Burlington). The Democrats renominated Meech. The major issue of the campaign seems to have been not Antimasonry but an accusation by the Nationals that Palmer was proslavery, this charge being based on his votes in the U.S. Senate during debate of the Maine-Missouri bills, 1819-1820, when he opposed any attempt to place slavery restrictions on Missouri, principally on constitutional grounds. In the October election, Palmer received 2,000 more votes than "Allen" (Griswold) but did not have a majority of the popular vote. Once again the legislature had to select a governor and did so on the ninth ballot, when Palmer was elected with 114 votes, compared with 36 for "Allen," 35 for Crafts, and 42 for Meech. Egerton, former assemblyman and currently serving as the town clerk of Randolph, became lieutenant governor, receiving 110 votes on the first ballot for that office.[12]

Biographical information about the nation's first Antimasonic governor is limited. Palmer was more moderate than other Antimasonic leaders and also had the advantage of being better known as the result of a long career in state and national politics. He ultimately served four consecutive one-year terms as governor, proving himself a competent executive who administered the state with impartiality. Born at Hebron, Connecticut, in 1781, of parents who had migrated from England prior to the Revolution, Palmer attended public schools in Hebron before moving to Chelsea, Vermont, in 1800. There he began to read and eventually to practice law, first in Derby, then in St. Johnsbury. In 1802 he moved to Danville in Caledonia County. Palmer began his political career when he was elected county probate judge in 1807. He served eight years (1808-1816) as county clerk, until he was elected in 1811 to the first of five one-year terms in the General Assembly. In 1816 voters placed him on the state supreme court, where he remained for only one term, preferring reelection to the legislature. He was a member of that body when he was chosen to fill the vacant U.S. Senate seat of James Fisk.[13]

Palmer's seven-year stint in the Senate revealed his willingness to support the Monroe administration in most matters but also an inclination to promote the principles of Clay's American system, which included the protective tariff, an issue dear to the hearts of Vermont's wool growers, of whom Palmer was one. In the Senate he also indicated a reverence for internal improvements and states' rights, and the latter might explain his position on the Missouri question, a stand that angered many of his constituents. This feeling contributed to the assembly's failure to reelect Palmer as senator in 1825. He went home, only to be returned to the assembly for two years, 1825-1827, and then for another term in 1829. During these later years in the legislature, Palmer promoted the interests of banks and canal companies but did, in 1827, advocate the abolition of imprisonment for debt. With that exception, his political career prior to becoming governor in 1831 was characterized by devotion to various special interests and evidenced no particular concern for the economically or socially disadvantaged.[14]

Palmer's four terms as governor belie the accusation of a local Democratic journal that the sole aim of the Antimasonic leadership was the winning of office "and that they care nothing about the *evils of masonry* . . . only as they serve as battle-cries to win a victory." The office of governor in Vermont, as in most states during that period, was not a position of power, for the governor did not possess a final veto. If he did veto a bill, the assembly could repass it during the next session, and it would become law without his signature. In the realm of appointments, Palmer's policies were characterized by a spirit of moderation toward Masons, a spirit that did not apply to the governor's views on legislation to destroy Masonry. The appointment by the assembly of two "high Masons," Thomas Hutchinson and Stephen Royce, Jr., to the supreme court, with Palmer's concurrence, produced favorable editorial comment from the Nationals' major newspaper, the *Vermont Watchman and State Gazette*. It observed that these appointments, as well as the selection of many "adhering Masons" to the sheriffs' and other departments, indicated that this new administration had based its policy upon the doctrine of the public good rather than on the proscription of Masonry.[15]

In one category, nevertheless, Palmer remained loyal to the Antimasonic creed. As part of his first annual message (1831) to the legislature, the governor responded to editorials in the Antimasonic press denouncing Masonic oaths and demanding that they be prohibited. As it was obvious that Masons were not going to abandon the fraternity voluntarily, Palmer recommended that the legislature prohibit by law the administration or imposition of all extrajudicial oaths, vows, and obligations, permitting only the swearing of those necessary to "secure the faithful discharge of official trusts and to elicit truth in the administration of justice." The assembly, however, took no action in this session.[16]

Elected to Congress in 1831 on the third attempt was a man who now emerged as one of Vermont's most effective Antimasonic leaders —William Slade. A native Vermonter, a graduate of Middlebury College (1807), and an attorney and newspaper editor, Slade had served as secretary of state from 1816 to 1823, during which time he compiled the *Vermont State Papers,* then considered a major achievement. In 1824 Monroe appointed Slade as a clerk of the U.S. State Department, a position that he held until April 1829, when Jackson's new secretary of state, Martin Van Buren, removed him from office. This action made him extremely bitter toward the president and may also have contributed to his dislike of Masonry. As with many other converts, Antimasonry offered Slade a means of political advancement as well as an opportunity to attack the Jackson administration. As an Antimasonic congressman, his primary role came to be that of a practical, anti-Jackson politician, who emphasized support for Clay's American system and, after 1833-1834, aided the transition to Whiggery.[17]

Vermont Antimasons held two state conventions in 1832, the first being a poorly attended gathering in February that did little more than endorse the Wirt-Ellmaker ticket. The second convention at Montpelier in late June adopted a platform that, except for the usual denunciations of Masonry, was extremely National Republican in tone. It advocated maintenance of the protective tariff, the Bank of the United States, internal improvements, and the Supreme Court as a means of continuing the Union. It also contained a strong condemnation of nullification "as but another name for rebellion." Delegates again endorsed the Wirt-Ellmaker candidacies and then renominated Palmer, Egerton, and Clarke in addition to twelve candidates for councillor and seven for presidential electors. The months preceding the state election in October and presidential contest in November were enlivened by Jackson's pocket veto of an internal improvements bill dear to the hearts of Vermonters—one that would have improved navigation on the Connecticut River. In addition, Antimasons discovered a "secret scheme" of Clay's supporters whereby local committees would pressure individual voters who had previously voted other tickets to switch and support clay. This "plot," supposedly uncovered by a village postmaster, was given full coverage by the *North Star*.[18]

The election saw Palmer reelected to a second term, but once again he failed to achieve a popular majority, and the contest had to be settled by the legislature. The popular vote totals were: Palmer, 17,-318; Crafts (National Republican), 15,499; and Meech (Democrat), 8,210. It took the legislature six days and forty-three ballots in late October to declare Palmer the victor. Fourteen ballots were needed to reelect Lieutenant Governor Egerton, and thirteen trials occurred before selection of a clerk of the assembly. The *North Star* condemned these "obstructionist" tactics as a needless waste of time and expense and blamed thirty-eight recently elected "Jackson Antimasons" for the delay.[19]

The presidential contest produced less excitement in Vermont than the statewide races of the previous month. Declaring Wirt to be above reproach, the *North Star* exhorted voters to support the Antimasonic ticket on November 13 and to ensure "the preservation of our invaluable republican institutions and . . . the Supremacy of the Laws." On the eve of the election, the *State Journal* reminded Antimasonic voters of Jackson's and Clay's Masonic affiliation with a sly reference to "Most Excellent Royal Arch Companion Andrew Jackson [and] . . . Worshipful Master Henry Clay." Wirt did not win a majority of the popular vote in Vermont, but in a presidential election a plurality was sufficient to carry the state. He polled more than 13,000 votes, compared with more than 11,000 for Clay and some 7,800 for Jackson. Wirt's greatest strength was in Windsor, Orange, Addison, and Caledonia counties, all in the central and eastern portion of the state; he also did well in the northern counties of Franklin and Orleans. In the midst of this statewide victory but national disaster, the *North Star* urged the faithful never to abandon the cause, although a few weeks later it concurred with Wirt's refusal to accept a renomination for 1836. In contrast, the pro-Jackson *Vermont Patriot* declared that although it had anticipated Wirt's success, "We do not yet despair of our Green Mountain State. We still believe that she will redeem herself."[20]

By 1833 Vermont National Republicans and Democrats were sufficiently desperate to form a coalition, which first saw fruition when an amalgamation candidate defeated an Antimason in the Third Congressional District. Even in the face of this coalition, Antimasons were able to elect three of the state's five representatives. When 322 Antimasonic delegates met in state convention at Montpelier on June 27 to renominate Palmer, Egerton, and Clarke, they took note of the coalition and passed a resolution condemning it as "substituting the blindness of party zeal or the mandates of party leaders, for the honest conviction of truth and a laudable adherence to principle." Led by perennial Democratic boss and gubernatorial candidate Meech, one of the state's largest landowners, the Democratic and National Republican parties held simultaneous but separate state conventions at Montpelier on July 3, 1833, and produced a "Union" ticket. The parties nominated Meech for governor, Jedediah Harris, a National, for lieutenant governor, and Benjamin Swan, another National, for treasurer. In addition, eight Nationals and four Democrats were selected for the councillor posts. The *State Journal* later accused ten of the fifteen Union candidates of being Freemasons, including Meech and Swan. Vermont's National Republicans now declared that they could never unite with a party such as the Antimasons, whose motto was *"proscription,"* but they could join with an organization whose principles agreed with their own. This astounding bit of hyperbole was reiterated by Meech from his home at Shelburne, when, in endorsing the Union ticket, he stated that he now favored tariff protection for raw materials produced in the United States, a stand untypical of most Democrats.[21]

The coalition was unpopular with a number of Democrats, and several pro-Jackson papers, including the *Patriot,* "nominated" John Roberts for governor. Unhappy National Republicans promoted former U.S. Senator Horatio Seymour, but he declined, and most of his supporters returned to the coalition, which an Ohio Antimasonic press now described as "a fair array of freemasonry at the polls." All dissent was not on the coalition side, however, and rumors began to circulate among Antimasons that Governor Palmer had Jacksonian tendencies. The anti-Palmer movement was encouraged by Knapp, editor of the *State Journal,* and also by Slade, and was merely the latter's latest tactic to gain a stronger grip on the party and to elect a governor more indebted to him as well as one more committed to National Republican principles.[22]

The election of 1833 produced a complete triumph for the Antimasons, as their entire statewide ticket swamped the Union ticket. Palmer at last had a popular majority, receiving 20,565 votes compared with 15,683 for Meech. The two "dissenters," Seymour (National Republican) and Roberts (Democrat), received 1,765 and 772 votes, respectively. Instead of destroying Antimasonry, the coalition had strengthened it, and Palmer won 3,000 more votes than in 1832. Antimasons elected all twelve councillors and a plurality of the assembly; their candidate for speaker, John Smith, was selected on the first ballot. In terms of counties, the Antis carried nine of thirteen; the coalition won in Orange and Washington (Montpelier), and Chittenden was divided between the two parties. The *North Star* exulted in this victory over "a most unprincipled and cunningly devised scheme of the administration party to foist on the freemen a *Jackson* governor." A few weeks later that same paper declared that the recent election was the "triumph of *principle* over coalesced corruption." The *State Journal* also trumpeted about crushing this "monster half horse and half alligator . . . the miserable offspring of political Masonry."[23]

In 1831, following his first election as governor, Palmer had recommended to the assembly passage of an act outlawing "extrajudicial," that is, Masonic, oaths. He then asked "whether the cause of morality, and the general good, do not demand your interposition—even for the above purposes." Such a bill failed to become law in 1831 or in 1832. In 1833, encouraged by Palmer's election by a popular majority, Antimasons again demanded passage of a bill outlawing extrajudicial oaths. The governor requested it in his annual message to the assembly, which passed the desired statute on November 7, 1833, and the governor and council concurred on the same day. The law decreed that if any person was convicted of administering an oath or obligation not authorized by law, he would be subject to a fine of between $50.00 and $100. This did not apply to any "oath or affirmation to truth of any affidavit or any swearing in court." Although this statute was intended to intimidate Masons and to force them to abandon the fraternity, there is no record of its enforcement.[24]

By 1834 Freemasonry in Vermont was dying, and many who viewed the Antimasonic party as a temporary fixture—one that would go out of existence when the lodge disappeared—began to predict a speedy fusion with the National Republicans to form the new Whig party, as was happening in New York. Evidence that this change was already taking place seemed apparent at the Antimasonic state convention in late May, when observers noticed a number in attendance who were already identified with Whiggery. The majority of delegates, however, quickly rejected union with the Whigs because they were "too Masonic" and decided to nominate a separate slate of candidates, headed, as usual, by Palmer. To reassure the public that they were still Antimasons, the delegates passed several resolutions asserting that

Antimasons must "adhere steadfastly to our original principles, until Freemasonry is effectively abolished." The Whig influence prevailing in this convention showed itself in other resolutions, one of which criticized Jackson for an undue assumption of power and for removing federal deposits from the Bank of the United States. Another pledged resistance to encroachments against the supremacy of the laws and the U.S. Constitution, "whether perpetrated by the Masonic Order or the President."[25]

Vermont Whigs organized their party at a Montpelier convention in July 1834 from a core of the once-vital National Republicans, adding dissident Democrats and Antimasons who considered Jackson to be a greater threat than Freemasonry. Some eighty delegates nominated former U.S. Senator Seymour for governor and passed a resolution declaring "that Masonry and Antimasonry are not subjects which should identify or designate political parties." Seymour, of course, was not the only opponent of Governor Palmer, for the Democrats nominated William C. Bradley. The campaign brought renewed charges, this time from the Whig press, that Palmer, while serving in the U.S. Senate, was an "abettor of negro slavery . . . [and] a negro driver."[26]

In the gubernatorial election of 1834 Palmer once again won a plurality of popular votes but not the majority needed for a victory, and the contest had to be decided by the legislature. The governor received 17,131 votes; Bradley and Seymour each achieved slightly more than 10,000. The Antimasons had, however, elected the lieutenant governor and twelve councillors, although two of them, Silas Jenison and Henry F. Janes, were already regarded as more Whig than Antimasonic. The General Assembly now contained some 102 Antimasons, 57 Whigs, 49 Democrats, 7 "doubtfuls." Seymour and Bradley withdrew their names from consideration before the legislative balloting on October 10, 1834, and Palmer became governor with 147 votes to 13 for Bradley. The "willingness" of numerous Whigs and Democrats in the legislature to support Palmer was undoubtedly predicated on an early collapse of the Antimasonic party for "want of fuel," leaders of the other parties hoping to attract Antimasonic voters looking for a new home.[27]

Although the Antimasonic press, both before and after the autumn elections of 1834, voiced fears that Antimasonry was slipping into Whiggery, Palmer did nothing to quiet these fears with his annual message to the legislature, delivered on October 13, but instead inspired new anxiety concerning his proclivities for the Democrats. The governor's speech contained not one word on Masonry or Antimasonry, which upset the purists within his own party. Although he criticized the "tyranny" of Jackson, he also expressed his opposition to renewal of the charter of the Bank of the United States "in its present form." This statement infuriated the Whigs and Antimasons with Whiggish tendencies, including Slade, and they never forgave Palmer. Two weeks later, an Antimasonic legislative caucus meeting at the statehouse passed resolutions asserting the party's loyalty to Antimasonic principles and declaring that its purpose was the total destruction of Freemasonry. Delegates bound themselves to maintain the Antimasonic organization "while Masonry continues to exist among us." These same Antis, however, also strongly criticized Jackson for removing deposits from the Bank of the United States and for witholding certain nominations from the Senate.[28]

Influenced by the party's decline on the national level, internal dissent within the state organization, and the removal of Masonry as a threat, Vermont Antimasonry began to disintegrate rapidly in 1835, and both the Whigs and the Democrats stood by, attempting to woo distracted Antis into their respective camps. The sparsely attended Antimasonic state convention on July 1 (at most, 120 delegates were present), was filled with "distrust, fear and trepidation." Palmer was renominated for governor, but to please the "Whig-Antimasons," a moderate, Silas Jennison from Shoreham, was named for second place on the ticket. The convention passed several resolutions, including one that withheld any preference for an Antimasonic presidential nomination for 1836 until the next national convention. On the same day that the Antimasons held their convention, the Whigs also met in Montpelier and endorsed the Anti ticket. In addition, it was immediately apparent that leaders of both parties had arranged a coalition slate of nominees for councillor.[29]

The Antimasonic gubernatorial campaign of 1835 was enlivened by a split within the party over support of Palmer, although most voters seemed willing to go along with the Whig-Anti coalition councillor tickets. Whigs, and Antimasons with Whiggish inclinations, led by Slade and centered in Montpelier, were angry about the governor's opposition to renewal of the Bank of the United States charter, which he had expressed in his legislative message of 1834. In addition, rumors continued to circulate that Palmer would support Van Buren for president in 1836. On August 31, the *North Star,* still a firm advocate of Palmer's reelection, urged all "Democratic Antimasonic Republicans" not only to vote for Palmer but to "WATCH . . . VIGILANTLY . . . WATCH . . . THOSE WHO ARE CREATING DISUNION in your ranks."[30]

Although Vermont Whigs had, at their recent convention, endorsed the Palmer-Jennison slate, a number of Whig voters supported a "dissident" candidate, Charles Paine, who received 5,435 votes. Palmer had 16,210, and Bradley 13,254. Only in three counties, Windham, Caledonia, and Addison, did the governor outpoll both Paine and Bradley. Once again, no candidate had a statewide majority, and the election was sent to the legislature. There was, however, an election of a lieutenant governor, as Jennison, the "Whig-Antimason," defeated his Democratic opponent, Thomas Chittenden, 21,316 to 13,071, this vote being an indication of how the gubernatorial race might have fared if the Whigs and Antis had truly united behind Palmer. The Democratic *Patriot* concluded that the Whigs had not given Palmer their wholehearted support because of their inability to obtain a pledge from him "that he would oppose the elevation of Mr. Van Buren at all hazards. This was the condition upon which their support of him depended, and, as yet, the stipulation has not been performed, which leaves it clear that there are suspicions existing as to his attachment to the principles of modern Whiggery."[31]

Unfortunately for Palmer, "loyal" Antimasons in the legislature lacked sufficient numbers to reelect him to a fifth consecutive term. The lower house was divided between 110 Antis, 75 Democrats, and 35 Whigs. Although the entire coalition councillor slate had been elected, at least half were more Whig than Antimasonic. The balloting began on October 9 and lasted until November 2, 1835. The vote on the first ballot was: Palmer, 110; Bradley, 73; and Paine, 42. Palmer's highest total was 112, with some 117 needed for election. By the time the thirty-third ballot was taken, the *North Star* was blaming Masonry for the failure of Whigs and Democrats to unite behind Palmer. After sixty-three ballots had produced no result, the "joint assembly" voted 113 to 100 to dissolve, and Jennison became "acting governor" under terms of the state constitution. Had those assemblymen who had been elected as "Antimasons" given full support to Palmer, there would have been only one ballot, and he would have served a fifth term. As it transpired, a few voted for Bradley, and some supported Paine. Jennison, through a quirk of fate, thus became acting governor. In 1836 he was elected governor as a Whig and continued as Vermont's chief executive through 1841.[32]

Palmer was the only Antimason to serve as governor of the Green Mountain State, and by the standards of that day and of his party, he was a successful chief executive. With limited powers, he was able to secure the passage of laws canceling the civil charters of the grand lodge and grand Royal Arch chapter and prohibiting the administra-

tion of extrajudicial oaths. The public school system expanded during
his terms; the legislature chartered seven new banks; funds were
appropriated to improve transportation; and as the most lasting testimony to his administration, construction began on a new statehouse
at Montpelier in 1833. Perhaps Palmer's greatest failure was his inability to secure a statute abolishing imprisonment for debt. His four
terms "may have been characterized as an anomaly in politics, but his
civil administration attested to solid accomplishment of a program
and a philosophy." The governor kept Antimasonry a moderate
movement in Vermont and was able for a few years to draw support
in the legislature from the National Republicans-Whigs and Democrats as well as Antimasons, and this cooperation produced statutory
successes. When, however, the Whigs-Antimasons, as led by Slade,
decided that Palmer was a "nuisance," he was defeated for reelection,
and the party disintegrated.[33]

The year 1836 brought the fusion of perhaps two-thirds of Vermont's Antimasons into the Whig party. In January Whig members
of a state constitutional convention caucused to make plans for a
political convention, where all opposed to "Executive Tyranny"
would be welcomed "without distinction of party names." On February 24, two carefully orchestrated gatherings met simultaneously at
Montpelier, the Whigs convening at the Washington County courthouse, the Antimasons at the statehouse. Both parties nominated
Jennison for governor and passed a resolution condemning all secret
societies and monopolies. The *State Journal,* now exhibiting strong
Whig tendencies, praised the Whig convention for also adopting the
"Antimasonic" slate and declared that this "evidenced a spirit of
liberality which is highly creditable to them and which demands a
respectful recognition at our hands." In addition to these nominees,
both parties selected a presidential ticket, recommending William
Henry Harrison of Ohio for president and Francis Granger of New
York for vice president. The presidential issue sparked dissent in the
Antimasonic meeting, where Harrison received eighty-seven votes,
Webster (promoted by Slade), twenty-eight, Van Buren, twenty-
seven, and Granger, twenty. A second vote was taken, with Harrison
receiving 104 ayes and 40 nos. Granger was then nominated for vice
president and received all but one vote. The twenty-seven votes for
Van Buren reveal the approximate strength of the Democrats-
Antimasons, led at this convention by the radical, Barber. The *State
Journal,* trying to obscure Harrison's tepid support of Antimasonry,
declared that the the aging general's opinions on Masonry "are sub-
stantially the same as held by the Antimasonic party from its orga-

nization. He speaks out plainly of free-masonry, 'as an evil both moral and political'."[34]

The movement of Vermont Antimasons into the Democratic party began at the February 24, 1836, convention, when twenty-seven Antis seceded from the convention, moved to a Montpelier hotel, and held their own meeting, chaired by John S. Pettibone of Manchester. Also included in this group were Blodgett, Egerton, and Barber. The secessionists passed two resolutions, one condemning the nomination of Harrison as "a virtual disbanding of Antimasonry and a bold attempt to transform the antimasonic into a whig party." The other resolution proposed nominations for certain offices: Van Buren for president, Palmer for governor, Pettibone for lieutenant governor, Clarke for treasurer, plus seven presidential electors, including Barber and Egerton. The secessionists also took with them the state's most vocal Anti press and editor, the *North Star* and Ebeneezer Eaton. Several Democratic leaders declared their new-found hostility to Masonry, but John B. Hollinbeck, Democratic wheelhorse at Burlington, asserted that although he had no objection to "drawing out some of the Anti electors . . ., some of them are so slippery that they would not stay out unless they were proposed very strongly with a prospect of advancement by our party."[35]

The exact reasons for the defection of the Antimasonic minority to the Democrats, while most of their former associates were becoming Whigs, have dimmed with the passage of time and because of the scarcity of personal papers of those involved in the transition. Unhappiness with the Harrison nomination, refusal to support the stand of the Whig-Antimasons in favor of another federally chartered bank, opposition to all "monopolies," and dissatisfaction with Slade's leadership emerge as the principal causes of the Antimasonic movement to "The Democracy." That the union of the "Barber Antimasons" with the Democrats was imperfect at best was admitted by the *Patriot* in May 1836 when it observed that the party now had two distinct branches, "the original administration party and that portion of the anti-masons who had declared against Harrison and bank-whiggery." Former Governor Palmer was one of those Antimasons who eventually became a Democrat. Realizing that his gubernatorial candidacy on a pro-Van Buren Antimasonic ticket was divisive, Palmer withdrew from the race in early May to unite the Democratic party. He became a delegate to the Vermont constitutional convention of 1836 and voted for the change to a bicameral form of government that eliminated the council and established a senate. He continued in public office for another year, serving as one of two new state senators from Caledonia County and becoming the Democratic minority leader in that body. Palmer retired from public life in 1837 and reappeared only briefly as a delegate to the 1850 constitutional convention. He died in December 1860, his passing ignored by both the general public and the press. Abolition and temperance had replaced Antimasonry as the passions of reform-minded Vermonters, while political Antimasonry had receded into the dim past.[36]

The influence of the recent converts within the Democratic ranks was evident immediately. Several local Democratic conventions endorsed Antimasonic principles, one at Stowe declaring that "all secret combinations . . . are of the most fatal character to the liberties and institutions of our happy country." When Democrats met at their state convention on June 30, they nominated Pettibone, one of the twenty-seven secessionists, for lieutenant governor. Their candidate for governor was once again Bradley, long popular with some Antimasons because he had never joined a lodge. The Whigs nominated Acting Governor Jennison and endorsed Harrison and Granger for president and vice president, and both tickets carried the state. Jennison received 20,371 votes, compared with Bradley's 16,134; not all "Democratic" voters, however, supported Pettibone, whose tally was only 15,926. The Harrison-Granger ticket won Vermont by a margin of almost 7,000 votes, although Van Buren was successful in the national election. In the legislature, the Whigs had a slim working majority in both houses. The final steps toward complete amalgamation of the Slade Antimasons into the Whig party took place in July 1837 at a state convention at Montpelier, when former Antimasonic leaders Knapp and Milton Brown received appointments to the Whig state committee and the now-united party renominated Jennison for governor.[37]

The hostility that Masons had encountered in New York during the "excitement" was repeated in Vermont on a more fevered pitch. Although the motto of the state's official Antimasonic press, the *Montpelier State Journal,* was "THE MOST PERFECT POPULAR GOVERNMENT IS THAT, WHERE AN INJURY DONE TO THE HUMBLEST CITIZEN IS AN INSULT TO THE WHOLE CONSTITUTION," this platitude did not seem to apply to the Masons of Vermont or to their families. The controversy produced great divisiveness, even within family units. At a funeral at Danville in 1830, the Masonic relatives and friends occupied one room of a home, the Antimasons and their allies, another. At the burial each group stood on opposite sides of the grave, no words being exchanged, even between brother and sister. At Bristol, a gristmill jointly owned by a

Mason and an Antimason was patronized one week by the lodge brethren, the next week by the Antis. One Mason who lived through the "excitement" recalled in 1850 that Antis made "unhallowed efforts" to exclude every Mason from public office, juries, voting, church membership and preaching. Any brother "too honest to secede . . . was marked and pointed out, and vilified as a dangerous man." Mount Anthony Lodge at Bennington, chartered in 1824, became dormant in 1832 and probably did not meet again until 1848. At Royalton, Rising Sun Lodge kept no records from 1839 to 1848 because of Antimasonic pressure. The brethren held underground meetings, "moving from house to house and places outside, hiding their properties to avoid mob violence." The only lodge in the Green Mountain State during this era to perform degree work was Missiquoi Lodge at Berkshire, which initiated fifteen candidates during a twelve-year period. Weary of controversy, some Masons succumbed to pressure and urged abandonment of both the civil and Masonic charters of the grand lodge. In 1830 five Masons who publicly seceded from Green Mountain Lodge at Cavendish were subsequently expelled by that lodge for unmasonic conduct, which included "associating with the enemies of masonry and participating in their measures hostile to the masonic institution."[38]

Although in 1829 Deputy Grand Master Philip C. Tucker wrote a pamphlet urging the citizens of Vermont to ignore the Antimasonic persecutions, and the grand lodge printed and distributed some 2,000 copies of this tract, it had little effect. By 1831 even the grand lodge was beginning to falter against the pressure of the last three years. At its October 1831 convocation, with forty of seventy-one lodges represented, the brethren passed a resolution advising subordinate lodges to hold only two meetings a year, one to elect officers, the other for "good order, discipline and instruction in Masonry." At this same session, the delegates overwhelmingly defeated a resolution calling for surrender of all subordinate lodge charters to the grand lodge and for that body to abandon all functions as a Masonic entity. Although the resolution was killed, the general situation continued to worsen, and only ten lodges sent representatives to the 1832 convocation.[39]

In 1833, with the Antimasons in complete control of the state government, the grand lodge took even more drastic action, while the *North Star* was demanding that every Mason abandon Masonry, "immediately and forever." At the convocation at Montpelier in October, Brother Samuel Elliot, who had been in communication with Slade, introduced a series of resolutions calling for dissolution of the grand lodge and all local lodges. Elliot's resolutions were preceded by

a lengthy preamble declaring that Masonry's usefulness had ended
and that the great majority of Vermonters desired its abandonment.
The brethren defeated this proposal, seventy-nine to forty-two. Later
that day they passed a motion, introduced by Past Grand Master
Tucker, permitting the voluntary surrender of subordinate lodge
charters to the grand secretary. Failure to pass the more drastic Elliot
resolution produced a violent attack from the *State Journal,* which
queried, "Will the people of Vermont be satisfied with this new insult
on their common sense?"[40]

Although political Antimasonry in Vermont was virtually defunct
by 1836, so was the grand lodge. Undoubtedly influenced if not intimi-
dated by the 1833 statute outlawing extrajudicial oaths, only nine
Masons, representing seven lodges, attended the convocation of 1834.
This session urged those brethren still sympathetic toward Masonry
to continue as members, but "while we are ready to forgive those
whose fidelity has been shaken . . ., we are also ready to judge with
candor the *motives* by which they have been governed." There was
no convocation in 1835, and attendance at the 1836 meeting equaled
that of 1834. The 1836 gathering elected thirteen grand officers and
eleven district deputy grand masters, all of whom eventually served
ten-year terms, for the grand lodge did not officially meet again until
1846. By authority of an 1836 resolution, Grand Master Nathan B.
Haswell, together with the grand secretary and treasurer, met approximately every two years at Burlington and adjourned grand lodge. By
1846, Haswell had determined that the time was propitious to resume
Masonic activities in Vermont. In calling a meeting of the grand lodge
at Burlington for January 14, he declared, "We think it not best to
issue any public notice, as we wish not to give alarm, or see any but
true and faithful Masons." Thirty-four Masons, representing ten
lodges that had retained their charters during the crisis years, convened and reopened grand lodge. Delegates adopted a committee
report proposing reactivation of the fraternity by restoring forfeited
charters and returning brethren to the fold. Three years later, the
grand lodge declared the charters of forty-six lodges to be "extinct,"
and the rebuilding process continued. Haswell, who had served as
grand master continuously since 1829, was reelected for the last time
in 1846 and retired the next year. Masonry made a slow but steady
recovery in Vermont, and by 1849 thirteen lodges were "at work."
Between 1846 and 1894, the grand lodge granted eighty-six new charters, and by the latter year, Vermont had 101 active lodges with some
10,000 members.[41]

# 7. The "Union" Ticket of 1832

Pennsylvania was in the midst of a long era of political chaos when Antimasonry appeared on the scene. The Federalist party had declined, and the Adams party, never strong, was disintegrating. The Jacksonian Democrats, like their predecessors, the Jeffersonian Republicans, were so numerous that they remained fragmented. Pennsylvania historians generally divide them into two distinct groups: one, established about 1817, was known as the "Family party," so called because of the leaders' connections by blood and marriage. George M. Dallas, a Philadelphian, was considered the "brains" of the organization. The other faction, the "Amalgamators," included old-time Federalists as well as "Democratic-Republicans." The Amalgamators, or "Original Jackson" men, led by future president James Buchanan, were among the first Pennsylvania Republicans to support Jackson in his initial presidential race of 1824 and therefore believed that they should be preeminent in party affairs. During the Antimasonic era, the continued occurrence of factional strife among the Jacksonians, along with the inability of the Antimasons and National Republicans to "effect a complete coalition," produced constant instability in the Keystone State, and voters did not hesitate to cross party lines.[1]

As Antimasonry developed in Pennsylvania, it appealed largely to two groups: poor farmers in the western tier of counties, angry at being bypassed by the main canal system linking Philadelphia and Pittsburgh, yet desirous of branch canals for their counties; and the thrifty German sectarians of the central and southeastern portion of the state, who used the Susquehanna River and considered canals a needless expense but also found a religious appeal in Antimasonry. Most of the pietistic sects, such as the Mennonites, Amish, and Dunkards, as well as the Quakers, opposed the swearing of oaths or obligations. They also disliked the regalia, elaborate ceremonies, and secrecy associated with Masonry. In the Northwest, the inhabitants were mainly of New England stock and had Calvinist origins, and the area was geographically connected to New York, site of the Morgan affair. Accusations of Masonic influence in an 1818 court case at Pittsburgh may have established the basis for an Antimasonic movement in that locality.[2]

The creation of an Antimasonic press preceded organization of the party in Pennsylvania, as it had in other states. The *Rochester Anti-Masonic Enquirer* received wide circulation, and Whittlesey traveled to the Keystone State to do "missionary" work. The *Antimasonic Herald,* initially established at New Holland in Lancaster County in late June of 1828, was apparently the first Anti paper in Pennsylvania. Its editor was Theophilus ("Theo") Fenn, later state printer and party workhorse. For the paper's motto, Fenn cleverly lifted out of context a sentence from George Washington's Farewell Address of 1796: "Beware of Secret Associations, Under Whatever Plausible Character." Although at first claiming political neutrality, Fenn in September 1828 nevertheless accused Masonic postmasters of failing to deliver the *Herald* because of the influence of "Masonic *mystic ties.*" On April 1, 1829, the *Herald* moved from New Holland to the county seat of Lancaster, which was then emerging as the center of Antimasonic activity in southeastern Pennsylvania. The *Herald* was quickly followed by other presses in the Lancaster and Pittsburgh areas.[3]

Political Antimasonry emerged in July 1828 with organization of the party in Lancaster County and the subsequent nomination of William Hiester for the U.S. House of Representatives. Hiester, a kinsman of Ellmaker, was defeated by James Buchanan by a 1,500-vote margin. The few who called themselves "Antimasons" kept a low profile in the presidential contest of 1828, when Jackson defeated Adams in Pennsylvania by a two-to-one margin. Old Hickory once again displayed his great popularity among the voters of German ancestry, and the Adams party almost ceased to exist. The *Herald* warned Pennsylvania Antimasons to organize statewide immediately: "A firm and inflexible stand must be taken, unitedly, against the institution—temporising [*sic*] only enervates us."[4]

The organization of Antimasonry in Pennsylvania came quickly with the 1829 conversion of Thaddeus Stevens, who would be associated with the party for more than fourteen years. Stevens was born in Vermont in 1792. His father was an alcoholic and ran away; his mother was fanatically religious. Stevens entered life with a severely clubbed foot. As a young man he spent a few semesters at the University of Vermont before transferring to Dartmouth College at Hanover, New Hampshire, from which he graduated in 1814. While at Dartmouth, he was infuriated by his inability to gain admittance into the local Phi Beta Kappa chapter, then both a scholastic and a social fraternity but also a secret society. Moving to York, Pennsylvania,

Stevens taught at a local academy and read law in his spare time, only to discover later, when he applied for admission, that the county bar association had recently passed a resolution denying recognition as an attorney to anyone who had followed another vocation while studying law. Stevens was able to gain admission to the bar in nearby Hartford County, Maryland, where he was unknown, and then to practice in Gettysburg, Pennsylvania, under a reciprocal agreement between the two states. During this most difficult period of Stevens's life, it was rumored that he had been blackballed when he had applied for the Masonic degrees in Good Samaritan Lodge No. 200 at Gettysburg, although this charge has never been substantiated by scholars.[5]

It is difficult to determine Stevens's precise motivation in becoming an Antimason, largely because of the paucity of his personal papers extant today. Certainly, political opportunism and expediency played some part in this process—as a former Federalist, he really had no-where else to go in Adams County in 1829. In addition, his long-standing hatred of secret societies, combined with his strong belief in egalitarianism and in the absolute equality and supremacy of the law, made him receptive to Antimasonry. By 1829 he firmly believed that Masonry, a "vile institution," had degenerated into a "conspiratorial organization" whose purpose was to achieve political and economic power by every means possible. He also believed that Masonic governors such as George Wolf had been overly influenced by fraternal ties in making appointments.[6]

Stevens began his Antimasonic career in 1829 when he organized the party in Adams County, established the *Gettysburg Star*, and promoted the gubernatorial candidacy of Joseph Ritner. In 1830 he was a delegate to both the state and national conventions, and at the latter meeting in Philadelphia, he gave two speeches, one attacking Masonic influence over the American press, the other defending various exposés of Masonry as authentic. In this address Stevens asserted that Masons, who composed only one-twentieth of the population, controlled eighteen of every twenty offices of "high profit and honor." In 1831 Stevens was an ardent supporter of McLean for the presidential nomination, even after the Ohioan had declined. By this time, Stevens's role in Antimasonry was giving him the notoriety he always seemed to crave. In June of 1831 he gave a vindictive address at Hagerstown, Maryland, in which he described Masonry as "this feeble band of lowly reptiles" and asserted that politics was the only effective means of suppressing the fraternity. Publication of the "notorious" speech by editor Jacob Lefever in the pro-Jackson *Gettysburg Compiler,* accompanied by an unsigned letter denouncing Stevens, produced a libel suit and other legal entanglements that dragged on until 1835. Ultimately, Stevens was awarded damages of $1,800, which Lefever could not pay. The editor saw his property sold by the sheriff to Stevens, who, in an unusual gesture, returned it to Lefever. It was no wonder that Stevens's mother wrote to her son during this period that Antimasonry, although a good cause, was "a dangerous won [sic] because it creates enemyes [sic]."[7]

An Antimasonic meeting at Lancaster on April 23, 1829, attended by more than 800 citizens, called for a statewide convention as well as approving New York's proposal for a national meeting in Philadelphia. Those attending also appointed a six-man committee of correspondence, which included Ellmaker and Hiester. Three months later, a "state" convention of irregular composition met at Harrisburg, with thirty-five delegates representing eight of the fifty-two counties. Eight delegates were from Lancaster County alone. Whittlesey gave his usual long address, after which delegates nominated Joseph Ritner of Washington County in southwestern Pennsylvania for governor and produced an address to the people. Reflecting the rural and small-town composition of the party, this statement declared that the countryside looked upon the city as "overwhelming, arrogant and dictatorial." It especially indicated the Antimasons' dislike for Philadelphia, a city of 200,000 people, which also served as headquarters for the Grand Lodge of Pennsylvania. Angered by jibes of the Democratic press that Ritner was merely an "ignorant Dutch farmer," the *Lancaster Herald* asserted that he was one of the most popular men in the state, whereas his Democratic opponent, Wolf, would never have received the nomination had he not worn a Masonic apron.[8]

Ritner was born in Berks County (eastern Pennsylvania); his parents were impoverished Germans. He worked as a wool weaver until acquiring sufficient captial to purchase horses and a wagon. Then he crossed the mountains, moving westward to Washington County. In 1820 Ritner achieved election to the Pennyslvania House of Representatives and served six consecutive one-year terms. His fellow representatives selected him as Speaker in 1824 and 1825 without opposition. In the House he became a champion of the wool growers and the protective tariff. He also favored public education, temperance reform, and the abolition of slavery. Ritner had gubernatorial ambitions as early as 1823 and was told that he would be "up" for 1829. His career as Speaker was an unhappy one, however, for he broke with certain pro-Jackson representatives of the U.S. House who opposed the tariff bill of 1827 with its higher rates on wool. In 1828 Ritner supported Jackson for the presidency, as he had in 1824. After the election of 1828, he had a brief flirtation with the dying Adams party before becoming an Antimason. Because of the absence of personal papers, it is difficult to determine Ritner's precise reasons for becoming an Antimason; however, we may recall his German heritage, his fight with the Jacksonians about the tariff, and his probable realization that the only viable political alternative at the moment was Antimasonry. Throughout his career, Ritner was always able to maintain his reputation as a man of the people.[9]

Ritner's only opponent in the 1829 gubernatorial race was the Democrat, Wolf, as the National Republicans were too weak to promote a candidate. A prominent Mason from eastern Pennsylvania, Wolf had served three terms in the U.S. House of Representatives and was closely associated with the "Family" faction of the Jacksonian party. Ritner received the support of Antimasons, probably most of the National Republican votes, and quite likely some ballots from the Amalgamators, who hated Wolf more than Ritner. By Pennsylvania standards, the campaign was uneventful, notable only for the rather sudden conversion of Pennsylvania's Speaker of the House, Ner Middleswarth of Union County, to Antimasonry. Middleswarth now loudly proclaimed to all who would listen that certain Masons had recently approached him and had promised him the governorship if he would only join the fraternity.[10]

A few Antimasonic papers, including the *Lancaster Herald,* asserted that Wolf was the "CANDIDATE of MASONRY" and wondered, "Who can support such a candidate for Governor? Who can vote for a Freemason while he adheres to such an Institution?" Wolf won, nevertheless, although Ritner came within 17,000 votes of victory (almost 130,000 ballots were cast), polling nearly 40 percent and carrying seventeen counties; he and Wolf tied in one jurisdiction. Ritner's strength lay in the western and eastern portions of the state, excluding Philadelphia. The tallies of each candidate were: Wolf, 78, 138; Ritner, 51,776. The Antimasonic party was particularly successful in Lancaster County, which Ritner carried by some 1,600 votes, and the *Herald* now referred to his statewide defeat as a "triumph of principle." Most important of all, Antis elected Harmar Denny of Pittsburgh to the U.S. House. Denny, the son of Pittsburgh's first mayor, carried his four-county district (Allegheny, Beaver, Butler, and Armstrong) by almost 1,200 votes. He would soon become one of the few able and prominent Antimasons in the lower chamber.[11]

The years 1830-1831 were ones of gradual achievement for Pennsylvania Antimasons. In the legislature, the Antis, with help of the

Nationals, passed a law repealing the tax-exempt status of the grand lodge hall in Philadelphia. This was the first time that Masonry had encountered opposition in the General Assembly, and when the bill passed the house in February 1830, fifty-three to thirty-one, it was only after violent and angry debates. In both the legislative sessions of 1829-1830 and 1830-1831, Antimasons tended to vote with their sections rather than take a united party stand on the controversial and decisive issue of appropriations for the state works systems, in general voting for the main line against the branch canals. A sparsely attended party convention at Harrisburg in May 1830 reflected the Antimasons' continuing disunity and lack of organization. A total of 133 delegates should have been present, but there were only 64, representing 26 counties. Those delegates condemned Jackson for his Masonic affiliation, advocated that all judges acknowledge that they were not Masons and, in the convention's most controversial action, instructed the twenty-eight delegates selected to attend the national convention at Baltimore to give no support to Clay. The last resolution passed only after Clay's name had been deleted, although everyone knew who was meant. The autumn elections of 1830 reflected the party's drift and lack of purpose. Only six Antimasons were chosen for senate and twenty for the assembly.[12]

Other than support of Middleswarth for Speaker of the assembly, the only other action at this time that united Antimasons in the legislature was their unsuccessful effort to elect Richard Rush as U.S. senator, replacing the ailing Isaac D. Barnard, who had recently resigned. Rush's conversion to Antimasonry was announced to the world through several well-publicized letters written between May and November 1831. The theme of these letters was blame of all Masons throughout the United States for the Morgan affair. In his communication to an Antimasonic committee of York County (Rush was a native of York), he admitted that many years earlier he had taken the first degree of Masonry but had attended lodge only once after his initiation. In 1826 Rush withdrew, voluntarily, by letter (prior to Morgan's abduction), and by 1831 he firmly believed that the fraternity had subverted the free press and laws of the states and nation. The impact of the Rush letters in boosting the cause of Antimasonry was enormous; the support brought to the Antimasonry party by a man of such national importance could hardly be calculated. Desperate to have a prominent man in office, the Antimasons promoted Rush as a successor to Barnard. Rush's major opponent was George M. Dallas. Although Rush trailed Dallas by only one vote on the first ballot, the contest was decided on the eleventh ballot when another Democratic candidate, the Reverend Henry A. Muhlenberg, threw his support to Dallas, who was elected with 67 of 132 votes. Failure to elect Rush to the Senate deprived Pennsylvania Antimasons of a leader of national repute and evidently soured Rush on Antimasonry as well, for within a year he was a Jacksonian.[13]

The year 1832 loomed as a crucial one for Antimasonry in Pennsylvania, for it involved not only the presidential contest but the triennial gubernatorial election as well. The party's state convention assembled at Harrisburg on February 22 and renominated Ritner for governor. Delegates also selected a presidential electoral slate headed by Rush and pledged to support the Wirt-Ellmaker ticket. In addition, the Antimasons comdemned the Wolf administration in general, and Masonry in particular, with the following resolution: "Masonry encourages in the business and intercourse of life preferences for its own members, destruction of fair competition, and is deeply prejudicial to the industry of others. It creates in favor of Masons a monopoly of public offices and public honors injurious to the services of the Republic." In retrospect it seems surprising that one issue raised by a Lancaster paper friendly to Wolf during the gubernatorial campaign was not mentioned more often in the political wars of the Antimasonic era—whether or not the proscription of Masonry was a suitable subject for a political campaign. Was it "not in the teeth of the constitution, which looks to no such qualification for office, and if it is fair and proper to organize a party to put down Masonry, it will be fair and proper to organize one to put down other societies, say Episcopalians, Methodists . . ." Wolf's followers also circulated the rumor that Ritner had written a letter promising, if he was elected, to cut off funds for the branch canal projects and to limit expenditures to the completion of the main line between Philadelphia and Pittsburgh. This statement created such consternation that Ritner was forced to proclaim the letter a forgery in a communication to the chairman of the Antimasonic state committee.[14]

Wolf won reelection to a second term in October 1832, but by the narrow margin of some 3,000 votes, a considerable drop from his 1829 majority of 17,000. Although there had been a general understanding that the National Republicans, having no candidate, would support Ritner, many angry Antimasons thought the opposite had happened. The tallies were: Wolf, 91,385, and Ritner, 88,115. Once again Ritner's strength was in the southern, southeastern, and eastern counties. He carried twenty counties plus the city of Philadelphia (by 1,400 votes), where Antimasonry was normally the weakest. Ritner's success in Philadelphia, however, indicated that many Nationals had

voted for him. In the legislative contests the Antimasons elected from
thirty-two to thirty-four to the Pennsylvania House, from eight to
nine to the state senate, and approximately eight to the U.S. House.
Once again, Antimasons were forced to rejoice in a "triumph of
principle."[15]

Although in this Ritner-Wolf election there was only an understanding between Antimasons and National Republicans that the
latter would support Ritner, a more explicit arrangement was made
for the presidential contest to be held the following month. A union
or coalition electoral ticket, similar to the one organized in New York,
was suggested by the pro-Jackson Harrisburg *Pennsylvania Reporter*
in late July. The Nationals had held their state convention on May
5, 1832, and did *not* adopt a separate gubernatorial ticket. They did,
however, select their own electoral ticket of thirty names pledged to
Clay and placed these nominees under the authority of their state
committee. This committee initially declared its preference for Wolf,
but when Wolf announced his support for Jackson, now extremely
unpopular in Pennsylvania because of his veto of the bill to recharter
the Bank of the United States, the National Republican Committee
switched to Ritner, even promising Masonic support. The committee also called for another National Republican state convention to
meet on October 15, with the proviso that "if it shall appear that
we can not elect our own electoral ticket, and that by supporting it,
we shall render the success of the Jackson ticket probable, we are
prepared to abandon it." When the Nationals again assembled in
mid-October, they followed the advice of the committee. The hapless
delegates, with one dissenting vote, agreed to withdraw the electoral
ticket accepted in May, resolved to adopt the "anti-Jackson" ticket chosen by the Antimasons on February 22, "and earnestly recommend that ticket to the support of the National Republican Party."
Whether this ticket, if elected, would support Clay or Wirt remained
unclear, the Nationals possibly following the stand of their counterparts in New York but never specifically stating their position as
such.[16]

The action of the Nationals in withdrawing their electoral ticket
was not well received by all Antimasons. The *Gettysburg Star,* reflecting the opinions of Stevens, declared, "We are Anti-Masons, and
are as much anti-Clay as anti-Jackson. Down with the lodge! is our
motto—From this, we shall never be diverted." A week later the *Star*
warned that no "interlopers" would be tolerated in the Antimasonic
party. Fenn, now editor of the *Harrisburg Telegraph,* unofficial
spokesman of the party, cautiously observed that "the adoption of our

ticket by National Republicans *will almost* ensure its success." In Lancaster County, Ellmaker, the party's vice presidential candidate, was also unhappy. Prior to the Nationals' action of October 15, he had written to Stevens that any attempt of the Antimasons to cooperate with any other party would hurt their chances in the autumn elections. Those who had supported Clay "must be more inveterate in their opposition to anti-masonry than those who support Jackson." Ellmaker believed that Wirt would get more votes by maintaining a separate ticket, for this would convince the "most scrupulous and fearful that anti-masons are pure, single-hearted & upright, & give us increased numbers of votes from those who are adherents of Jackson." The prevailing general confusion among National Republicans was reflected by their leading journal in Philadelphia, the *United States Gazette,* which as late as October 23 carried the names of Clay and Sergeant on its masthead, followed by the anti-Jackson, or Antimasonic, electoral ticket, headed by Rush.[17]

The so-called "union" of Antimasons and National Republicans behind the Antimasonic electoral ticket produced bickering, suspicion, and complaints on both sides. The absence of any genuine prior cooperation between the two parties certainly did not make the situation easier for 1832. On the vital question of whether the anti-Jackson ticket was actually pledged to vote for Wirt and Ellmaker, the *Telegraph* attempted to obtain statements of loyalty from the thirty men on the ballot. It was able to publish six positive pledges of support for the Antimasonic candidates if the electors were victorious. No statement was obtained from the remaining twenty-four candidates. The major problem the Antimasons faced in Pennsylvania, however, was their inability to hold the wavering German vote. Although the Germans had at first been flattered that the Wirt-Ellmaker slate appeared to be "all-German," they were also torn by their strong loyalties to Jackson, whom most had supported in 1824 and 1828. Why the United States' principal war hero of that era, a man of Scots-Irish descent, should have had such a strong attraction to these people, many of whom were strong pacifists, remains unclear. On the eve of the election, the *Boston Advocate* reported a warning in a New York newspaper that the German Antimasons of central Pennsylvania were deserting "en masse" to Jackson. Many who had voted for Ritner now voted for Old Hickory, and he carried the Keystone State by only 24,000 votes out of some 157,000 total ballots, in contrast to his 7:1 majority of 1824 and 2:1 margin of 1828. Jackson was unpopular with many of his earlier non-German supporters because of his Bank veto, and Pennsylvania Democrats had refused to accept Van Buren for vice president, supporting favorite son William Wilkins of Pittsburgh, who had been nominated by a state convention.[18]

Although it was clear that many of the German Antimasons had deserted the cause and had voted for Jackson, what the Nationals did at the polls remains a moot point. The *Telegraph* charged that 5,000 Clay Masons had supported Wolf over Ritner, and "thousands of these same men voted for Jackson." The anti-Jackson ticket nevertheless polled only 66,706 votes, some 21,409 fewer than Ritner's total of October. The ticket won in only eight counties—Adams, Beaver, Bucks, Chester, Delaware, Erie, Franklin, and Lancaster—and the city of Philadelphia. In Lancaster County, the anti-Jackson slate triumphed over the Jacksonian, 5,140 to 4,061. The anti-Jacksonians' poorest showing was in western Pennsylvania, where the Antimasons had carried nine counties, including Allegheny (Pittsburgh), in October's gubernatorial election. In November, only Erie and Beaver counties, among the western tier, went *against* Jackson. The coalition, if it can be so called, met defeat, not only because of Jackson's great popularity, especially with the Germans, and the alleged desertion of the Clay Masons, but also because of the defection of some Antimasonic purists who believed that the anti-Jackson ticket, if elected, would have voted for Clay in the electoral college. As 1832 ended in a dual failure, Pennsylvania Antimasons, watching earlier stages of the party's disintegration in other states, must have wondered whether victory and success had eluded them forever. They did not anticipate that the advent of Stevens into the General Assembly in 1833 would accelerate both the cause and the party and would keep them alive for another decade.[19]

For three years following the elections of 1832, Pennsylvania's Antimasonic party had accomplished almost nothing. Another senatorial contest late in 1832 saw the Antis once again support Rush in a futile effort. Antimasons did close ranks with the Nationals in 1833 to elect William Patterson of Washington County as Speaker of the House, and the two parties also worked together in both chambers to support resolutions favoring recharter of the Bank. It was in behalf of such efforts that Stevens, the new representative from Adams County, made several speeches lauding the Bank and Antimasonry at the same time. He reserved most of his legislative energies, however, for his personal war on Freemasonry, which began in this session of the General Assembly.[20]

# 8. Pennsylvania, 1834-1843

On February 6, 1834, Stevens introduced a resolution in the Pennsylvania House of Representatives calling for creation of a committee to examine the expediency of: (1) making Masonic affiliation a "good cause" for a preemptory challenge of jurors in all cases where one party was a Mason and the other was not; (2) disqualifying Masonic judges from hearing cases where the judge and one party were Masons; and (3) applying similar restrictions upon Masonic sheriffs in the summoning of jurors when the sheriff and one party in the case were Masons. He also requested that the new committee be given the power to subpoena papers and witnesses but became enraged when, on February 10, the resolution failed, forty-five to thirty-one.[1]

Undaunted by defeat, Stevens one week later presented memorials from citizens seeking the appointment of a committee with subpoena power to inquire into the "evils" of Freemasonry and the "extent and influence of its oaths and obligations upon the community." The speaker referred these petitions to a committee chaired by Stevens, but the house refused to give it the needed subpoena power. Denied this weapon, the members had to content themselves with a report that was little more than a typical Antimasonic propaganda document. Stevens read the report to the house on March 20, 1834. It declared that it was the duty of the government to see "that in the future none of our respectable citizens should be entrapped into such a degrading and painful thralldom [as Masonry]." The committee next introduced a bill prohibiting the administration of Masonic and all other secret "extra judicial oaths, obligations and promises in the nature of oaths." The legislature had 2,000 committee reports printed in English and 1,000 in German, but outside pressure could not effect passage of this bill; it was never even brought to a vote.[2]

By the time the legislature adjourned in mid-April 1834, Antimasonry had become the dominant political organization among the anti-Jackson forces, and Stevens had emerged as a figure of power and prominence. The new Whig party evolved at a May 27, 1834, convention at Harrisburg, with several prominent Antimasons as recruits, including Joseph Lawrence from Washington County, who became

convention president. Middleswarth was also present as a Whig delegate and was selected one of the vice presidents. In contrast to events
in New York, the transition from National Republicanism to Whiggery in Pennsylvania represented little more than a name change, and
the Whigs became a minor third party that lacked a permanent state
organization and held no convention in 1835. They maintained an
uneasy alliance with the Antimasons, allowing the Antis to dominate
in areas where they were strong, while the Whigs ran the coalition in
Philadelphia and Pittsburgh. The Antimasonic-Whig coalition
suffered a serious defeat in the state elections of 1834 when the Democrats won a majority in both the senate and the house.[3]

During the 1834-1835 session of the General Assembly, thirty-three
memorials were introduced calling for the proscription and destruction of Freemasonry. At the beginning of the session, on December
10, 1834, Stevens introduced a resolution containing what is generally
regarded as one of his most famous denunciations of Masonry. He
condemned the fraternity as "injurious to the rights and dangerous to
the liberties of the people." It imposed "oaths and obligations unau-
thorized by and inconsistent with the laws of the country." Stevens
also accused Masonry of being "Anti-republican, and an insidious and
dangerous enemy to our democratic form of government." He added
that the lodge had corrupted legislatures, governors, and courts. "Its
whole tendency is to cherish a hatred of democracy and a love of
aristocratic and regal forms of power." He then proposed that the
house judiciary committee draft a bill outlawing all "extrajudicial"
oaths, but this motion was laid on the table and produced no results
during the 1834-1835 session, although he attempted to reintroduce
similar bills on at least seven separate occasions.[4]

By 1835, when Pennsylvania faced another gubernatorial contest,
it remained the only state where Antimasonry was still a vital force.
Governor Wolf, "resting on his laurels" of completing the main line
of the state works and establishing a tax-supported public school
system in 1834, desired a third term, the maximum allowed by the
constitution. The Democrats were badly split over the school law.
Many of their German supporters, including Lutherans and other
sectarians who strongly believed in the support of parochial schools,
bitterly opposed taxation for public schools and blamed Wolf for it.
Early in 1835 hostility to the new law forced its repeal in the senate.
In the house, however, a rousing speech by Stevens prevented repeal,
which garnered only 34 of a possible 100 votes, and public education
was saved in Pennsylvania. Stevens's views were not shared by many
of his fellow Antimasons in the General Assembly, for five of six Anti

senators favored repeal, and twelve of twenty-seven Antimasonic representatives took a similar stance. Stevens's motives may not have been entirely altruistic, for by pressing the school issue, he hoped to widen the breach in the Democratic party and thus enable the Whigs and Antimasons to elect Ritner as governor.[5]

Animosity among Democrats regarding retention or repeal of the public school law and the large expenditures occasioned by construction of the state works, as well as the usual divisions within the party, were magnified at the Democratic convention in the Dauphin County court house at Harrisburg on March 4. The initial fight between the pro-Wolf forces and those favoring the Reverend Henry A. Muhlenberg concerned the seating of eleven contested delegates. After much argument and confusion, the delegates voted to dissolve and to reassemble at Lewistown. Ignoring the adjournment, the Wolf faction, with help from some of the legislators, assembled in the supreme court chamber of the state house on March 7 and nominated Wolf for a third term with only two dissenting votes. Muhlenberg's partisans denounced this meeting as a "Wolf Caucus" and "sham convention," and they met in Lewistown on May 6 and nominated their leader without opposition. Muhlenberg, scion of a long-prominent Pennsylvania family, had served as pastor of Trinity Lutheran Church in Reading from 1803 to 1829. He achieved election in 1828 to the U.S. House of Representatives, where he served until February 1838. Avoiding adoption of a platform, the Muhlenberg Democrats criticized the Wolf administration for assorted acts of wrongdoing, which received an emphasis and an interpretation that varied throughout the state. In northwestern Pennsylvania, Wolf was pilloried for failing to extend a branch canal line from the main line; in the southeastern counties, the Muhlenberg forces concentrated upon opposition to the public school law. The "Mules," as they became known, adopted a battle cry of "no third term" as they desperately attempted to deny the "Wolves" continued control of the executive branch. The Wolves, in turn, predicted that Muhlenberg's election would lead to a union of church and state in Pennsylvania. Both sides attempted to drag Jackson into the furor, but without success.[6]

Antimasons and Whigs both gleefully witnessed the disintegration of the Democratic party and savored the distinct possibility of victory. The Antimasons assembled in convention on March 4, 1835, and renominated Ritner. The delegates also agreed to support creation of a joint Antimasonic-Whig state committee to supervise the campaign. Whig leaders such as Joseph Chandler, a distinguished Mason and editor of the *United States Gazette*, blocked plans for a Whig state convention; instead, they promoted city and county meetings to endorse Ritner, whose recent statements in favor of the Bank of the United States pleased the Whig hierarchy. Most of Ritner's Antimasonic partisans confined themselves to charges of waste, corruption, and extravagance by the Wolf administration and downplayed the usual vendetta against Masonry. Even Stevens temporarily shelved his crusade and in mid-August 1835 made a calculated but judicious appeal for Masonic support: "Let no other test be required than a cordial support of our candidates. That will be conclusive proof that they consider their obligations to their country superior to their secret oaths to a foreign power. That is all Antimasonry requires."[7]

The split in the Democratic party and the resulting dual candidates for governor, along with the Whig support of Ritner, made the Antimasons' victory likely. Although Ritner received 94,023 votes, compared with 65,804 for Wolf and 40,586 for Muhlenberg, the two Democrats together polled 12,000 more votes than the victor. Ritner's tallies actually varied little from those of 1832, and in 1835 he rarely gained more than 300 votes per county. He carried thirty counties, including usual Anitmasonic strongholds in the southern, central, and western portion of the state, together with the Whig bastion of Philadelphia and Pittsburgh. In the General Assembly, the Whigs and Antimasons together now controlled seventy-two seats and returned Middleswarth to his job as Speaker. Although it was a minority in the Senate, the coalition could control both houses on a joint ballot.[8]

Some two months after Ritner's election, the Antimasons held a state convention at Harrisburg that revealed the divisiveness within their own ranks. The more vocal of the two factions was the Stevens-led "Exclusives," who opposed formal union with the Whigs. They once again refused to consider any moderation of the stand against Masonry and also hoped to block in 1835 the presidential nomination of William Henry Harrison, an Antimasonic fence straddler. The Exclusives favored Webster, who had been making increasingly Antimasonic statements since 1834. In addition to Stevens, prominent Antis identified with this clique included Ellmaker, Fenn, Burrowes (the newly-appointed secretary of the commonwealth), and Joseph Wallace of Harrisburg (the state party chairman and the new deputy secretary of Pennsylvania). The other faction was the more moderate, pro-Harrison "Coalitionists," who advocated a formal relationship with the Whigs in order to control the legislature and to distribute patronage. Leading members of this group included Governor Ritner, Attorney General James Todd of Fayette County, Speaker Middleswarth, and state treasurer Lawrence.[9]

The rancor and animosity and between the Exclusives and Coalitionists exploded at the Antimasonic state convention, which assembled at Harrisburg on December 14, 1835. By intent, the Democratic
Whigs also met at Harrisburg on the same day, and leaders of both
the Coalitionists and Whigs were primarily interested in producing a
single presidential nominee—Harrison. Every county in Pennsylvania
was represented at the Antimasonic meeting, where the Harrison
supporters successfully opposed a resolution to send delegates to a
national convention. Faced with this defeat and an earlier one regarding a contested delegate, nine pro-Webster delegates including Stevens, Ellmaker, and Denny, the convention president, read a formal
statement of protest and seceded from the meeting. In their "Address
to the People," the seceders referred to the Antimasonic convention
as a "Masonic plot," declaring that it contained among its delegates
twenty-four Whigs, one Mason, and sixty-four applicants for office.
They condemned this blatant attempt at Antimasonic amalgamation
with "Masonic Whiggery" and passed several resolutions damning
the Whig party. The Coalitionists, now in full control of the convention, reorganized, selected Lawrence as presiding officer, and the next
day nominated Harrison, rather than Webster, for president by a vote
of eighty-nine to twenty-nine. They then chose Granger of New York
for vice president. The Whigs, who had been adjourning from day to
day, waiting for the Antimasons to act, now nominated Harrison and
Granger, adopted the Antimasonic electoral ticket, and adjourned
sine die.[10]

Ritner's inauguration address on December 15, 1835, disappointed
the Exclusives. Its only reference to Antimasonry was a simple pledge
to maintain supremacy of the laws and equal rights of the people,
followed by this assertion: "The people have willed the destruction of
all secret societies, and that will cannot be disregarded." A little more
than a week before the governor's speech, Stevens, obviously ex-
hilarated by the recent Antimasonic-Whig victory at the polls, on
December 7 introduced a bill to suppress secret societies "bound
together by secret and unlawful oaths." On December 19 he was
appointed chairman of a five-man committee to investigate the "evils"
of Freemasonry. Somewhat lost in the furor of the subsequent investigation was a motion known as House Bill No. 4. Intended to eradicate
Masonry by outlawing extrajudicial oaths, it passed the lower chamber on February 27, 1836, forty-six to forty-one. During debate of
House Bill No. 4, Stevens, pleased by the tone of the speeches, declared that genuine Antimasonry was being destroyed by the Ritner
and Harrison supporters in the coalition. He predicted that the people

would soon learn "that there is no safety for them but in pure and undefiled antimasonry—that that alone can protect them from the power of the lodge." House Bill No. 4 was reported to the senate on March 12, but various parliamentary tactics delayed consideration until June 6. On that day, the senate adopted a report from the committee of the whole negating the first section and, in effect, killing the entire measure.[11]

Antimasons in Pennsylvania's General Assembly had failed to enact proscriptive legislation against Freemasonry during the sessions of 1834-1835 and 1835-1836. Although they lacked sufficient strength to pass bills outlawing Masonic oaths and suppressing secret societies, Antimasons did muster enough pressure to launch a legislative inquiry of the fraternity, a tactic that in Massachusetts and Rhode Island had proved to be most effective in escalating public opposition to Masonry. Most important, the Antimasons possessed in Stevens a dynamic and determined, albeit vitriolic, spokesman who had the ability to motivate people and was eager to begin the inquiry. Little in the way of leadership came from Ritner, who had no legal training and little administrative experience and rarely acted as a formulator of policy. The governor was no "rubber stamp," however, and legislators lived in fear that his stubbornness, when sufficiently aroused, might result in a veto.[12]

The committee appointed to investigate Freemasonry began its work on December 23, and ultimately its activities focused the eyes of the state and the nation upon Harrisburg. Chaired by Stevens, the committee met originally in the supreme court chamber, but the investigation attracted such crowds that on January 18 the hearings were moved to the house chamber. The proceedings were alleged to be costing the commonwealth the then unheard-of sum of $1,000 a day, which included the expenses of those witnesses who came to the little captial city of 4,500. Stevens's committee first considered a large number of petitions and memorials from Pennsylvanians containing charges against Freemasonry that, if proven true, "could not fail to render them dangerous to every free government; subversive of all equal rights, social order, morality and religion." The members then decided to investigate the charges, which, they claimed, had been ignored by the legislature for several years. They composed eleven questions to be submitted to each witness, inquiring of each whether he was a Mason; how many degrees he had taken; whether an oath or obligation had been administered during these degrees; whether the witness could repeat the obligations; whether he would listen to them as read from (Avery) *Allyn's Ritual*, an Antimasonic exposé, and whether he would point out any variations; whether there were Masonic obligations other than those contained in Allyn's *Ritual* or Bernard's *Light on Masonry;* and whether Masonry was essentially the same type of organization everywhere. The committee then issued subpoenas to some 100 witnesses, including all the present and past officers of the Grand Lodge of Pennsylvania.[13]

On January 12-13, an angry debate took place in the house about a resolution, offered by Stevens, to issue attachments or subpoenas to the 100 witnesses summoned by this committee, thereby forcing them to appear. Rep. William B. Reed of Philadelphia, a Masonic Whig, offered the most rational arguments in favor of Stevens's resolution. He argued that the house's power to investigate was "coextensive" with its power to legislate, and powers of subpoena and attachment were "inevitable corollaries." He also asserted the supremacy of the legal process over personal, religious, or ethical obligations and insisted that Masonic obligations "did not confer a privileged position." The house voted, fifty-nine to twenty-six, to issue the attachments; of the 100 witnesses summoned, however, fewer than 30 appeared, and only 4 agreed to testify—3 Masons and 1 Odd Fellow. One of the Masons, a seceder, James H. Shedd of Dayton, Ohio, claimed to have played a minor role in Morgan's abduction. Damaging testimony came from Dr. Robert May of Chester County, who related that he had once been asked by lodge members to vote for a Mason; that he knew of a crime of forgery concealed under a Masonic obligation; and that his brethren had requested that he favor a Mason in an arbitration proceeding.[14]

Far more exciting to spectators at the "Stevens Inquisition" was the refusal of certain prominent Masons to testify. These men, through a prior agreement between Dallas and Wolf, had decided on a policy of passive resistance that would serve as an example to others. Several, including Wolf, sent letters to the committee denying its authority to compel them to appear. Wolf inquired as to which article in the Pennsylvania constitution authorized this investigation or forbade people from associating together in a fraternal body in the pursuit of happiness. He called the investigation an inquisition, asking, if a man has once been a Mason in this nation of equal rights, "is he to be placed beyond the pale of the laws, and persecuted and prosecuted as an outlaw?" Wolf declared that he must be excused for declining to lend himself as a "willing instrument to gratify an idle curiosity, or minister to the prying inquisitiveness of a superstitious prejudice and ignorance on the one hand or the designing artifices of a reckless demagogism on the other." He then gave a stirring defense of Masonry, declaring the fraternity to be unrelated to contemporary political conflicts and possessing not the slightest influence over elections and judicial proceedings. Wolf did appear in person before the Stevens committee on January 14 and, risking imprisonment, declined to be sworn in, citing the reasons contained in his letter. Stevens then politely informed Wolf that the committee would take no immediate action but indicated that the former governor might be cited for contempt at a later time. The *Gettysburg Star* commented a few days later that it was to be regretted that Wolf "should hold his Masonic obligations paramount to those" of his gubernatorial office.[15]

Past Grand Master Dallas, later vice president of the United States under James K. Polk, also arrived to testify. On his way to Harrisburg from Philadelphia, he stopped at Lancaster, where he allegedly received the offer of 500 men ready to march to the captial at an hour's notice. Once before the committee, Dallas declared that never in his life had he violated the laws of Pennsylvania, although he had been a Mason for more than twenty years. He asserted that the entire investigation was illegal under the ninth article of the state constitution, which established the essential principles of liberty and free government. The Reverend William T. Sprole, one of the "deacons" of the grand lodge, appeared and infuriated Stevens when he explained his refusal to testify, saying that the intent of the committee was to gratify personal antipathies rather than to secure information and that the committee, by resolution, had already implied that Masonry was evil. Sprole then declared: "Gentlemen, if you are willing to convert yourselves into a modern Juggernaut, roll on!" At this point, Stevens screamed: "Silence! Sit down! You have insulted the legislature—not another word!"[16]

As other Masons gave similar reasons for declining to testify, the committee seemed surprised and helpless in finding a way out of its dilemma. Then, on January 21, 1836, Stevens asked the house to remand the twenty-five witnesses who had refused to answer the committee's questions to the custody of the sergeant at arms; the witnesses were to be brought to the "bar of the House" to answer for contempt. Much bitter debate followed, with Stevens proclaiming that the Masonic order had found friends in the legislature to "protect and defend it against all its foul trickery." The motion failed, fifty to forty. Reed moved that the witnesses who had refused to testify be declared guilty of contempt of the house and be reprimanded by the Speaker. This proposal also failed. On a motion, Speaker Middleswarth, now more Whig than Antimason, received authorization to request the witnesses to present a defense, either by themselves or through counsel. Dallas rose and thanked the house but declined to take the representatives' time by supplementing the reasons already given to the committee. The next day, January 22, the twenty-five nonjurors were rounded up at various hotels and rooming houses by the sergeant at arms and were brought to the canal commissioner's room in the statehouse. According to Chandler's wry observation, they entered the building in a "Masonic procession." As the representatives and crowded galleries were preparing for a battle royal, Spackman of Philadelphia suddenly proposed discharging the witnesses, and a majority of the house concurred, fifty to thirty-seven. Weary of spectacle and controversy, all but one Whig voted aye with the Democrats; all but two Antimasons voted against release. On January 26, the twenty-five nonjurors issued a sworn statement in which they justified their refusal to be sworn. They denied that Masonry was an "engine" of political or religious sectarianism and insisted that nothing in Masonic ritual or teachings was at variance with "Charity, Friendship, Virtue, Knowledge and Industry."[17]

The failure of the Stevens inquiry to produce any positive accomplishments brought recriminations from all sides. A number of Democrats believed that the Whigs had initially agreed to support the investigation in return for Antimasonic votes needed to pass a bill chartering the Bank of the United States in Pennsylvania. The introduction by Stevens on January 19 of such a charter, buried in an omnibus bill, confirmed the suspicions of many Jacksonians. Democratic papers, both in and out of state, condemned the investigation. The *Albany Argus* declared, "Pursuing its ends by unheard of proscription, it served as a terror and warning to citizens not within its inflictions, to avoid it as a pestilence." In only one sense could the inquiry be considered a success for the Antimasons: Stevens had forced a number of prominent Masons, including Wolf, to appear before his committee. Stevens remained undaunted, however, and discharge of the witnesses did not end the inquiry, for public sessions were held on January 28 and March 3, with more testimony being given by three seceding Masons. On March 5, Stevens presented a stirring speech defending Antimasonry before the house and declared that the Masonic question was still the paramount issue of the day.[18]

Most of the time and effort of both the General Assembly and the governor from 1835 to 1838 was spent in dealing with matters that had little or nothing to do with Antimasonry. The Whig-Antimasonic coalition survived the inquistion, although the session of 1835-1836 marks the beginning of Whig domination of the coalition and the decline of the Exclusives in the assembly. After electing Thomas S.

Cunningham as Speaker of the senate and Middleswarth as Speaker of the house, the coalition moved ahead with the Bank proposal. The federal charter of the Bank of the United States, which had not been renewed in 1832 because of Jackson's veto, was to expire in March 1836, and bank president Nicholas Biddle was determined to continue operations with a charter from the Pennsylvania General Assembly, an action favored by all of the Whigs and by most of the Antimasons in that body. On January 19, Stevens, as chairman of the inland navigation and internal improvements committee, introduced an omnibus bill that appropriated state funds for a number of transportation projects, including Stevens's own Gettysburg railroad, repealed the state tax on real and personal property, and chartered the U.S. Bank of Pennsylvania. Biddle was reputed to have spent $130,000 through lobbyists (known as "borers") to help the legislators see the "advantages" of this bill for the state, including a $4,000,000 bonus to be paid by the Bank, several hundred thousand dollars for the new public school system, a readily available loan of $1,000,000 at 4 percent interest, and numerous other "benefits." The bill passed the house on January 22 and the senate on February 10, when eight pro-Bank Democrats joined Whigs and Antimasons to approve it, nineteen to twelve. Ritner signed the bill into law on February 18.[19]

The coalition was less fortunate in both the state and national elections of 1836. Many voters, angry about the legislative investigation of Masonry and suspicious about the new state charter for the Bank of the United States, returned to the Democrats. The coalition lost half its representatives in the General Assembly, including Stevens. Following his defeat, Stevens made peace with both Ritner and Whig-Antimasonic presidential candidate Harrison, whom Stevens had considered a weak supporter of Antimasonry because of his avowed refusal to use the presidential office to proscribe Masonry. Stevens's last minute support was insufficient, however, for Harrison lost Pennsylvania to Van Buren by the narrow margin of 87,235 to 91,466.[20]

Throughout 1836, Stevens, briefly bereft of his power base in the legislature, attempted to keep Antimasonry alive as a distinct entity. Under his direction a "Democratic Antimasonic" convention assembled at Harrisburg on May 22, 1837, to issue a call for a national convention to meet in Washington in September to nominate candidates for president and vice president. With reference to state politics, neither the Antimasonic or Whig elements of the coalition seemed to have much interest in a campaign for legislative offices. The coalition was able, however, to elect some nineteen members to the senate and to retain its majority in that body, primarily because of a redistricting effort carried out in 1836 under Stevens's direction, which so favored the Antimasons that it has been called a model of gerrymandering. In the house, the Democrats now held fifty-six seats, and Adams County voters once again returned Stevens to the lower chamber. Antimasonry remained a minor issue in Pennsylvania throughout 1837, briefly emerging in the constitutional convention of that year in which the Whig-Antimasons possessed a majority of one vote. Stevens attempted to have the delegates adopt an amendment forbidding the existence of secret, oath-bound societies, but both the Whigs and Democrats refused to support this proposal, and nothing came of it. Neither the Whigs nor the Antimasons acted in coordinated fashion either for or against the constitution as eventually amended, and it was ratified by a small majority in the autumn elections of 1838. Antimasonry also briefly reemerged in the governor's message to the legislature of December 6, 1837, in which Ritner once again urged that body to pass a statute outlawing extrajudicial oaths. The recommendation was referred to a committee chaired by Stevens, but no action was taken.[21]

Time was running out for both Antimasonry and Ritner when the governor was renominated for a second term by an unenthusiastic Antimasonic convention on March 5, 1838. Once again the Whigs declined to nominate a separate candidate and later gave Ritner modest support through a series of county conventions. To win more votes from both the Whigs and the Antimasonic Exclusives, Ritner in the spring of 1838 appointed Representative Reed as attorney general and Stevens as canal commissioner. This was the first time that Stevens had been a recipient of the governor's patronage. These appointments were among the final positive actions of Ritner's administration, one soon remembered for little else than the gerrymandering of the senatorial districts and the thirty-year charter for the U.S. Bank of Pennsylvania, which went out of business in 1841, during the panic of 1837-1842.[22]

By the time of the 1838 gubernatorial elections, the Democrats had been reunited, thank to the efforts of Sen. James Buchanan, who was successful in obtaining federal appointments from Van Buren for both Wolf and Muhlenberg and thus moved them out of the way. The Democratic convention of March 4, 1838, was therefore able to nominate a former legislator, David R. Porter, an iron manufacturer from Huntingdon County. Because Porter was of Scots-Irish descent, the Whig-Antimasons, led by Theo Fenn, attempted to discredit him with the German voters through accusations of gross immorality and dishonesty. Ritner, on the other hand, was described by the Democrats as the "old Dutch Farmer Governor" and was accused of everything from deism to full responsibility for Pennsylvania's bankrupt treasury and overbuilt internal improvements system. Rush, furious about the state charter issued to Biddle's bank and true to character, deserted Ritner and openly supported Porter. Interestingly, none of the issues in this gubernatorial campaign, often described as the dirtiest in Pennsylvania's history, involved Masonry or Antimasonry. When the votes were counted, Porter had clearly won, albeit by a slim margin of some 5,000 votes. Although control of the house of representatives was in doubt because of eight disputed seats from Philadelphia County, the senate was dominated by the Whigs-Antimasons.[23]

The eight contested seats, a result of fraud and deception practiced by both Democrats and Whigs-Antimasons, determined which party would have a legislative majority on a joint ballot, and the General Assembly would in turn certify the vote for governor. Antimasonic leaders believed that if they controlled the legislature, they could invalidate the 5,000 votes that separated Ritner from a second term. Six Whig election judges refused to accept the decision of the Democratic majority on the election board, which had rejected returns from an area of Philadelphia County known as the "Northern Liberties." These Whig judges drew up a minority report indicating Whig victories in the disputed district, a decision that presumably would lead to coalition control of the house and domination of the joint ballot. Secretary Burrowes, manager of Ritner's recent campaign, accepted the Whig returns and also issued a report to "The Friends of Joseph Ritner" calling for an investigation of the election. Until the inquiry was completed, he urged, coalition supporters should "treat the election as if we had not been defeated and in that attitude abide the result." Harrisburg now became tense with excitement as the crisis deepened and evolved into the final spasm of Antimasonry in Pennsylvania.[24]

On December 4, 1838, Stevens assumed leadership of fifty-two Whig-Antimasons and had them organize the "Cunningham House" (named after Speaker Thomas S. Cunningham), as though the doubtful eight members had been certified. The Democrats did likewise with their fifty-six men, producing the "Hopkins House" (named after their Speaker, William Hopkins), and for a brief time, Pennsylvania had two houses of representatives. Neither chamber had enough uncontested seats to constitute a majority. The Democrats, fearing that the coalition-dominated senate would recognize the Cunningham House as the legitimate chamber, disturbed the afternoon session of the senate as it organized. The threat of violence from a hostile crowd that had assembled in the senate chamber caused a fearful Speaker Charles Penrose, as well as Burrowes and Stevens (the latter two present as spectators), to escape through a window in a small room to the rear of the speaker's desk and to flee to the governor's mansion. Stevens later declared that he had never seen "any lawless body of men so thoroughly organized, desperate, daring and dangerous." Ritner now mobilized the state militia, and Maj. Gen. Robert Patterson ordered the troops to assemble with thirteen rounds of buckshot cartridges and seventeen rounds of ball cartridges. This controversy, which produced many heated arguments but no bloodshed, became known as the "Buckshot War." The troops arrived at Harrisburg on December 9, and the senate resumed deliberations on the twenty-fifth. By a vote of seventeen to sixteen (the seventeen yeas included five Whigs-Antimasons), the upper chamber recognized the legality of the Democratic Hopkins House after the transfer of three members from the Cunningham House, giving the former a majority of the full chamber membership. The new house then declared Stevens's seat vacant because of "malconduct," an action protested by Antimasonic citizens of Lancaster County as "the last outrage of Masonic Locofocoism," but Stevens was soon duly reelected by his loyal constituents in Adams County.[25]

Four years later, Stevens moved from Gettysburg to Lancaster, where he retained his bachelor's residence until his death in 1868. He never lost his zeal for Antimasonry. In 1867, while serving in the U.S. House as a Radical Republican and plotting the impeachment of President Andrew Johnson, a Mason, he referred to certain agencies with "invisible powers" that protected a man like Johnson. On June 26 of that year, he asked his friend, Edward McPherson, to see that he was furnished with the names of all congressional Masons. Although no reason was given, this request undoubtedly related to the forthcoming impeachment trial, Stevens fearing that the Masons in Congress would conspire to prevent the indictment and removal of a brother.[26]

After the Buckshot War, most Pennsylvanians still considering themselves Antimasons made a rapid transition into the Whig party, if for no other reason than to influence the selection of Harrison as the Whig presidential candidate for 1840. Occasionally, vestiges of political Antimasonry would reappear, as when the senate in June 1839 briefly considered another bill to suppress secret societies, "bound together by secret and unlawful oaths." This bill failed by the surprisingly narrow margin of one vote and was not considered by the heavily Democratic house. During the previous month, Antimasons held a state convention and endorsed an electoral ticket pledged to Harrison and Webster. In June, a poorly attended Whig convention at Chambersurg passed resolutions favoring a Clay nomination. That the two parties were at last coming together was apparent when seventeen Antimasons seceded from the meeting and called for a convention of all forces opposing Van Buren to meet at Harrisburg on September 4. This "Unity and Harmony Anti-Van Buren Convention," dominated by the Antimasons, briefly praised Clay but endorsed Harrison as the only candidate who could win Antimasonic votes and could beat the New Yorker in 1840. Showing the Antimasons' influence, the national Whig convention at Harrisburg in December 1839 ultimately nominated Harrison for president. During the campaign, Pennsylvania Whigs and Antimasons continued to maintain separate organizations, although they created a joint electoral ticket, with twenty-three of thirty candidates being Antimasons. Burrowes became chairman of the Harrison state committee, and for purposes of the campaign, the Antimasonic remnant styled itself the "Democratic Harrison" party. These organizational tactics were successful, for Harrison carried the Keystone State by the tiny margin of 350 votes, although winning by a landslide in the electoral college.[27]

Support of Harrison in 1840 by the Antimasons produced little federal patronage for those who had ever considered themselves members of the party. Although Granger of New York became postmaster general in the Harrison cabinet, Stevens, who was also expecting that office, received nothing. The old National Republican clique dominated Harrison's appointments to the post office and custom's house in Philadelphia, but no Pennsylvanian was chosen for the Harrison cabinet, supposedly because of the divisiveness between the two Whig factions in the state and Harrison's fears of offending either group. Whig rebuffs to Stevens and other Antimasons led to continuation of separate organizations in Allegheny and Lancaster counties. This situation produced one last-ditch Antimasonic effort to influence the course of politics in an attempt by Stevens and other Antis, mainly in Lancaster County, to promote Gen. Winfield Scott as the Whig-Antimasonic candidate for president in 1844. Nothing came of this intrigue, and Clay utlimately received the nomination, only to lose to Polk in the general election. The Antimasons now lost control of Lancaster County to the Clay Whigs.[28]

The effect of Antimasonry upon the Masonic institution in Pennsylvania was parallel to that on its counterpart in New York but was not as devastating as in the case of Vermont. There were approximately 113 chartered lodges in operation in Pennsylvania when the crusade began (membership statistics are not generally available for this period). Typical of attitudes in other grand lodges, Past Grand Master Thomas Kittera naively wrote to the Pennsylvania Grand Lodge Committee of Correspondence, "A Society based upon the principles of Masonry has nothing to dread from the attacks. Let us but oppose their clamour with silence and their malevolence with abundant [*sic*] and the result will be such as rarely fail to attend the efforts of the virtuous." Local lodges began to collapse as early as 1829-1830. Good Samaritan Lodge No. 200 at Gettysburg, chartered in 1825, ceased in December 1832. Lodge No. 43 in Lancaster, one of six in that county, remained open, although under great difficulties. The reduced membership of thirteen considered surrendering the charter in May 1830 but ultimately decided against such a course of action. The lodge nearly became extinct between January 1832, and November 1833, when no meetings were held because of insufficient attendance. After November, 1833, attendance did improve, and Lodge No. 43 acquired new vigor. In 1834 it initiated seven and affiliated two new members.[29]

Antimasonry quickly took its toll on the fortunes of the Grand Lodge of Pennsylvania. Attendance at quarterly convocations, poor even before the advent of Antimasonry, declined predictably although not consistently. Forty-one subordinate lodges were represented at the 1828 convocation (these figures represent the maximum attendance at the *quarterly* convocations); thirty-eight in 1829; twenty-nine in 1830; and twenty-four in 1831. Then attendance began to increase surprisingly: to twenty-nine in 1832 and to thirty-eight in 1834. In 1835, the year of Ritner's election as governor, only twenty-seven lodges were represented, followed by twenty-four in 1836 and twenty, the nadir, in 1837. This, of course, was the year after Stevens's inquisition. After 1837 attendance gradually began to increase and by 1839 had reached twenty-six lodges. Loss of membership and lack of degree work on the local level meant a reduction in the assessment (dues) and fees paid to grand lodge, which showed a deficit of $1,500 in 1834, $975 in 1835, and $3,749 in 1836. Because of financial difficulties, in 1835 the grand lodge sold its building on Chestnut Street in Philadelphia, in use since 1820, for $20,000. A smaller structure, known as Washington Hall, was then purchased as a meeting place.[30]

Most devastating was the large number of subordinate lodges that surrendered their charters during the crisis years, some seventy being "vacated" in this period, so that by 1839, only forty-five lodges were in good standing. In contrast, only three charters for new lodges were

granted between 1828 and 1839. In 1836-1837, forty-seven charters
were lifted because of accounts past due to the grand lodge. At this
time, the officers of lodges No. 45 and 113 at Pittsburgh concurrently
requested the grand lodge to waive all delinquent dues, amounting to
some $3,000, with the plea: "We presume it is well known to you the
persecution we have labored under for several years, which has been
the cause of many of our luke warm [*sic*] members withdrawing their
aid and Support from us; there is still a worthy few who adhere to the
Good cause in this city and are determined that the [*Masonic*] Institution shall revive among us." As in other states, a Masonic resur-
gence began once Antimasonry had waned. In 1839; the secretary of
Tioga Point Lodge No. 70 in Bradford County (northwestern Pennsylvania) wrote to Grand Secretary Michael Nisbet: "Antimasonry in
this quarter of the state is either dead or asleep. If asleep, we shall not
by any boisterous exaltation wake the *monster* up to any new vituperation, but endeavor to preserve the *even tenor of our way* in peace and
quietness." Because Antimasonry had survived longer in Pennsylvania than in any other state, the Masonic revival was later in commencing. The grand lodge chartered four new lodges in both 1846 and
1847, followed by eleven in 1848 and five in 1849. Masonry continued
its upward course, and by 1856, Pennsylvania had 130 lodges; more
than when the crusade began. By the late twentieth century, the state
was second only to Ohio in its number of Masons.[31]

# 9. Massachusetts, 1828-1836

Massachusetts vies with Pennsylvania in claiming the site of the first Masonic lodge in colonial America. The Bay State had previously witnessed a brief outpouring of sentiment against Masonry during the Bavarian Illuminati scare of 1789-1800, and although no direct connection existed between the Antimasonic movements of 1798 and 1828, there remained "the tradition of Masonic intrigue and a vague but repellent feeling to hold some men aloof from Masonry." Between 1800 and 1827, however, many men of high social, economic, and political standing became Masons, and the lodge recovered its prominence of the pre-1798 period, reaching a membership of more than 4,300. Nevertheless, many citizens, especially in the rural southern and western counties, inherited from their Puritan ancestors a dislike of secret, "oathbound" societies.[1]

Influenced by events in other states, Antimasonry began with the establishment of newspapers and country organizations in 1828-1829, with most of the activity being in Bristol (Fall River), Plymouth, and Norfolk counties. Following the pattern of development exhibited elsewhere, county conventions quickly led to the assembling of the first state convention at Faneuil Hall in Boston on December 30, 1829, with 243 delegates representing eight of fourteen counties. Those present selected delegates to the national convention at Philadelphia, passed the usual resolutions condemning Masonry, and appointed a state propaganda committee, henceforth known as the Suffolk Committee (Boston is located in Suffolk County). Although not as able as its counterpart in New York, the Rochester Morgan Committee, the Suffolk Committee became noted for its energy and intense hatred of Masonry. The best-known committee members were the wealthy physician Dr. Abner Phelps and Amasa Walker. This first Massachusetts convention requested that the Grand Lodge of Massachusetts disfellowship the various "grand" Masonic bodies of New York for "embracing the perpetrators of violence upon William Morgan." It also called upon the grand lodge to "renounce the system, and the oaths of Free Masonry." Of course, the only response to these suggestions from the Massachusetts Grand Lodge was complete silence.[2]

The Antimasons made slow progress in 1830, electing some twenty-five men to the house of representatives of the General Court and three to the senate. Other than the state elections in April, the only event of note was a disturbance at an Antimasonic meeting on August 31 at Faneuil Hall, where Masons had been invited to discuss "freely" the issue of whether a man who had sworn the Masonic oaths could discharge the duties of public office in an impartial manner. One local Mason, angered by the presence of two Antimasonic "foreign visitors," the Reverend Henry Dana Ward of New York and Judge Samuel W. Dexter of Michigan Territory, asserted that Bostonians could manage their own affairs. When Dexter and Ward attempted to speak, they were heckled and were forced to sit down. Although Mayor Harrison Gray Otis eventually restored order, the meeting adjourned because of continuing confusion, ending one of the few documented cases in which an Antimasonic gathering was broken up by Masons and their friends.[3]

Political parties in Massachusetts faced a difficult year in 1831, for the General Court had just passed a statute transferring state elections to the autumn to coincide with national contests. This change meant that for 1831 only, there would be two gubernatorial elections—in April and in November. The Antimasonic state committee supported the incumbent of seven years, Levi Lincoln, whom they hoped was sympathetic to their cause. With Antimasonic help, Lincoln swamped his Democratic opponent, Marcus Morton, 31,875 to 12,694. An Antimasonic convention assembled at Boston on May 18, following Lincoln's reelection. In addition to selecting representatives to attend the second national convention at Baltimore, the 245 delegates from ten counties passed several resolutions demanding: that Masonic affiliation be made sufficient reason for challenging jurors when only one party to a case was a Mason; that extrajudicial oaths be declared illegal; and that "all zealous adhering Masons" be disbarred from holding any state or federal offices. Between their first convention and a second statewide meeting in the autumn, the state committee, headed by Phelps, attempted to secure some type of commitment to their cause from the governor, asking for his views on the "character, influence and tendency" of Masonry as well as inviting him to attend Antimasonic meetings and rallies. Lincoln replied to these entreaties on September 13, declaring his disapproval of Masonry and desire for its abolition but adding at the same time, "*as the chief magistrate for the commonwealth, I can unite myself with no combinations of men,* in [a] means of its suppression."[4]

These difficulties provided a background for the Antimasons' second convention of 1831, which met on October 5 at Worcester. Furious with the tone, if not the content, of Lincoln's response, the delegates first nominated John Quincy Adams, who declined, saying he approved of Lincoln's views and would not run against him. The convention then turned to Samuel Lathrop, a Yale graduate and former member of the U.S. House of Representatives (1819-1827) and of the Massachusetts Senate (1829-1830). Lathrop was one of the organizers of the National Republican party in the Bay State, and his only drawback, in the eyes of the Antimasons, was his continuing adherence to Clay. Lincoln won another term with 28,804 votes, but Lathrop received more votes (13,357) than the Democrat, Morton (10,975). Lathrop carried Franklin and Hampshire counties on the Connecticut River and polled a substantial vote in Bristol County, indicating the movement of many rural National Republican and old-time Federalist voters into the Antimasonic ranks. The Antimasons also claimed to have elected 150 men (out of 490) to the Massachusetts House of Representatives. The results of this contest were sufficient to make Daniel Webster believe that Antimasonry was gaining strength in New England as a "sentiment," but he still did not believe that as a party, it was "broad enough to save the Country & maintain the Govt."[5]

Bay State Antimasonry received added impetus when, in 1831, journalist Benjamin Franklin Hallett returned from Rhode Island to edit a new Antimasonic paper, the *Boston Daily Advocate.* The *Advocate* became the foremost Antimasonic journal in New England and was famous not only for the bitterness of its attacks on Masonry but also for the extremism its editor showed in causing factionalism and divisiveness within the party. In a state in which the Antimasons possessed no truly effective leaders, Hallett became the most notable (if not notorious) of the lot and never ceased to be a center of controversy. Born in Barnstable County (Cape Cod) in 1797, the son of an evangelically minded owner of shipping lines, he attended Brown University. Remaining in Providence to study law, he was admitted to the Rhode Island bar in 1819. Law did not interest Hallett as much as politics or journalism, and he practiced his profession only intermittently. From 1821 to 1831 he edited several newspapers in Providence, including the *Daily Advertiser.* He became a political Antimason in 1830 and in 1831 served as a delegate to the party's Baltimore convention.[6]

Ninety-four Antimasons contributed $10,000 to help establish the *Advocate,* including Henry Gassett and George Odiorne, the latter being one of several wealthy bankers who gave money to Hallett. First appearing on December 27, 1831, the *Advocate,* like its editor, was a late arrival in the field of Antimasonic journalism. In the initial issue, the sponsors, after alleging that five of Boston's seven newspapers were Masonically controlled, proclaimed that the "dissemination of truth and the overthrow of dangerous secret combinations are the grand object of the whole Antimasonic party."[7]

Concurrent with the founding of the *Advocate* was the appearance of the "Declaration of 1,200 Masons" (later 1,400), a proclamation signed by one-third of the lodge members in Massachusetts. Its proponents believed the declaration exerted a major influence in checking the growing hostility toward Masonry. It was, however, ineffectual in light of the subsequent proscriptive legislation passed in Massachusetts and Rhode Island and attempted in Connecticut. The declaration was written by Charles W. Moore, a printer by trade, editor of the nation's most influential Masonic newspaper, the *Masonic Mirror* and, after 1834, secretary of the Grand Lodge of Massachusetts. In the "Declaration" Moore asserted that although Masons might eventually be deprived of their civil rights through Antimasonic pressure, the great majority would remain true to their convictions. Masonry, he said, insisted on a strict obedience to the laws of God and man, and there was nothing in Masonic teachings that would violate the principles of morality and good citizenship.[8]

The third Antimasonic state convention, which met at Worcester on September 5-6, 1832, was considerably larger than its predecessors, with 319 delegates representing eleven counties. Desperate for a gubernatorial candidate, the Antimasons once again turned to Lathrop, an avowed admirer of Clay but also a friend of Wirt. The delegates also selected electoral candidates pledged to support the national Antimasonic ticket of Wirt and Ellmaker. Although they had high hopes for both their national and their state candidates, the Antimasons were bitterly disappointed with most of the results except the election of 100 men to the house of representatives. In the gubernatorial race, which brought out 10,000 more voters than in 1831, the incumbent National Republican, Lincoln, won with 33,946 votes. Morton, the Democratic candidate, received 15,197, and Lathrop ran a close third with 14,755 votes, although this was 1,100 more than he had polled the year before. The Antimasons did slightly better in the presidential contest, Wirt coming in second with 14,692 votes, compared with Clay's 31,396 and Jackson's 13,933. The major issue with Massachusetts voters in 1832 was not Antimasonry but Jackson's veto of the bill to recharter the Bank of the United States, an action obviously unpopular with the majority of the electorate. Hallett sought solace in defeat with the observation that the "identity of the party is established and its integrity is insured by its being kept a minority." Searching for a better known and more attractive gubernatorial candidate, the Antimasons began to lay plans for 1833.[9]

The most prominent officeholder ever to affiliate with the Antimasonic party was former president John Quincy Adams, who was elected to the U.S. House of Representatives from the Twelfth (Plymouth) District in 1830 with Antimasonic support. The Twelfth District, which became a stronghold of Antimasonry, was rural in character, consisting of small towns and villages far different from metropolitan Boston. Adams had always run well in country areas and was therefore well suited to represent this district and a likely prospect for Antimasonry, with its rural orientation in the Bay State. Adams's dislike of Freemasonry was partially inherited from his father, and after the elder Adams's death on July 4, 1826, it was necessary for the son to deny on several occasions that John Adams had ever been a Mason or had even been friendly to the institution. When, in 1827, asked by New York congressman Tracy to state *his* views on Masonry, John Quincy declared "that I am not, never was, and never shall be a Freemason." His hostility to the lodge, like that of many nonmembers, greatly increased with the lurid revelations of the Morgan affair, which, he observed, "has at length brought a mass of obloquy upon the institution of Masonry itself." Adams, as president, remained publicly neutral on the Antimasonic issue, but the heavy support that he received from Empire State Antimasons in 1828 impressed him with the political significance of the movement. In contrast, his overwhelming defeat by Mason and Grand Master Andrew Jackson did nothing to increase Adams's fondness for the lodge.[10]

John Quincy Adams was deeply concerned about the Masons' alleged monopoly of three-fourths of all public offices, this dominance having been one of the first major "discoveries" made by the Antimasons. Among the most fascinating "allurements" of Masonry, he noted, "has been her influence in promoting the political advancement of the brethren of the Craft: Silent and secret in her operations, she raised them . . . to place and power." He also felt a genuine revulsion for the oaths, obligations, and penalties used in the Masonic degrees. "The Masonic oaths and mysteries give a tenfold power to the Knot of the association, and by the secrecy vital to the institution, it becomes a conspiracy of exclusive privilege to the members at the expense of all the rest of the community." Masonry was also a "foul blot" upon the morals of a community. In May of 1831, the former president decided that the time had approached "when it becomes the duty of a good citizen" to take a stand, and he indicated his own position by visiting the Antimasonic state convention at Boston on May 20. He also visited a poorly attended Antimasonic gathering on July 4 at Faneuil Hall, which caused him to comment in his diary on the lack of popular feeling for Antimasonry in this city of 61,000. By December 1831, when he took his seat in the House of Representatives for the opening of the Twenty-second Congress, Adams considered himself a full-fledged Antimason, one of eighteen in that chamber.[11]

To prominent Massachusetts Antis, Adams appeared as their means to success in the gubernatorial election of 1833. Although generally unpopular nationwide, he retained a large following in his native state among National Republicans and old-line opponents of Federalism. He had publicly announced his views on Antimasonry and was the only nationally known figure the Bay State party could claim. Hallett and Gassett visited Adams in Washington on July 10 and found him most reluctant to accept a nomination, although Hallett hinted that a "portion" of the National Republicans wanted him as well. On the last day of that month, Adams received two members of the Middlesex County Antimasonic committee, who also urged him to run. Again he declined, saying he could be of more service in the House and suggested, to no avail, the names of Lathrop and the incumbent lieutenant governor, Samuel T. Armstrong, previously elected as a National.[12]

Some 419 delegates attended the Antimasonic state convention at Boston, September 12-14, 1833, and selected John Bailey, a good friend of Adams, as presiding officer and Hallett as first vice president. Six men were considered for governor, including Adams, Lathrop, Edward Everett, Bailey, Henry Shaw, and Marcus Marton, the perennial Democratic candidate. Lathrop, Everett, and Bailey declined on the first day, after which the delegates nominated Adams, who received 219 of 288 votes. They wanted to nominate the Nationals' lieutenant governor, Armstrong, for that position, but he declined, saying he would never use public office to proscribe Masonry. William Reed of Marblehead was selected for second place on the ticket, but he withdrew and the state committee named Lathrop in his place. Visited by a group that included Pliny Merrick and Gassett, Adams gave an informal but reluctant acquiescence. In his official letter of acceptance, the former president did not address the Antimasonic party per se or make any reference to Antimasonic principles. Instead, he wrote to the "people," saying that personal considerations would not permit him to evade his duty as a citizen by refusing the nomination. If elected, he would "heal the divisions of party . . ., promote the harmony of the Union, and . . . maintain the industry of freedom, and the purity of the Constitution." To his diary, however, Adams bemoaned his acceptance "which casts me again upon the stormy ocean of political electioneering when I hoped and believed I was snug in port."[13]

John Quincy Adams accepted the Antimasonic gubernatorial nomination with the knowledge that throughout the commonwealth, the Antis at most formed only 20 percent of the voting population, except in Boston, where they were 10 percent. For public consumption, he wrote that he had agreed to run because the Antimasonic crusade was the "cause of truth and pure morals; it was an abused and calumniated cause, it was a cause deeply interesting to my constituents, to my fellow citizens, to my country." Privately, Adams expected the endorsement of the Nationals, who would meet in convention at Worcester in October. The *Advocate* declared, "If the National Republicans are now willing to prove what they often assert, that their party is not identified with Masonry, they shall find no obstacles thrown in their way by us." Prior to the Worcester convention, however, the *Boston Atlas,* the leading journal of the Nationals, referred to Adams as "that tired soldier and renowned renegade," who had permitted himself to be made "the tool and dupe of a desperate faction." When the Nationals did convene with thirty-five of their sixty-three delegates from Boston reputed to be Masons, they did not endorse Adams but instead nominated John Davis, a congressman from Worcester and the brother-in-law of historian (and Democrat) George Bancroft. Davis also had the support of retiring Governor Lincoln. Adams blamed the Nationals' state committee chairman, William Sullivan, for what had transpired, observing that "Sullivan has the double venom of Hartford Convention federalism and of spurious Masonry in his blood." The Democrats, also refusing to consider a temporary coalition with the Antis, again nominated Morton, who stated that he would not participate in any public discussion concerning Freemasonry.[14]

The Massachusetts gubernatorial campaign of 1833 was a tense and bitter one, most of the obloquy being heaped upon Adams by the Nationals, many of whom regarded him as a traitor. Alexander Everett, brother of Anti sympathizer Edward Everett, reported to Adams that the Boston Masons, many of whom were National Republicans, were "in a complete combustion" over his nomination. The Nationals' "Address to the People" described the aims of Antimasonry as being

"UTTERLY UNWORTHY OF THE COUNTENANCE OF AN INTELLIGENT PEOPLE." The *Atlas* attacked Adams for leaving Boston to go to Washington for the opening of Congress before conclusion of the campaign, implying that he knew his race was a futile effort. Even the pro-Democratic *Boston Post* commented upon the treatment that Adams had received from the *Atlas,* which "has for months applied the coarsest epithets and vilest political scourging to Mr. Adams, and unceasingly heaped the most savage and vulgar personal vituperation upon the Ex-President." Charles Gordon Greene, editor of the *Post,* nevertheless accused Adams of being an eccentric. "His has been the mad track of the comet. . . . Massachusetts has been his friend—and she must now pass upon the requittal he has made." As the election date of November 12 approached, the Antimasons were hopeful of success, and various campaign broadsides and articles in almanacs and other journals urged every man to do his duty: "See that an abundant supply of votes are carried to the polls. Ammunition is everything in war."[15]

Fragmentation of the vote between parties prevented any candidate from achieving the majority necessary for victory. Davis (National Republican) had a plurality with 25,149 votes; Adams (Antimason) was second with 18,274; Morton (Democrat) had 15,493; and Samuel Allen (Workingmen's) had 3,459. Adams, always the minority candidate, carried only Norfolk, Bristol, Franklin, Middlesex, and Plymouth counties in eastern Massachusetts and secured 29 percent of the popular vote, largely at the expense of the Nationals. The Democrats carried two counties and secured 25 percent of the votes; the Nationals won seven counties and 40 percent of the votes. With no candidate having a majority of the popular votes, the decision would be made by the legislature, with the house selecting two names from the four candidates and sending them to the senate for consideration. This situation created a marvelous opportunity for political machinations.[16]

On November 26, Edward Everett called upon Adams, urging him, in an oblique way, to withdraw in favor of Davis. Everett was concerned that if the house chose Adams and Morton as the two names to be supplied to the senate, that body would select Morton. The former president replied that he "should be much obliged to them if they should." Adams feared a heated dispute in the senate and hoped that Davis, by tactful negotiations, might attract most of the Antimasons to the National Republican party. Feeling an obligation to the people of his congressional district and fearing that if elected, Hallett and John Quincy's son, Charles Francis, would attempt to control his administration, Adams resigned from the legislative balloting at the end of December, 1833. John Quincy Adams sent a note to the Speaker of the house and requested that his name be withdrawn, stating that he preferred not to be chosen by the legislature if he could not be elected by the people. The Massachusetts House balloted on January 9, 1834, giving Davis 377 votes, Morton, 199, and Adams, against his instructions, 18. The senate acted on the same day and elected Davis over Morton, 30 to 4. No one was surprised at the outcome, as the Nationals dominated both chambers of the General Court.[17]

After the senate's election of Davis, Charles Francis Adams released to the press his father's "Address to the People of Massachusetts," which gave the former president an opportunity to justify his withdrawal in more detail and to repeat his now familiar charges against Masonic oaths and penalties. In this address Adams indicated that he had hoped to unite Antimasons and Nationals behind his candidacy but that the effort had failed, and he did not wish to face a hostile legislature dominated by the Nationals. The address marks the beginning of the end of Adams's brief flirtation with the Antimasonic party, for he soon lost interest in it, although he continued to write letters for publication denouncing Masonry and to consult with Antimasons in the House of Representatives. Two meetings with Antimasonic congressmen in March and April of 1834 and the subsequent failure to produce any definite program or course of action convinced him that political Antimasonry was a doomed cause.[18]

Legislative battles about Masonry in Massachusetts began in 1831 and involved the proposed erection of a new grand lodge temple in Boston. Lodge officers purchased land and began construction of a new building on Tremont Street. By terms of its act of (civil) incorporation in 1817, the grand lodge could hold real estate not to exceed the value of $20,000 and personal property not to exceed $60,000. Wishing to amend the charter and to revise the above figures to permit the new construction, the grand lodge naively went ahead with its building plans, and then in March 1831 its officers petitioned the legislature to revise the charter, changing the maximum real estate value to $60,000 and personal property to $120,000. This request produced a violent reaction from the Antimasons, who strongly protested that amending the charter would be another means of increasing the already enormous power of the Masonry. The grand lodge petition was referred to the house judiciary committee, which reported favorably. The house nevertheless rejected the petition after a stormy debate by the close vote of 133 to 128, and nothing further transpired during the 1832 legislative session concerning the petition. The grand lodge completed its new building in 1833, technically having exceeded its corporate limitations, and Masons now uneasily awaited the legislative session that would begin in January 1834.[19]

The controversy actually commenced in December 1833, when a sheriff handed a summons to the grand lodge officers demanding revocation of the 1817 charter. On December 27, a grand lodge committee, with Grand Secretary Moore as the principal member, recommended turning over the charter to the state and presenting an explanatory memorial to the General Court. The grand lodge, then in session, unanimously agreed to the surrender, which took place on January 1, 1834. Grand Master John Abbot pointed out that the grand lodge had no desire to see the legislature embroiled in a fight over the charter issue, something the Antimasons obviously desired, but he emphasized that by handing in its civil charter, the "Grand Lodge has relinquished none of its Masonic attributes or prerogatives." Shortly before the charter was delivered to the legislature, the grand lodge sold its new temple to Brother Robert G. Shaw, a local merchant, for $35,000. He in turn sold it to a board of trustees, who maintained control of the building until the controversy had passed.[20]

The Massachusetts General Court had come close to conducting an investigation of Masonry during its 1833 session, but failure of the senate to concur with the house on this issue produced a stalemate. When the legislature convened on January 1 for the 1834 session, it faced some 120 petitions from Antimasons demanding an official investigation of Freemasonry and passage of a statute prohibiting the administration of nonjudicial, that is, Masonic, oaths. One of the attorneys for the Antimasonic petitioners was Hallett. Sen. Daniel Webster and Congressmen Edward Everett and John Quincy Adams urged Massachusetts National Republicans to conciliate the Antimasons by supporting their legislative demands; perhaps then most Antis would return to the National fold rather than affiliate with the Democrats, thus ensuring that party's victory in 1835 and 1836. Webster sagely suggested to an influential Boston merchant, Stephen White, that several Antimasons, perhaps John Bailey and Timothy Fuller, be placed on the governor's council. The senator believed that the Antimasonic party was about to lose its separate identity, and he urged that the door be left open for the return "of such as may prefer the association of old friends, to that of new ones." The breach in the legislature, largely a result of the Nationals' furor over the separate Antimasonic tickets of 1832 and 1833, was not healed, however, and the Antimasons gradually drifted into the arms of the friendly, opportunistic Jacksonians.[21]

The willingness of both the National Republican and Democratic parties to placate the Antimasons by supporting their legislative demands of 1834 largely explains why Antimasonic proposals passed with so little opposition. Both parties wished to include the Antis in their ranks; Adams, for example, believed if the Nationals in the legislature would support an investigation of Masonry, then the Antimasons would in turn vote for a National-sponsored resolution condemning Jackson's removal of deposits from the Bank of the United States. Governor Davis indicated to Adams that while he would not recommend to the legislature any particular measure proscribing Masonry, he would favor passage of a statute outlawing extrajudicial oaths, and he requested that two Antimasons be placed on his council.[22]

The Massachusetts legislature finally authorized an investigation of Masonry in January 1834, and although the house on February 19 favored granting full subpoena powers to the ad hoc committee of inquiry, on the following day the senate blocked the proposal, which ensured that the committee would be powerless. Before the investigation began, notices were sent to four grand lodge officers and to thirteen other Masons, inviting them to attend the hearings, but none accepted the invitation. A five-man committee conducted the investigation and produced a seventy-three-page report replete with the usual Antimasonic arguments. The committee concluded that Masonry was a moral, pecuniary, and political evil that utilized oaths intended to strike "terror" into the hearts of initiates and to confound their ability to distinguish between right and wrong. It therefore advised the "necessity of legislative action, directly and equivocally declaring Masonic oaths to be unlawful" and recommended passage of an act outlawing such oaths.[23]

The most detailed account of the 1834 legislative session comes from a diary kept by a Masonic member of the house, the Reverend E. H. Cobb, then minister of the First Congregational Church at Malden. He noted that the original bill to outlaw extrajudicial oaths did not include the word "Masonic" in its text. An Antimason then amended the bill to add the phrase "Masonic and other" before "extra-judicial," whereupon a Masonic representative inserted "Anti-Masonic," so that the bill now read "Antimasonic, Masonic and extra-judicial oaths." The intent, of course, was to kill the bill with absurd amendments, and the representatives rejected the bill as

amended on January 27 by a vote of 170 to 160. Cobb then moved
to amend the bill by striking all previous amendments, restoring it to
its original form. He addressed the house, directing his remarks to the
other Masonic representatives, saying that although "such a law
might suppress the public exhibition of a class of non-sensical and
ridiculous oaths which might be regarded as public nuisances, it
would not—it could not—among honorable Christian men—touch
the quiet exercise, in retirement, of any natural and unalienable
right." Cobb then urged approval of the bill, hoping this would hasten
the demise of Antimasonic political agitation. The house passed the
bill on January 30, 437 to 37, and the senate concurred on February
27. Davis signed the bill into law on March 13. Those who might be
found guilty of administering extrajudicial oaths, or any person allowing such an oath to be administered to him or her, "shall forfeit a sum
of not less than five dollars nor more than two hundred dollars."[24]

Within a few months, Antimasonic legislators were declaring the
new law to be a sham because some Masons had insisted that it did
not apply to Masonic degrees or ceremonies. Thirty years later, Cobb
asserted that he knew of no enforcement of this statute, and attorneys
consulted by Massachusetts Masons observed that the legislature had
never possessed the constitutional power "to prohibit individuals
from binding themselves, in retirement, to solemn obligations to each
other in the manner of an oath."[25]

The gubernatorial candidacy of John Quincy Adams in the autumn
of 1833, surrender of the civil grand lodge charter, and subsequent
passage of the statute prohibiting extrajudicial oaths during the winter
and early spring of 1834 signify the zenith of Antimasonic activity in
Massachusetts. The party struggled on for another two years before
disintegrating prior to the election of 1836. The task of attracting the
Antimasons into the camp of the National Republicans-Whigs was
taken up with vigor on the federal level by Webster, Adams, and
Caleb Cushing. They received almost no cooperation from their colleagues at home, particularly in the legislature, where Antimasonic
votes were needed on some occasions, such as when a futile attempt
was made to pass a resolution condemning Jackson's removal policy.
Points of contention included: refusal of the Nationals to vote for a
subpoena power for the committee to investigate Masonry; the vote
of the Nationals to table the investigating committee's report; and
continued refusal of the Nationals to support the addition of Antimasons to the governor's council and to the senate. By late February
1834 Adams had abandoned his attempts to reconcile the two parties,
firmly believing that the National Republican legislators had done

everything possible to "fret and exasperate" the Antis: "It was impossible to do anything more with them, and I did believe they would go over to Jacksonianism."[26]

By 1834 the Antimasons and National Republicans-Whigs were definitely acting more as rivals than as allies against the Jacksonians. Through 1833 Massachusetts Democrats had appeared as no genuine threat to National-Whig domination. The state Democratic organization, concerned mainly with receiving patronage from the Jackson administration, was "weak" and the leadership "incompetent." The Democratic hierarchy consisted primarily of supreme court justice Morton, a candidate for governor for more than ten years until he finally achieved victory in 1839, and David Henshaw, a banker appointed in 1829 by Jackson as collector of revenue for the port of Boston. By February, 1834, both Henshaw and Morton were aware of the antagonism between the Antimasons and Whigs and were also receptive to the overtures of Hallett and his *Boston Advocate.* In addition, many Antimasonic stalwarts had once been Democrats, including Odiorne, Phelps, Walker, and Merrick. An alliance or merger with the Antimasons might actually give the Democrats a chance of victory at the polls and might change their status from that of a minority party that seemed likely always to remain so. Morton wrote to J. K. Simpson, president of the Commonwealth Bank (one of Jackson's "pet" banks) and a U.S. pension agent, that he had no objection to an "understanding" between the Democratic and Antimasonic parties "so far as to secure their cooperation against a common enemy ... if it can be done without compromising our principles. It has said to have worked in R. I." Statements from certain Antimasons also indicated the possibility of a coalition ticket headed by Morton for governor and Lathrop for lieutenant governor.[27]

The Antimasons were extremely confused as they prepared for their fifth state convention at Boston in early September. There were some behind-the-scenes maneuverings by Adams through intermediaries, who aimed at reconciling the Antis to Davis's reelection. These negotiations failed when Davis refused to condemn Masonry satisfactorily in the eyes of the more radical Antimasonic leaders such as Hallett. Adams commented that "the only alternatives were to vote for Morton, which would merge Anti-Masonry in Jacksonianism, or to nominate a candidate of their own with a certainty of defeat." The 419 delegates who gathered at Boston on September 10, 1834, faced a difficult task. Hallett was unquestionably the dominant figure at this meeting, and at his request the delegates unanimously passed a resolution requiring the selection of a "true and distinct" Antimason for governor. In what would later be called a keynote address, the editor declared that Massachusetts Antimasons must now rely upon their own resources and must select "able and sound and efficient candidates from their own ranks." From a field of seven, the delegates then nominated Bailey for governor on the third ballot and Heman Lincoln of Watertown for second place on the ticket. Bailey, a native of Dorchester, was a graduate of Brown University and had served in the U.S. House of Representatives (1824-1831) and in the state senate (1831-1834).[28]

Bailey's gubernatorial candidacy was the last independent nomination on this level for the Antimasons, and it proved to be a fiasco. Amid assertions that there could be no cooperation or conciliation with the National Republicans-Whigs, Hallett worked with the Democrat Bancroft to influence voters against Whig candidates. In mid-November, however, the *Advocate* did publish a disclaimer, denying statements by certain "enemies" in Fall River that Antimasonry and Jacksonianism were one and the same and that Hallett and Bailey were "working in the traces for *Martin Van Buren.*" When the votes were cast in November, the results were disastrous for Antimasonry. Davis, now classified as a Whig, had 43,757; Morton, 18,683; Bailey, 10,160; and Allen (Workingmen), 2,602 votes. Bailey's total votes were 8,000 fewer than Adams had received in 1833, whereas Davis's vote was more than 18,000 greater than in the previous election. The great upsurge in Davis's total was largely a result of the decline of Antimasonry and the return of some of its supporters to the Nationals-Whigs; but the Whig victory was primarily a manifestation of the great dislike many Massachusetts voters felt for Jackson's political and fiscal policies, especially removal of the Bank of the United States deposits. About the most the Antimasons could claim was that three of the state's twelve congressmen were of the Antimasonic persuasion. Adams, however, had resumed his status of a political independent with occasional Whig inclinations, and Nathaniel Borden was acknowledged as a Van Buren supporter. This situation revealed the true dilemma of Antimasonry in the Bay State by the end of 1834.[29]

In 1835 the Whigs in Massachusetts hoped to maneuver the Antimasons into supporting Edward Everett for governor. Governor Davis planned to seek election to the U.S. Senate to replace Nathaniel Silsbee, who did not desire another term. When the time came in February for the legislature to select a senator, the Antimasons attempted to promote Adams. Although the house supported Davis, the senate favored Adams until it was learned that the former president was backing Jackson's "get tough" stand on the question of the French spoliation claims in Congress, whereupon Whigs in the upper chamber switched to Davis, who was elected. The Antimasons were furious because they had already nominated Everett for governor through a legislative caucus on February 25, an action taken largely at the urging of both John Quincy and Charles Francis Adams. Hallett, who had previously opposed any Antimasonic support of Everett, now favored it, and he served on the committee that offered the nomination to the congressman. Two days later, on February 27, a Whig legislative caucus endorsed Everett's nomination.[30]

At first glance it appeared that by endorsing the same gubernatorial candidate, the Antimasons and Whigs were effecting a merger, as had happened or would happen in other northeastern states. This was not the case in Massachusetts, however, for when the Antimasonic state convention met in October with meager attendance, the delegates asserted that the previous nomination of Everett in no way bound the party to support other Whig nominees or Whig principles. The Whig candidate for lieutenant governor, George Hull, was repudiated because of his alleged Masonic membership, and the Antimasons endorsed Democrat William Foster for second place on the ticket. As a further indication of their leanings toward the Democratic party, the delegates refused to endorse Webster, Massachusetts's adopted son and senator, for president, and instead nominated Van Buren. It was not, as is sometimes stated, Webster's opposition to Jackson's stand on the French claims issue, nor was it the Democrats' alleged reputation as a reform party, that attracted the Antimasons; it was, rather, the failure of the Antimasons to force the National Republicans into accepting "second place" in the new Whig coalition that eventually propelled the Antis toward the Jacksonians. As Ershkowitz has observed, the Whigs were less able to "accommodate" the Antimasons because they "would have had to abandon the absolute power they already possessed in the state." Apart from their desire to destroy Freemasonry, Massachusetts Antimasons were hardly reform minded, except for Hallett and a few others who quietly favored the antimonopoly views of New York's radical Locofocos, and they were always afraid of offending conservative financial backers such as Odiorne. Nor was the Jackson party, as led by that conservative "spoilsman" Henshaw and his cohort Morton, a collection of crusaders. The union of Democrats and Antimasons that took place from 1835 to 1838 largely proceeded from a desire by those two parties to void their seemingly permanent minority status and to win elections, a goal ultimately achieved when Morton became governor in 1839.[31]

The gubernatorial election of November 9, 1835, produced a victory for Everett, who had 37,555 votes, compared with 25,227 for Morton. Foster, Morton's running mate, who had the endorsement of the recent Antimasonic convention, received 30,183 votes, or some 5,000 more than Morton, indicating the influence of Antimasonic votes in that race. Although Morton lost the election, he had gained 6,500 votes from his 1834 contest. In contrast, Everett, the victor, received 6,200 votes fewer than Davis had in 1834. Clearly, the Democrats had attracted many if not most of the remaining hard-core Antimasons into their party and had made considerable gains from their poor showing of the previous year. The transition of Antimasons into the Jackson party naturally infuriated those Antis with Whig inclinations and produced a feud between Hallet and Pliny Merrick.[32]

By January 1836 the bulk of the Antimasonic party had clearly become an adjunct of the Democrats. In January, a fifteen-man committee recommended the nomination of Van Buren for the presidency before what proved to be the last genuine Antimasonic convention, which met at the statehouse in Boston on January 29. According to the *Advocate,* this convention approved Van Buren's nomination with only one dissenting vote. Hallett justified this tactic some two months later, saying that Massachusetts Antimasons favored the New Yorker, not because he was an Antimason or a Mason, but because he was a Democrat without "moral blemish" and was opposed to monopolies, "among which Masonry stands conspicuous." The selection of Van Buren by the convention produced a bitter protest from Whig-Antimasonic members of the legislature. Meeting on March 9, they described the nomination of Van Buren as a "surrender" of Antimasonic principles to a "party which hurled that distinguished Antimason John Quincy Adams from the Executive Chair and filled it with a *worthy brother* who acknowledges the 'jurisdiction' of the lodge room and stoops from the elevated station of a Chief Magistrate . . . to enact, with his gilded hammer, the part of a mock artificer in a Masonic ceremony." These legislators then nominated Webster for president and Francis Granger for vice president. They attempted to prove that Webster was at last an Antimason by citing a recent letter from the senator to some Antimasons in Pennsylvania that condemned Masonry and all secret societies and requested the statutory prohibition of all secret oaths.[33]

Antimasonic support of Governor Everett faded quickly between 1835 and 1836. Angered by the governor's alleged appointment of Masons to office and proscription of the anti-Webster, pro-Van Buren faction of Antimasons, Hallett inferred that Everett should be abandoned and that the party should back Morton. In August 1836 Morton wrote to Hallett asserting that the Democratic and Antimasonic parties were in agreement on all important principles, and there was no reason why they should not act together in "all things," especially in opposing the "common enemy." He did not say whether the enemy was Masonry or the Whig party. On August 31 what the *Advocate* described as an "Anti-masonic convention" met at Lexington and endorsed the Democratic slate of Morton and Foster. Hallet now declared that all Massachusetts Antimasons were "honor bound" to vote for Van Buren, Morton, and Foster, and he reminded them that George Hull, Whig candidate for lieutenant governor, was a Mason, as was William Hastings, Whig candidate for Congress. A joint Democratic-Antimasonic electoral ticket was arranged by a committee of thirteen selected from the legislature. All electors pledged to support Van Buren, but the Antimasons were not bound to support Richard M. Johnson, a Mason, for vice president. When the votes were counted, Everett was reelected over Morton by a margin of 6,100 votes of a total of 78,000 ballots. In the presidential race, Van Buren received 33,486 votes, compared with Webster's 41,201. Much to Webster's chagrin, the Bay State was the only state he carried. Although the Democrats had lost Massachusetts, had done much better than anticipated, thanks to infusions of support from the Antimasonic and Workingmen's parties. Interestingly, Van Buren's vote, 45 percent of the total, slightly exceeded that of Jackson (21 percent) and Wirt (22 percent) combined, in 1832. In other states, Antimasons-Whigs were livid with rage concerning the transition of Bay State Antimasons into the Democratic party, and Thurlow Weed, revealing a short memory, now referred to his fellow opportunist, Hallett, as the "Boston Benedict Arnold." The Antimasonic party in Massachusetts nevertheless ceased to exist as a separate entity after 1834.[34]

In June, 1836, Hallett gleefully announced that in Massachusetts, Masons "have run so low, that we understand they could not get a quorum for a Grand Lodge meeting the other night. Have we not killed the monster!" Unfortunately for the Antimasons, the "monster," that is, Masonry, was not dead, although it was extremely ill. Unfortunately for historians, membership statistics for the Grand Lodge of Massachusetts are unavailable for the years 1827-1844. As of 1826, there were 101 lodges with 4,312 members; by 1844 only fifty-two lodges were operating. In 1834 the grand lodge forbade Massachusetts Masons to secede from the fraternity at public meetings, asserting that there are "more becoming methods of withdrawing." By 1837, conditions had begun to improve, and the first public installation of grand lodge officers was held since the "excitement" had begun eleven years before. The installation included a public procession, and some 1,500 ladies and gentlemen attended this "gala occasion." It was not until 1845 that a revival of defunct lodges began to take place, with sixty-six working as of 1850. By the Civil War, Masonry had recovered the membership and influence in Massachusetts that it had enjoyed prior to the Morgan affair.[35]

# 10. Coalition Politics
## in Rhode Island

In February 1834 Hallett hailed Rhode Island as the only state in which Antimasonry had fully asserted the "supremacy of the laws" over Freemasonry. He was essentially correct, but what is surprising is not that these stringent laws were passed but that they emanated from a small minority party that never polled more than 16 percent of the vote. The Antimasons in the nation's smallest state would never have achieved any success had their votes not been sought by the power-hungry leaders of first the National Republicans and then the Democrats, each party eager to achieve domination in a state where politics was characterized by instability, shifting coalitions, and low voter participation.[1]

Rhode Island was still operating under the colonial charter of 1663 when political Antimasonry arrived in 1829. The principal officials were elected on a statewide basis, a majority vote being necessary for victory. The seventy-two members of the house of representatives were chosen in either April or November at town meetings. Some 400 offices were filled by a majority vote of the legislature on an annual basis. Obviously, control of that body meant domination of state patronage, and this became the common goal of virtually all Rhode Island politicians. Voting in the state was done by the "prox" system, in which the "towns" (townships) conducted the elections, using a printed ballot known as a prox. Representatives to the federal Congress and presidential electors were chosen at large, increasing the importance of the state as an election unit. Three state offices—treasurer, attorney general, and general secretary—were usually regarded as nonpolitical, and the incumbents retained them for long periods.[2]

In addition to the prox system, other features of political life in Rhode Island made the state seem almost Byzantine in character. Party loyalty was virtually nonexistent, for leaders frequently switched sides, and occasionally rival factions would jointly support a single candidate. Coalitions and sudden changes of allegiance were a way of life, as was political corruption. Voter participation was

usually low, rarely exceeding 30 percent in state elections during the
1830s. Participation in state contests was higher than that in presidential elections, for, as noted, control of the legislature and its substantial patronage distribution was the primary aim of all parties. Both the
Democrats and National Republicans were relatively free from ideological commitments, although each adhered to support of Clay's
American system, with its emphasis on the protective tariff and on the
Bank of the United States.[3]

Freemasonry had arrived during the colonial period, when some
brethren established St. John's Lodge at Newport in 1753, and four
years later a lodge was chartered at Providence. By 1826 there were
nineteen working lodges in the state with a total membership of some
3,000, about 75 percent of the number of Masons in neighboring
Massachusetts, a state with a much larger population. Masonry in
Rhode Island was obviously a successful and flourishing institution
when the Antimasonic crusade began in the late 1820s.[4]

Antimasonry was slow to develop in Rhode Island, and the impetus
predictably came from Massachusetts in November 1828, when the
*Pawtucket Herald* printed "A Candid Appeal" from "Roger Williams," urging Rhode Islanders to read and listen about the evils of
Freemasonry and to "see if the influence has not become immense and
alarming." Taking up this challenge, an eccentric Newport physician,
Dr. Benjamin W. Case, began to edit the *Anti-Masonick Rhode Islander* in April 1829, with the motto on its masthead "Thou Shalt Do
No Murder." Case, a seceded Mason, had been elected master of St.
John's Lodge No. 1, Newport, in 1817, but he subsequently became
involved in a series of complicated lawsuits with Masons from other
lodges over control of lodge property and turned against the fraternity, which he then attacked in a series of vindictive editorials. Running out of money and forced to cancel his paper after only six months
of publication, Case used one of the last issues to publish lists of
"sworn Masons" in six towns with the intent of humiliating them.[5]

The promotion of Antimasonry in the *Anti-Masonick Rhode Islander* instigated several town and county conventions in 1829, after
which the party organized on the state level with a convention at
Providence on March 25-26, 1830. Moses Thatcher of Massachusetts
and the Reverend Henry Dana Ward of New York attended, along
with some fifty delegates. They passed resolutions urging voters not
to support Masons for any public office, selected representatives for
the national convention at Philadelphia in September, and appointed
a state executive and correspondence committee. The delegates made
no nominations and listened to an address primarily concerned with

Masonry as a subversive force in the United States. Present as a spectator at this convention was Hallett, still a National Republican and wary of political Antimasonry. Currently serving as editor of three newspapers in Providence, he had become angry with the Antimasons for allegedly aiding the Jacksonians in the April election, which had resulted in a Democratic victory. He also opposed the political decisions of the national convention at Philadelphia and showed no signs of sympathy toward political Antimasonry until mid-November. On November 16, 1830, he declared that although he had hoped to keep the Masonic issue out of Rhode Island politics, he now had no choice but to accept the assistance that the Antimasons were offering to the National Republicans. The alternative was abandoning hope of ever defeating the Democrats, "merely to uphold a private institution of doubtful utility, and dangerous tendency."[6]

Because the Antimasons had accomplished so little at their March convention, they held a second one on December 30, 1830, with some seventy delegates present. By a vote of thirty-one to eleven, the convention adopted a prox, headed by John Brown Francis, a maverick National Republican from Warwick, for governor. Francis had no previous association with Antimasonry, and the nomination was evidently made without his consent or knowledge, for he was out of the state at the time. The delegates also issued a challenge to several Masonic organizations of Rhode Island by requesting that the legislature summon their officers and demonstrate why the civil charters of these bodies should not be canceled. The Antimasons also demanded passage of a law prohibiting extrajudicial oaths.[7]

Francis, also nominated for governor by the Nationals, waited more than a month before declining both nominations, saying that he had "acted dispassionately and disinterestedly." Always a reluctant candidate, he did not wish to run against James Fenner, the Democratic nominee, although his reasoning is unclear. The Antimasonic convention now had to reorganize its prox and eventually agreed to support Gov. Lemuel Arnold, the incumbent National Republican. On March 3, 1831, Arnold wrote to the Antimasons, saying that he had accepted their nomination but pointing out that he was "neither a mason nor an antimason." If ever called upon to act concerning the issue of Masonry, he would do so "as candidly and impartially as I should [with] any question relating to any other subject." All seemed to be going well until the eve of the election when, as was typical of Rhode Island politics, a "pure" Antimasonic prox appeared, naming wealthy cotton manufacturer William Sprague, Sr., for governor and Case for lieutenant governor. This last-minute effort, attributed to some rene-

gade Antis in Scituate, failed. Hallett (in contrast to his own later
actions in Massachusetts) pleaded for unity, saying that this was no
time to split hairs and to create internal divisions. Arnold achieved
victory over Fenner by a majority of 903 votes, 3,780 to 2,877.
Sprague, Sr., evidently received only a handful of votes, which were
not generally recorded. Six senators nominated jointly by the Nationals and Antimasons received an average of 509 votes more than those
nominated by the Nationals alone. Thus the purely Antimasonic vote
of April 1831 can be tabulated at slightly more than 500 of a total of
about 6,600 ballots cast.[8]

Rhode Island Antimasons assembled at the statehouse in Providence on September 14 for what proved to be a decisive convention.
Eighty-five delegates attended, including Hallett, serving for the first
time as a duly elected Antimason. The convention also appointed a
new executive committee, with four of its eight members from Providence. Hallett, who now seemed to be everywhere, emerged as a
member of this committee, which was to run the party throughout the
state. The delegates also passed nineteen resolutions, one of which
described the Jackson administration as being "totally Masonic;"
another expressed approval for Clay's American system. They then
declared that "in this sense the anti-masonic party is strictly National
Republican." A staunch pro-Clay newspaper, the *Providence Journal,*
strongly disagreed, responding that the Antimasons are "our political
foes, not less so than the partisans of President Jackson." The pro-
Jackson *Providence Herald,* not to be outdone, also asserted that
Antimasonry was an enemy of the Democratic party.[9]

The Antimasons' "war" upon Freemasonry began in earnest in
January 1831, when a committee memorialized the General Assembly, urging that body to revoke the civil charters of twenty-two Masonic bodies and to pass a statute prohibiting extrajudicial oaths. Of
the twenty-two charters, thirteen were revokable if the corporation
rules were determined "repugnant" to the law of the land; the remaining nine were subject to repeal or amendment. The petitioners declared that revocation was justifiable on the grounds that these
charters were the only ones ever issued by the Rhode Island legislature without "a full knowledge of the design, relations, operation and
constitution" of such organizations. Another reason for demanding
revocation was that the "unlawful oaths" required by these bodies
encouraged serious legal violations. This memorial now received
strong support from Arnold, who was eager for Antimasonic votes in
the forthcoming April election. The petition was assigned to a three-

man select committee, on which no one of prominence wished to serve, and nothing more was heard of it for several months.[10]

On November 5, 1831, James F. Simmons, a close friend of Arnold, introduced the Antimasonic memorial to the house, claiming pressure from his constituents. A six-man committee was appointed to evaluate the charges embodied in the petition. None of the members were Masons, but four were known to be hostile to Antimasonry, especially the vocal and vituperative National Republican leader, Benjamin Hazard. The composition of this committee and the investigation it subsequently conducted during a three-week period produced so much animosity between the Antimasons and the National Republicans that it prevented any alliance between these two parties and eventually drove the Antis into a coalition with the Democrats.[11]

The investigation began on December 6, 1831, at Providence, and then, after ten days of testimony, it moved to Newport for an eleven-day session (both cities were considered state capitals). The committee listened to 110 witnesses, including Thatcher of Massachusetts, who talked for more than twelve hours. Fifty-seven of the witnesses were Masons "of varying degrees of fervor," thirty were neutral on the issue, and thirteen were Antimasons. The Masonic witnesses, including those in good standing as well as secessionists, were principally questioned about oaths. Thatcher, who had taken seven degrees (Blue Lodge and Royal Arch chapter) in Rhode Island, declared that after due deliberation, he had concluded that Masonic oaths interfered with both his politics and religion, "and he considered them so far unlawful . . . [that] he had no moral right to bind himself under a barbarous penalty to keep secrets such as Masonry." After reviewing the testimony of Thatcher and other seceding Masons, the *Journal* commented that its editors had "discovered no injury that Masonry had inflicted on the community and no danger to be apprehended from the institution."[12]

The investigating committee was torn by dissension from the beginning of its deliberations. Its members allegedly adopted a rule that Masonic witnesses would be questioned not on the passwords, signs, and grips used for identification purposes among members but only on oaths or obligations. William Sprague, Jr., like his father an Antimason, later said that he had never agreed to this policy. Most of the internal problems, however, emanated from Chairman Hazard, a non-Mason who dominated the hearings and attacked the Antimasonic witnesses with vigor, on one occasion declaring, "The Masonic dunghill has produced a great many Antimasonic vermin." Hazard accused the Antimasons of being so starved for political office that they were proscribing "a portion of our fellow citizens," and he said that the party would not live for one hour if Masonry were ever abandoned.[13]

The Hazard committee issued its report in January 1832. Although the committee found no evidence of criminal conspiracy or activity on the part of Rhode Island Masons, it recommended that the fraternity be abandoned on the grounds that Masonic charities had been superseded by acts of general welfare among the people; that there were no longer any valid reasons for continuing Masonry; and that *all* Masonic organizations were responsible for the "crime" against Morgan. The committee then concluded that the "masons owed it to the community, to themselves, and to sound principles, now to discontinue the masonic institutions."[14]

Only four of the six committeemen signed the report. Elisha R. Potter had become ill and never really met with the committee, and Sprague later issued his own minority report. The majority report was actually incomplete when the General Assembly met on January 9, 1832, but many legislators, eager to dispose of this controversy, accepted it and ordered that it be made public as a document one-third complete. Sprague's report proved to be far more troublesome than the majority document. He said that he issued it because of his disagreement with the committee's decision *not* to force Masonic witnesses to reveal *all* secrets and ceremonies and to explain the "true construction" on Masonic oaths. He claimed that a secret arrangement had been made with certain Masons by Hazard, exempting them from answering specific questions. Hallett, at last an Antimason, was also infuriated with Hazard's actions and unhappy with the majority report for the same reasons as Sprague, and he produced a third report, based on the notes he had taken at the hearings.[15]

The Masons of Rhode Island responded to the legislative report through two resolutions passed by the grand lodge in 1832. One declared that no good could come of the recommendation for self-abolition, for "it is not the Institution of Masonry they are contending against; that it is merely the pretense; political favor is the object." The second resolution asserted that although Rhode Island Masons might "regret" the present state of society, they declared their determination "peacefully to adhere to an institution through evil as well as good report." The following March (1833), some 634 Masons, including 170 from Providence, from a total of approximately 1,000 remaining in the state, signed a declaration similar to that adopted in Massachusetts. Although the *Journal* seemed to believe that this document would "allay the excitement that has been raised against masons, and masonry in this quarter," it had no visible effect in deterring either the progress of Antimasonry or the decline of Freemasonry in Rhode Island.[16]

The legislative controversy regarding adoption of the Hazard report precluded any further cooperation between Nationals and Antimasons, and both parties went their separate ways in 1832. With another state election approaching, the Nationals renominated virtually all of their incumbents, including Arnold. The Democrats likewise repeated their slate of 1831, which was headed, as usual, by Fenner. The Antimasons, meeting in February at their fourth state convention, first passed thirteen "substantive" resolutions, nine relating to the conduct of the Hazard committee and its report. The delegates then nominated their own prox, with Sprague, Sr., for governor, but accepted the National Republican nominees for secretary of state and attorney general and the Democratic choice for treasurer. Sprague, Sr. (William Sprague II), was an unpretentious, hard-working man who had devoted most of his time to his family's successful textile business. Antimasonry was his first foray into politics, but his precise motives for becoming active in the party remain unclear.[17]

The gubernatorial campaign of 1832, even by Rhode Island standards, was unpleasant. The National Republicans believed the aim of the Antimasons was to defeat them, not to win the election. The *Journal* asserted that the Democrats have "most magnanimously come out in support of the consumptive cause of anti-masonry, and in return for the honor, the anti-masons support the Jackson party." The evils resulting from this alleged Antimasonic-Democratic coalition became the major theme of the Nationals' campaign, one hotly denied by the Antimasonic *Rhode Island American*, which declared, "There was never fabricated or circulating a more scandalous falsehood in the world." The election of April 18 resulted in no majority for any candidate, and according to a recently passed "Perpetuation Act," the incumbent remained in office until the voters produced a majority. The tallies, as reported by the canvassing committee, were: Arnold, 2,711; Fenner, 2,283; Sprague, 592. The number of votes necessary for a choice was 2,793; therefore, on this first attempt, Arnold lacked only 82 votes. Although Sprague was the poorest vote getter of the candidates, the Antimasons did increase their proportion of the total from more than 7 percent in 1831 to 11 percent in 1832. This election also indicated that Providence and Newport counties were now the centers of Antimasonry. The Antis indicated that the price of their cooperation in future elections was proscription of Masonry through the repeal of Masonic civil charters and prohibition of extrajudicial oaths. "But be it known, that none but such a Governor as the Antimasons approve will ever again be elected in Rhode Island, until the voice of the dead [Morgan] ceases to cry or until masonry has ceased its career of infamy."[18]

The state held four subsequent election "trials" for governor, with no majority being achieved. On May 16, 1832, the results were: Arnold, 3,319; Fenner, 2,954; Sprague, 709. Arnold needed 319 more votes for victory. Three subsequent "trials" were held, on July 18, August 28, and November 21, with approximately similar results and no majority, the Antimasons garnering about 14 percent in each contest.[19]

Almost unnoticed amid the continuing furor over the gubernatorial race was the Antimasons' election of eight men to the Rhode Island House, with two being incumbents. This group gave the Antis sufficient representation to act with a coherent voice, but it also enabled them to hold the balance of power between the Nationals and Democrats, neither of which had a majority. In the presidential election of 1832, the Antimasons of Rhode Island attempted no union with either major party, and their four-man electoral ticket remained pledged to Wirt and Ellmaker. One day before the election, the Antimasonic *American* reminded voters that there were only two valid choices, Clay and Wirt, both being advocates of the American system. Clay, however, was a "duelist," whereas Wirt was a true Christian, "a meek and lowly follower of Him that 'led captivity captive.' " In spite of that warning, Rhode Island voters still preferred Clay. Election tallies vary, but the votes were approximately: Clay, 2,871; Jackson, 2,051; and Wirt, 819, the Wirt ticket receiving 14.3 percent of the popular vote.[20]

When the General Assembly convened in January 1833, Rhode Island Antimasons enjoyed their first statutory triumph over Freemasonry. The legislature received a petition with 1,200 signatures demanding that Masonic corporations have their officers appear and show why their civil charters should not be revoked. In addition, the memorialists called for passage of a law prohibiting extrajudicial oaths. Little information remains concerning the debate of these proposals, but one result of the new Antimasonic-Jacksonian coalition was a surprising speech by Christopher Allen, a Masonic Democrat. Allen declared that the issue was not political Antimasonry but Masonry, and he (Allen) believed that Masonic oaths not only were unnecessary for a charitable institution but also tended to foster "evil" where none had previously existed. With both Democrats and National Republicans eager for Antimasonic support in the spring gubernatorial election, a bill prohibiting extrajudicial oaths passed the house on its first reading by a unanimous vote. The senate, which contained a proponderance of Nationals, concurred on January 22, adding two amendments: a $100 fine upon conviction for the first offense (the house had originally set the fine at $50.00) and disqualification from holding any state office after conviction for a subsequent offense. It now seems clear that many legislators from both major parties believed this new law would be unenforceable and therefore supported it unanimously as a concession to Antimasons that would produce political advantage for the future. Disregarding such views, Hallett declared that he hoped to see such a law passed in every state in the Union: "It is cheering to our cause, and a strong incentive in rooting out this noxious institution."[21]

The oft-predicted Democratic-Antimasonic merger began on January 17, 1833, when the fifth Antimasonic state convention nominated three Jacksonians and seven Antimasons for ten senatorial seats and Sprague, Sr., for governor. The following day, the Democrats renominated Fenner for governor, but as a portent of events to come, eight of ten senatorial nominees were identical to those of the Antimasons. The leaders of the coalition movement among the Democrats, Elisha R. Potter and Allen, had wished to nominate John Brown Francis for governor, but fears that Fenner's supporters would defect to the Nationals prevented such action at this time. Although Fenner was officially the nominee of the Jacksonians, the movement toward Francis was apparent when the *Herald* ceased to publish the Democratic prox, headed by Fenner, after January 23.[22]

Once again Francis appeared interested but reluctant to run for governor. He disliked the idea of leaving his family and estate, "Spring Green," and particularly seemed to fear being considered disloyal to Governor Arnold, whom he had nominated at the 1832 National Republican convention. Notwithstanding these minor problems, by February 1833 the power brokers of both parties were hard at work to produce a Francis candidacy: Benjamin Cowell and Dutee J. Pearce represented the Antimasons; Potter and John R. Waterman acted for the Democrats. In view of the impending coalition, Francis was an ideal choice, for he had no previous connection with either of those parties but had served as a National Republican in the Rhode Island House of Representatives (1821-1829) and the Rhode Island Senate (1831). He was born in Philadelphia in 1791, but his father had died when he was five, and Francis had moved to Providence, where he was raised by his wealthy maternal grandfather, John Carter

Brown. He attended Brown University, graduating in 1808, and then studied law. Taking little interest in his grandfather's extremely successful mercantile business, he moved to Spring Green and became heavily involved in experimental farming.[23]

On March 9, 1833, both the Democratic and Antimasonic parties published proxes headed by Francis for governor in a move to force a decision from the hesitant gentleman farmer. This effort produced violent reaction from Hazard, who wrote Francis, "I am very certain you will take effectual measures to suppress the unwarrantable liberties that are taken with your name." In spite of Hazard's rage, both the Democrats and Antimasons still wanted Francis and agreed to his condition that he run as an independent, or uncommitted, candidate. By March 20, the negotiators could announce in the *Herald* (the Antimasonic *American* had ceased publication on January 15) that "the public good required the union of two of the parties, to secure an election, and thereby prevent the harassing recurrence of the events of the last political year." Sprague, Sr., having withdrawn, the major obstacle proved to be Fenner, who refused to step down until the Antimasons removed their candidate for lieutenant governor and replaced him with Jeffrey Hazard, the Democratic choice for that office. When this move was accomplished, Fenner indicated on April 1 to Sprague, Sr., that he would withdraw, and two days later he made an official announcement through the *Herald:* "I withdraw from the contest solely on public consideration, without intimating to the Convention, in the slightest degree any feeling or with respecting composition of the prox." His principal reason, he said, for dropping out was to reduce the number of candidates from three to two, thereby producing a decision at the April election.[24]

Both the Democrats and Antimasons made earnest efforts to rationalize the new coalition, which was based solely on a quest for power and not on ideology. The pro-Jackson *Herald* declared, "They have but a common object and a common interest. These unite them. Their object is to restore harmony to the people, which the misrule of Lemuel H. Arnold has disturbed and interrupted." On the Antimasonic side, the *Microcosm* (edited by Daniel Mowry III of the defunct *American*) declared that Antimasonry was attempting to destroy the Masonic institution and not to persecute individual Masons; and because such persecution was a common tactic of National Republicans in the senate, the coalition with the Democrats was justified. The *Herald* gave a curious twist to this thrust at the Nationals when it stated that Masonry was an inherently good institution that had been perverted by certain unscrupulous members, especially those National Republicans who had attempted to transform the lodge into a political organization. Candidate Francis privately viewed Antimasonry with "detached amusement," although he was extremely serious about winning the forthcoming election. He nevertheless believed that the Masons, especially those in the National party, "have put on too much steam and thereby endangered their boiler." Throughout the campaign the *Herald* simply avoided any reference to Antimasonry, promoting Francis's candidacy as a means of curtailing corruption and the free spending habits of the Arnold administration. The *Microcosm* continued to publish the standard Antimasonic denunciations of Freemasonry, portraying the Jacksonians as fellow warriors against a common enemy—the Nationals—and at no time attempting an ideological union between the two parties.[25]

In April 1833, for the first time in more than a year, Rhode Islanders were able to elect a new governor. Francis won the election with 4,025 votes (55 percent), compared with 45 percent for Arnold, who had 3,292 out of 7,317 total ballots. Francis's victory should not be interpreted as a triumph for Antimasonry per se or for any position associated with the Jacksonians. He won because of his popularity with the rank-and-file voter, his ability to attract certain National Republicans, and the general frustration with the stalemate in the gubernatorial race. In addition to electing Francis, the coalition also carried to victory eight of ten senators and a majority of the house. In the case of the third senate seat, the Antimasons, Democrats, and Nationals all ran separate tickets, and the Antimasons' share of votes in this contest may be estimated at slightly more than 15 percent.[26]

Like all coalitions, the one in Rhode Island was fraught with tension. When examined closely, the alliance was actually formed with only the faction of the Democrats that was led by Potter. Opposing the coalition were Fenner and his followers, who included most of the recipients of federal patronage. The Fennerites wished to keep the Jackson party "pure" and abhorred the thought of any dealings with that former National-turned-Democrat-turned Antimason Dutee J. Pearce. Unfortunately for the coalition, the Fennerites generally controlled the editorial policy of the leading Democratic newspaper, the *Herald*. In the late summer and autumn of 1833, the coalition endured a severe test as Pearce sought to achieve reelection to the U.S. House of Representatives, a move favored by Governor Francis. An Antimasonic convention of July 1833 appointed a new fifteen-man executive committee, which in turn selected a nominating committee to name two candidates for the forthcoming election. Obviously unable to reach an agreement with the Democrats on this issue, the

Antimasons nominated Sprague, Jr., and Pearce; four days later, the Jacksonians named Nathan B. Sprague and Wilkins Updike. Allegedly the Democrats were angered by the strong protariff views of (William) Sprague, Jr., and Pearce. The coalition was now proving impossible to maintain with respect to candidates for national office, for in terms of economic philosophy, the Antimasons were advocates of Clay's American system as much as the Nationals.[27]

The Antimasons' fortunes in the congressional elections received a major blow when Sprague, Jr., resigned from the contest at the eleventh hour, writing Francis that his continuing in the race "would have a tendency to destroy the good feeling that now existed between the Antimasonic and the Jackson party." He evidently hoped that his supporters would vote for Democrat Nathan Sprague, thereby denying victory to the National candidate, Tristam Burges. To the Antimasonic state committee, however, Sprague, Jr., merely wrote that it had been inexpedient for him to accept the nomination. The Antimasons did not attempt to replace him but, through the *Microcosm,* continued to promote Pearce as the choice of both the Antimasonic party and a majority of the Democrats. On August 24, that paper declared, "We know that some of the Nationals are now boasting that they have good a wedge in to split us. We know the great body of the Jackson party are with us heart and soul. . . . LET THE UNION OF THESE TWO PARTIES BE PRESERVED."[28]

In the August election, Burges defeated Nathan Sprague for the "northern race" by a 2:1 vote (3,162 to 1,499). In the "southern race" (although Rhode Island was not divided into official districts, these terms were used), none of the candidates received a majority. When the Democratic candidate withdrew two days before the November election, leaving Pearce and National candidate Nathan F. Dixon as the only contenders, Pearce easily won, 2,152 to 1,705.[29]

Three months after Francis's election as governor, at the June 1833 session of the legislature, Antimasonic representative Jonah Titus called up the memorial concerning Masonic charter repeal from the roster of unfinished business. Titus's proposal, supported by Democrats Allen and Potter, passed, receiving three-fourths of the assembly's votes, and the senate quickly concurred. In permitting the Democrats to do most of the work needed to pass this memorial, the Antimasons may have been testing the strength of the new coalition —or perhaps, more plausibly, they were seeking experienced legislators who were able to handle such a volatile subject and ferocious opponents like Hazard. The legislature nevertheless took no formal action to repeal the charters until the session of January 1834.[30]

On January 22, George Turner began the Antimasonic offensive with a broad attack against Masonry in general, not confining himself to the charter issue. National Joseph L. Tillinghast objected, but several Democrats, including John R. Waterman, defended Turner. Turner then spent four days in attempting to prove his major contentions: Masonic corporations had broad and "ominous" connections throughout the world; Masonry was extremely strong in Rhode Island (he estimated that there were 1,500 members and thirty-one lodges); the Masonic civil charters did not exert adequate state control over the chartered bodies; and Masonic initiations involved the administration of oaths that imposed immoral and unpatriotic requirements upon the candidates. During a second week of testimony, Samuel Y. Atwell, attorney for the Masons, attempted to defend the lodge. A number of Masonic Democrats were called as witnesses, a situation that upset the *Herald,* which now seemed to fear that this would be the undoing of the fragile Democratic-Antimasonic coalition.[31]

On February 1, 1834, Christopher Allen, a staunch member of the coalition, introduced a bill intended to end the tortuous debate that had gone on for almost two weeks. According to its provisions: (1) six Masonic charters (of three Blue lodges, one council, one chapter and one commandery of Knights Templar) containing revocation clauses were to be repealed, with one year being granted the corporations to liquidate their property; (2) the remaining sixteen Masonic corporations were to report annually in May to the General Assembly, giving the number and names of their members and officers, the number and names of initiates, "with the mode and manner of their admission, and the form of the promise or obligation which such new members have taken on their admission, the place and times of all meetings, and an inventory of all funds and property belonging to the corporation." The original bill declared that if the above conditions were not met, the charters were to be forfeited to the Supreme Court of Rhode Island, but Titus amended this by changing the penalty to a fine of $100. Two National Republicans, Hazard and Henry Y. Cranston, attempted to have the vote postponed but failed, and the bill passed the house thirty-seven to twenty-six, with eight abstentions. The senate concurred on the same day.[32]

The Grand Lodge of Rhode Island responded to this punitive law on March 18, 1834, by voting to surrender its civil charter of incorporation, and it recommended that all subordinate lodges possessing such charters do likewise. At the annual convocation on June 24, however, a committee chaired by Grand Master Joseph S. Cooke made it clear that abandoning the civil charters did not mean the abandonment of Masonry. The committee explained that the grand lodge preferred giving up its corporate charter to submitting to the act of February 1, 1834, requiring annual returns, and in doing so, the grand lodge had surrendered nothing more to the General Assembly than what it had received from the assembly, that being a "naked charter of incorporation" that enabled it only to hold property and to act as a corporate body without conferring any Masonic powers or privileges. Eight Blue lodges followed suit (two of them in Providence County, two in Newport County), and in May 1834 they petitioned the legislature for surrender of their charters of incorporation, this being a viable alternative to making annual returns to that body.[33]

Undoubtedly influenced by the militant stand of the grand lodge, the legislature took further action in late 1834 and early 1835. In November, 1834, Antimason Gideon Spencer of Warwick proposed a bill to require *all* Masonic bodies, regardless of their status of incorporation, to make annual returns similar to those outlined in the law of February 1. Failure of a lodge to make the required annual returns would lead to a fine of $1,000. Cranston, now classified as a Whig, pleaded with Spencer to postpone the bill to the January 1835 session, declaring that he would support any Antimasonic proposal if only the Antimasons would not vote with the National Republicans-Whigs on matters of highest interest to the nation. Spencer agreed to the postponement, and during the interim, the Antimasons announced that they would withhold support from any candidate for the U.S. Senate until the Spencer bill passed. On January 21, 1835, it became law, receiving only three negative votes in the house. The senate agreed unanimously. Its passage went virtually unnoticed in the local press and was largely the result of a new source of support for the Antimasons—the Whigs, who were eager to undermine the Antimasonic-Democratic alliance, which was now showing signs of severe stress.[34]

Within a few months, however, delegates attending an Antimasonic state meeting in Providence complained that the laws requiring annual returns to the legislature from all Masonic bodies were *not* being enforced; thus it appears that, like previous Antimasonic legislation in Massachusetts and Vermont, this latest set of laws intended to destroy Masonry was proving unworkable.[35]

Antimasons in Rhode Island received a severe shock when, at the end of March 1834, Mowry's *Microcosm* ceased publication. The party now lacked a newspaper in the state and depended on the *Herald* for publicity—hardly a reassuring development, for that newspaper usually reflected the views of the pro-Fenner, anticoalition wing of the Democrats. Economic difficulties attributed to Jackson's removal of deposits from the Bank of the United States and reflected in the closing of several cotton mills caused a rift between the Antimasons, who had previously endorsed Clay's American system, and the Jacksonians, who did not. Much to the anger of many Antimasons and the "Francis wing" of the Democrats, the *Herald,* in March and April 1834, attempted to convince voters of the evils of the Bank. Further strain was placed on the coalition with the advent of another party, the "Liberty and Union," in reality the Whigs under an assumed name, who nominated a prox headed by Nehemiah R. Knight for governor.[36]

As the election of April 1834 approached, the Antimasons, still holding the balance of power, found themselves propositioned by both the Democrats and the Liberty and Union party-Whigs. The *Herald* reminded Antimasons that it was Democratic support that had made possible the laws restricting Masonry, while warning that if the opposition came to power, "another administration may so modify or repeal what has been done for the Antimasons as to render a surrender of the charter of Grand Lodge unnecessary." The paper also praised the Antis for their continued support of the coalition. The Whigs, via the *Journal,* likewise courted the Antimasons, reminding them of "common" financial interests and that "arbitrary acts of the National Executive" were a more powerful enemy to the rights and interests of Rhode Islanders than Masonry ever had been. On their part, the Antimasons published a prox, headed by Francis, in the *Herald* on April 5, together with an address aimed at Democratic adherents of the coalition. This statement asserted that Masonry was still the one and only issue, and while it existed, so would Antimasonry. Francis, who again received the Antimasonic endorsement, was not in accord with the fiscal policies of the national Democratic administration and let his opinions be known through private correspondence. These views, together with Antimasonic support, carried the day, although Francis won by only a 156-vote margin. Running one separate senatorial candidate, the Antimasons polled some 16 percent of the 7,200 votes cast, their best performance to date. In the gubernatorial election, the Antis' 16 percent, when added to the Democrats usual 38 percent, had produced the necessary margin for victory.[37]

Although the coalition had won the governor's race in April, the tide began to turn in the August legislative election when, largely because of increasing economic distress, the Whigs were able to win a majority in the Rhode Island House, electing thirty-eight representatives. The Democrats had twenty-eight, while the Antimasons retained their six seats from the previous session, four being from Warwick. The Jacksonians, who held nine of the coalition seats in the senate, needed the Antimasons' six votes to control the "Grand Committee," or joint session, which selected U.S. senators. Because of this situation, the *Herald* continued to court Antimasonic favor, going so far as to describe the Bank of the United States as being more dangerous in its operation than all the Masonic organizations that had ever existed. The coalition remained in business long enough to reelect Sprague, Jr., as Speaker of the house, but not long enough to elect Potter to the U.S. Senate in January 1835.[38]

The coalition had been in effect for more than a year, but the Antimasons and Democrats were still unable to hold a joint convention. Meeting simultaneously on January 16, 1835, at the Providence statehouse, each party appointed two committees, one to nominate a prox, the second to confer with the other about a prox. With little difficulty, the committees endorsed a coalition prox headed once again by Francis. Omitted from the prox were several Antimasons who had not favored Potter's election to the senate and were now being punished for their opposition. By the end of March 1835, when the Whigs published their prox, the coalition had begun to disintegrate. After renominating Knight for governor, they included three "identifiable" Antimasons among their nominees for state senator. Within two weeks, still another prox appeared, the "Free Antimasonic Prox," an effort of renegade Antimasons in Providence led by Edward S. Williams. This ticket, in terms of senatorial nominees, clearly indicated collusion with the Whigs. Hastily recalling that the Antimasons were indeed part of the coalition, the *Herald* finally mentioned this fact three days before the election, but then only to declare that Rhode Island's Antimasons would never be "beguiled" by the Whigs.[39]

In the election of April 1835 Francis achieved reelection over Knight, but only by the tiny majority of 106 votes, 3,880 to 3,774. The lieutenant governor and four of the five senators who achieved majorities were Whigs, elected by margins of fewer than twenty-six votes. The election itself indicated that Rhode Island's parties were in their normal state of disorganization, Antimasonry was falling apart, and the trend toward success at the polls was slowly moving in the direction of the Whigs. The Whigs, now controlling the grand committee, were able in May to elect Knight to the U.S. Senate over Potter by a vote of forty-one to thirty-eight (Potter, despondent at this latest defeat, died before the year was out). The only bright spot for this coalition was its support of Sprague, Jr., and Pearce for the U.S.

House of Representatives. The Antimasons were infuriated by the Whigs' nomination of Cranston for this office, although they seemed to take no particular offense at Whig support of incumbent Tristam Burges for reelection. In this contest the coalition made a brief come-back, the Antimasons being angered and spurred on by Cranston's nomination and by the first public appearance of Masons in Providence since 1831: on June 24, 1835, 200 had marched in procession to celebrate St. John's Day. The Antis turned out in force at the polls, and Sprague, Jr., and Pearce won by narrow margins.[40]

The election of Sprague, Jr., and Pearce to Congress in August of 1835 was the "last hurrah" of the Antimasonic-Democratic coalition. Many Antis now indicated that since their legislative goals had been achieved, there was no longer a need for political Antimasonry. Others felt closer to the Whigs on economic issues such as tariff and opposition to Jackson's banking policies. Several attempts were made during 1835 to reestablish a purely Antimasonic newspaper, but these failed and Antimasons still had to rely upon the *Herald,* a paper that, as Allen observed, was governed by "Fenner's fools." The solidarity of the Jackson party at this time, a shortage of funds, and the almost total decline of Masonry as a political issue were the primary reasons for the continued absence of any Antimasonic press in Rhode Island.[41]

By 1836, Antimasonic strength in the nation's smallest state appeared to be equally divided between those inclined to the Democrats and those favoring the Whigs, and what was left of Antimasonic party existed merely to lend support to the two major parties at election time. Both the Democrats and Antimasons held conventions in late January, the Democrats on the twenty-seventh, the Antimasons on the twenty-eighth but the nearly identical proxes they developed were not made public until the first week in March in an attempt to harmonize the nominations. When published, Francis, as usual, headed the ticket, with Democrat Jeffrey Hazard running for lieutenant governor. The Whig prox, headed by Burges for governor, was published less than two weeks before the election and contained no Antimasons on its slate. Francis easily trounced Burges, winning by more than 1,100 votes, and the coalition continued to dominate both houses of the General Assembly. Antimasonry ceased to be of interest in Rhode Island for the remainder of 1836 and only achieved notice when Van Buren carried the state over Harrison, 2,962 to 2,710. Obviously, a number of the Antimasons who had supported Clay in 1832 remained loyal to the post-1832 coalition and voted for Van Buren four years later.[42]

The year 1837 opened with the two coalition factions once again holding separate but simultaneous conventions and producing nearly identical proxes, both headed by Francis, who was seeking his fifth consecutive term as governor. The Whigs for some unclear reason failed to nominate a prox for the April election, and therefore the coalition's only opposition came from the Constitutionalists, who favored replacement of the colonial charter. In an election characterized by extremely low voter participation, Francis won by an overwhelming margin, 2,716 to 946. The Whigs had no qualms about running candidates for Congress and in June nominated Robert B. Cranston and Tillinghast, whereas the coalition renominated Sprague, Jr., and Pearce. All seemed well until late June, when Sprague, Jr., suddenly told Francis that he would not run because he had become a Whig and did not wish to embarrass his former Antimasonic colleagues. Sprague's declination did not totally surprise the governor, who believed that most Antimasons would eventually become Whigs. Sprague apparently intended to retain some degree of affiliation with the Antis, for he did not withdraw as a delegate to the party's forthcoming national convention. Within two weeks, the name of Jesse Howard, a favorite of Francis, had been substituted for that of Sprague, Jr., on both proxes. On July 22, the *Herald,* obviously angered by Antimasonic defections to the Whigs, ceased publication of the Antimasonic prox. Sprague, now attempting to justify his political shift, asserted that in transferring to Whiggery he had not changed his principles at all: "As an Antimason, I have been connected with the Jackson party. . . . the whigs of this state opposed . . . the Antimasons—The consequence was a union of the antimasonic and Jackson parties. IT WAS A UNION OF MEN AND NOT OF PRINCIPLES." Sprague believed the Democrats had become, in terms of economic programs, more "loco focoish" and he was determined to oppose such measures as Van Buren's independent treasury bill. In the August election, both coalition nominees suffered defeat at the hands of Cranston and Tillinghast, who each won with a 400-vote majority. Antimasonic defections and economic disaster in the form of the panic of 1837 were taking their toll, and the Whig victory in these congressional races was merely a prelude to winning the governor's office in 1838 and the presidency in 1840.[43]

Sprague, Jr., who had shown Whiggish inclinations since 1834, was as prominent a convert as the Whigs could attract, and his defection from the coalition was the turning point in the disintegration of Rhode Island Antimasonry. From 1832 to 1835, he had served as the coalition's Speaker of the Rhode Island House; from 1835 to 1837, he represented the coalition in the U.S. House of Representatives. In January 1838 he accepted the Whig nomination for governor, which caused the *Journal* to declare, "The question of antimasonry is at an end in this State. There are high national interests in jeopardy, and neither masons nor antimasons, but good and patriotic Whigs, are engaged in the support of Mr. Sprague and Mr. Clay." The coalition, now reduced to the Democrats, nominated a reluctant John Brown Francis. Antimasonry was derelict, and both the Whigs and Democrats openly courted Masonic votes. New social issues included temperance and antislavery, and Sprague was able to appeal to advocates of these reforms more effectively and successfully than Francis. Sprague won the 1838 election over Francis with 53 percent of the vote, 3,984 to 3,504. All ten members of the Rhode Island Senate were now Whigs, as were forty-five of the seventy-two representatives.[44]

Rhode Island's Antimasonic party faded away during 1838. The loss of the governorship in the April election, in which the party had ceased to function, the inability to hold a convention, and the failure of several key leaders to vote were all signs of its moribund condition. By December of that year, even insurgent leader Williams would not deny the assertion of some of his Democratic friends that he constituted the "entire" Antimasonic party in Rhode Island, for he had been named as the state's sole delegate to the November national convention at Philadelphia. The party in Rhode Island had always been an association of men, bound together not by principles but by desire for office and patronage. Devoid of any ideological commitments and seeking union with one of the two major parties in order to legislate against Freemasonry, the Antimasons first crossed swords with the National Republican leadership in 1831–1832 but quickly found the friends they were seeking among the Jacksonians, who needed the Antimasons as much as the Antis needed them. The resulting coalition permitted the Democrats to control the governor's office, the legislature, and patronage for five years. It also allowed the Antimasons a share of the patronage and, most important, the opportunity to pass the harshest laws against Masonry of any state in the Union.[45]

Although the laws passed by Rhode Island in 1834–1835 with the intent of subverting Masonry were unusually severe in context, they were no more successful in obliterating the fraternity than the less stringent statutes of other states. Masonry in Rhode Island emerged in somewhat better condition than in New York, Vermont, and Massachusetts. Although the reasons are difficult to pinpoint, possibilities include the nonideological nature of the party, as evidenced by the

long five-year coalition with the Democrats, in which Antimasonic
principles, rhetoric, and propaganda were subdued through a mutual
desire for electoral success. Another factor was the general weakness
of the Antimasonic press in the state. With the demise of the *Rhode
Island American* in January 1833, only the weekly *Microcosm* remained, and its collapse in March 1834 meant that Rhode Island
Antimasons had to rely on the hostile Democratic *Providence Herald*
to "spread the word."

In Rhode Island, unlike other states of the Northeast affected by
Antimasonry, not one of the established lodges surrendered its Masonic charter during the time of difficulty. Masonic membership in
Rhode Island in 1825 had stood at about 3,000, but by 1835 only some
950 Masons remained in the state, a loss of two-thirds. No new lodges
were chartered from 1825 to 1856, and almost no degree work took
place during this period. Once the most severe phase of this crisis had
passed, the grand lodge began to clear out the dead wood and forced
eight lodges to surrender their Masonic charters in 1843. Three of
these were restored the following year. The grand lodge met each year
during this period, with the lowest point of attendance being 1834,
when only eleven lodges sent representatives. During that year, when
the General Assembly was busy attempting to legislate Masonry out
of existence, only two subordinate lodges, Temple No. 18 at Smith-
field and Lafayette No. 19 at Cumberland, failed to make their annual
membership reports and to pay the yearly per capita assessment to the
grand lodge. In 1834 Grand Master Cooke, in reflecting on the state
of the "Craft," observed: "Not withstanding the enactment of the laws
herein referred to, and the vexations they have otherwise had to
encounter, yet Masons do not despond, and we hope and trust they
will continue to stand firm and united by an indissolvable chain of
sincere affection." Recovery was slow and barely complete with the
advent of the Civil War. On March 4, 1861, a little more than one
month before the Confederate bombardment of Fort Sumter, the
General Assembly ended a conflict of another nature when it restored
to the grand lodge its civil charter of incorporation that had been
surrendered in March 1834. The Antimasonic crusade in Rhode Island was officially at an end.[46]

# 11. Coalitions on the Periphery

The Blessed Spirit, originally confined to western New York and New England, quickly expanded into areas settled by emigrants from these states. Ohio was the first state on the periphery to attract Antimasonry, which developed quickly in the state's northeastern corner, known as the Western Reserve. Located near western New York, the Reserve proved to be fertile soil for Antimasonic missionary endeavors. Including ten entire counties and portions of two others, it had been the stronghold of the National Republican party in Ohio. Two of these counties, Portage and Ashtabula, were the sites of the first Antimasonic activity, the latter being the location of the first Antimasonic newspaper, the *Ohio Luminary,* which began publication at Jefferson during the summer of 1828. Although the *Luminary* was the first Antimasonic press to be established as such, the *Painesville Telegraph and Geauga Free Press,* a paper already in existence, joined the Antimasonic ranks in March 1829, when its editor and publisher, Eber D. Howe, declared that because of its wealth, political power and influence, Masonry "ought no longer to have an abiding place among us."[1]

In the summer and autumn of 1829, Antimasons held numerous county conventions in the Reserve to nominate candidates for the legislature and for various county offices. In the October election, Antimasons were successful in Ashtabula County, where their candidates received the largest majority of any party's nominees to that time. On February 25, 1830, the first all-county Antimasonic gathering assembled at Chardon, Geauga County, and the 300 delegates who attended helped organize the party on a statewide basis. They created a number of new committees, including the central committee of vigilance and correspondence, established to unite the party and to appoint other committees when needed. In addition to the Antimasons present at Chardon, some sixty Masons also attended and attempted to cause a disturbance about passage of a resolution disapproving of "all secret combinations." One prominent Mason declared that this phrase could be interpreted to include "banking institutions and religious societies." The resolution passed nevertheless, 133 to 127.[2]

Ohio's first Antimasonic state convention assembled at the Stark County courthouse in Canton on July 21, 1830, with only thirty delegates present, fewer than half of the number chosen to attend. Because of the sparse representation, seven men from the audience were invited to take seats as delegates. Although no nominations occurred, four seceding Masons witnessed to their "conversion" to Antimasonry; a delegate from each county testified as to what was being done to stamp out the "evil" of Masonry in his jurisdiction; and delegates established a new and powerful correspondence committee to be headquartered in Portage County. In a departure from these usual activities, the delegates declared their approval of the principles of the Workingmen's party, for "they tend to disseminate light and knowledge, to preserve our equal rights, and to destroy all secret, monopolizing and designing parties." The *Telegraph* observed after the convention that Antimasonry was now "beginning to stand erect and ... the great state of Ohio in due time, will show herself a powerful auxiliary in the present warfare against Freemasonry."[3]

In the October election, the Antimasons, who did not have a candidate for governor, suffered defeat in their efforts to elect Jonathan Sloane to the U.S. House from the district including Portage, Geauga, and Trumbull counties. They did, however, elect state representatives from Portage, Geauga, and Ashtabula counties and won a number of county offices in the Reserve. Although the Antis made gains in the legislature, having some fifteen men in both houses, their voting record made them indistinguishable from the Nationals.[4]

It took the leading National press, the (Columbus) *Ohio State Journal* almost two years to recognize the existence of Antimasonry in the Buckeye State, and it eventually did so with only a brief notice stating that the party's second state convention had assembled at Columbus on January 11, 1831. Twenty-six delegates attended from fifteen of seventy-three counties. For the first time there were delegates from Franklin County (Columbus) in central Ohio and one each from Adams, Athens, and Highland counties in the southern part of the state. The delegates chose Darius Lyman of Portage County as presiding officer, passed a resolution asserting that Masonry was opposed to truth, justice, religion, and equal rights, enlarged the central committee, and gave it the authority to appoint delegates to the September national convention at Baltimore. Like its predecessor, this convention made no nominations. Candidates for office were selected either by the central committee or by county conventions or committees. The autumn election of 1831 produced results for the Antimasons similar to those of the 1830 contest, with six men achieving election to the Ohio Senate and nine to the Ohio House of Representatives.[5]

The "Blessed Spirit" was not producing the same excitement or the same results in Ohio as it had in some of the northeastern states, and therefore local Antimasons attempted a new tactic—they attempted to link Freemasonry with Mormonism. The Mormon community at Kirtland, led by the founder and prophet of the church, Joseph Smith, was only ten miles from Painesville and was a source of irritation to Howe, editor of the *Telegraph,* who was as opposed to Mormonism as he was to Masonry. In February 1831 Howe, who became well known as an early anti-Mormon writer, expressed grave doubts about the "new sect" that had sprung up "in this vicinity." He demanded that the Mormon church be "investigated, and if found to be a base counterfeit, like freemasonry, let it be nailed to the counter and ranked among the thousands of impositions which have arisen in the world, under the authority of a dream or vision, to deceive mankind." This attempt to agitate against Masonry failed, and no more was heard of the connection with the Mormons.[6]

In March 1832 the Antimasonic central committee announced a state convention at Columbus for June 12 for the purpose of nominating a governor and a presidential electoral ticket. This year, unlike previous years when the party had unofficially supported the National Republican gubernatorial candidates, as the *Ravenna Star* observed, "Antimasons must go alone." The delegates who assembled at the state capital represented only eighteen counties, the actual number described as merely "very small." After two declinations, they nominated state senator Lyman, who accepted, and a twenty-man electoral ticket pledged to support Wirt and Ellmaker. Each elector was later sent a circular by the state committee requiring him to vote for the national Antimasonic ticket if elected, but three resigned rather than do so.[7]

Meeting one month after the Antimasons, a group of National Republicans attending a federal court session at Columbus on July 12 renominated Gov. Duncan McArthur. On September 10, McArthur told his friends that he would withdraw from the race and would urge the Nationals to support Lyman if the Antimasons in turn would form a fusion electoral ticket. The nominees on this ticket must remain *unpledged* to either Clay or Wirt but must be free to prevent Jackson's election in whatever manner was most feasible. McArthur now asserted that there were no Masons but at least three Antimasons already on the National ticket. The request that they support Lyman was declined by a number of the governor's National friends, many of whom were Masons, on the grounds that Lyman was an Antimason and could not win, even with National support. McArthur then announced his candidacy for the U.S. House, Seventh District, and two other Nationals withdrew from the race to open the way for him. When the election took place in the fall, he lost to Democrat William Allen of Chillicothe by one vote.[8]

Ohio's Antimasonic presses lauded Lyman's nomination, the Columbus *Ohio Register* admitting that although he was not well known throughout the state, Lyman was one of the first Ohioans to take a stand against secret societies. Elected to the senate some five years before by an overwhelming margin, he had proved himself a capable legislator. The *Star* predicted that National Republican voters throughout Ohio would "generally" support him, citing meetings in Lorain and Medina counties, where Nationals had indicated that they would vote for Lyman for governor and Sloane for Congress. Several National presses also registered their approval of Lyman. On September 29, 1832, Judge John Bailhache, editor of the *Ohio State Journal* and chairman of the Nationals' central committee of correspondence, in accord with the "wishes of public sentiment," declared his support for Lyman, referring to the candidate as being "morally without stain" but also noting his attachment to the "great principles" of the National Republican party. Bailhache declared that Lyman should receive the vote of every man interested in "rescuing our common country from the ruthless grasp of Jacksonianism and its attendant evils—corruption, misrule and political intolerance." He did not once in his endorsement, however, refer to Lyman as an Antimason or as the candidate of the Antimasonic party.[9]

On October 5, 1832, the *Telegraph* urged all voters to support Lyman, saying that to vote for "other names will only help to proclaim the triumph of Freemasonry. . . . vote to extirpate the masonic institution, and you will vote to preserve your own rights and those of posterity." It also accused the Masons of trying to perpetrate various types of fraud in the forthcoming election, such as the printing of forged Antimasonic ballots with the names of candidates omitted. McArthur's withdrawal and the support of several National Republican newspapers and leaders came too late to save Lyman. Although twenty-nine counties gave him a majority, he was still virtually unknown in the southern part of the state. Lyman lost to Democrat Robert Lucas, a hero of the War of 1812, 63,213 to 71,038, and Lucas became the first Jacksonian governor of Ohio. Three National Republican congressman suffered defeat, but the Antimasons elected two men to the federal House—Sloane in the Fifteenth District and Elisha Whittlesey in the Sixteenth District. Both districts were located in the Western Reserve, and voters selected these men over Democratic and National Republican opponents by large margins. Ohio's next delegation to the U.S. House would include eleven Democrats, six Nationals, and two Antimasons. Throughout the state, Antimasons and National Republicans together cast 5,000 more votes in the congressional races than did the Jacksonians. This situation caused some Ohio Antimasons to remark, as their compatriots were doing in Pennsylvania, that the Clay Masons had defeated them in the gubernatorial contest.[10]

Part of the bargain for securing McArthur's withdrawal from the governor's election was a pledge by the Antimasons to cancel the Wirt-Ellmaker electoral ticket and to support the unpledged ticket nominated by the National Republicans. The Antimasonic central committee met at Columbus on October 15, 1832, and withdrew the Wirt ticket, adopting the National's unpledged ticket and urging Antimasons to support it. The committee, headed by Sloane, declared that the political situation had changed since formation of the Wirt ticket. Committee members had previously believed that the National electors were pledged to Clay, but upon investigation this ticket revealed no Masons but several Antimasons. The committee also observed that should the unpledged ticket win, its members "under certain circumstances" would be honor bound to vote for Wirt and Ellmaker.[11]

Following withdrawal of the Wirt ticket and announcement of this action through an address to the people, the central committee sent circulars to the men named on the unpledged ticket, asking them if they would feel free to vote for those candidates most likely to defeat Andrew Jackson, "even for Wirt and Ellmaker." Although the circular was a move in the direction of conciliation, the more radical Antimasons were furious at withdrawal of the Wirt ticket and bitterly opposed the unpledged anti-Jackson slate. Among the "ultras" or radicals was Andrew McElvain of Franklin County, irreconcilable member of the central committee, who denounced the action of his fellow committeemen as a "coalition by which it is attempted to transfer our whole strength to the support of Grand Master Clay." On October 24, those Antimasons opposed to the unpledged ticket met in Columbus and agreed to vote for Wirt and Ellmaker, declaring it to be "inconsistent" for an Antimason to support an elector who preferred Clay to any other man and suggesting that all friends of the party stand "firm and true to the cause." McElvain issued a statement of protest, endorsed by thirty-two Antimasons, declaring that the central committee had violated its trust, since all the committeemen knew that the electors on that ticket would never support Wirt over Clay. The *Star,* which now upheld the unpledged ticket, decried McElvain's action, declaring that he was far more a "Jackson man" than an Antimason and should have never been appointed to the committee.[12]

The Antimasonic press of the Western Reserve generally supported the action of the central committee and promoted the unpledged ticket, believing it to be the only practical course of action. The *Telegraph* asserted, "Let Ohio also do her duty, in support of the unpledged ticket, and the Constitution will be snatched from destruction." The *Star* also lauded the ticket, saying that nine-tenths of Ohio's Antimasons approved of the committee's actions. "Clay cannot be elected, but . . . Wirt may, if the Anti-Jackson ticket is successful in Ohio." National Republican presses, such as the *Journal,* attempted to conciliate Antimasonic voters, reminding them that the electors, if victorious, would support either Clay or Wirt, whichever stood the best chance of defeating Jackson.[13]

In the presidential election of 1832, Ohio voters had the choice of an electoral ticket pledged to Jackson, the unpledged National Republican ticket endorsed by the Antimasonic central committee, or a separate Antimasonic ticket pledged to Wirt and containing the names of four candidates who were also on the unpledged ticket. As in Pennsylvania and New York, the fusion ticket went down to defeat as Jackson won a narrow victory, 81,247 to 76,539. The Antimasonic vote for the Wirt ticket ranged between 509 and 538, or about 0.3 percent of the total. Almost one-third (173) of the separate Wirt vote came from Ashtabula County. The *Journal,* in conducting a postmortem of the election, observed that the Democrats had been united and determined to win, while "the opposition was divided into parties which could not be brought to act in concert without much difficulty." The *Star* attempted to console its readers by noting that the "result does not disappoint us. Ohio has never been set down by our paper as an anti-Jackson state."[14]

The union of Antis and Nationals in both the state and presidential elections of 1832, although never referred to as such, continued, with certain Antimasons attempting to disrupt it. On December 29, 1832, Franklin County Antimasons met and recommended that the central committee set a date and site for a state convention. They also suggested that the party reorganize in each county and appoint from one to two men to a committee of correspondence as a means of maintaining communications with the committee. These recommendations went unheeded; the committee failed to call a state convention, and the party quickly disintegrated. In the county and state elections of 1833, Antimasonry showed a marked decline in all counties except those in the Reserve, where it barely held its own.[15]

During 1833 the Antimasonic party in Ohio faded from the scene. Although in April the *Star,* citing an article from the *Ohio Register* about the national revival of Masonry, naively inquired, "Are We Ready? The Battle with Freemasonry has just begun," it was increasingly obvious that in the Buckeye State Antimasonry was ready only to die. Many Antimasonic presses were suspending publication, and those in existence, including the *Star,* were turning to other reform movements. In Portage County "Democratic Antimasons" were able to nominate candidates for legislative and county offices through a convention held at Ravenna on September 12. This meeting also passed resolutions declaring that the prospects for Antimasonry "were never more flattering than at the present time," and delegates admonished local Antis "not to be weary in well doing" but to imitate the vigorous and successful efforts of Antimasons in Vermont. Antimasons in Geauga County held a convention at Chardon on September 10 and nominated candidates for state representative and for several county offices. Two weeks later, Geauga and Ashtabula Antis selected former Ohio chief justice Peter Hitchcock as a candidate for the senate.[16]

During the autumn elections of 1833, the Democrats and National Republicans in Geauga County (Painesville) united to drive the Antimasons out of existence. The *Telegraph* complained, "Look at the coalition which has formed in this county and look at its avowed object. There is no secrecy about it—it is for the sole purpose of sustaining Freemasons." This coalition was no more successful in Geauga County, Ohio, than its counterpart in Vermont that year, for the Antimasonic slate won by a small majority, except for Hitchcock, who carried his senate seat by a vote of 2,112 to 1,112. The *Telegraph* declared that Hitchcock's victory was undeniable proof that Antimasonry was far from finished, but its pages told a different story—after November 1833 its main theme gradually switched from Antimasonry to antislavery—even in the Western Reserve, Antimasonry was dying.[17]

In Franklin County, Antimasons, meeting at Columbus in November of 1833, suggested a state convention be held in that city on February 22, 1834. The delegates assembled on the appointed date for what proved to be the Antis' fourth and last convention in Ohio. They nominated no candidates but passed a number of resolutions, proceeding as though it were the party's first convention. They resolved that the party be reorganized in Ohio; that the object of Antimasonry be the destruction of Masonry; that a law be passed supressing all extrajudicial oaths; and that the central committee call a convention to meet in the winter or spring of 1835. These resolutions were ignored and quickly forgotten, and the 1835 convention never materialized. By autumn, most Ohio Antimasons had made a rapid transition into the new Whig coalition organized by John McLean's supporters from National Republicans, anti-Jackson Democrats and, of course, Antimasons.[18]

Antimasons acknowledged their final obligation to the party when they memorialized the legislature in the winter of 1835 with numerous petitions calling for an investigation of Freemasonry and the prohibition of extrajudicial oaths. These petitions were referred to a committee that, at the end of March, reported that "under the present circumstances, the whole subject as heretofore, should be left to the solitary action of enlightened public opinion." This innocuous statement was the swan song of the Antimasons, most of whom, without noticeable controversy, became part of the Whig organization.[19]

The inroads of Antimasonry upon Masonry are more difficult to assess in Ohio than in other states, and the statistics available do not always correlate. Of approximately 104 chartered lodges in operation as of 1830, 41 ceased to work during the Antimasonic era, and 63 maintained a troubled existence. As many as 1,000 Masons may have seceded from the fraternity. The number of subordinate lodges represented at grand lodge sessions declined perceptibly, from fifty-five in 1830, to thirty-five in 1832 (with the top two grand lodge officers being absent), to seventeen in 1837. Some lodge buildings in Ohio were defaced during the crusade, and "sticks and stones were thrown at Masonic processions, with hoots and yells, even upon the occasion of funeral processions." Public Masonic processions and observances continued to be held in Ohio, in contrast to other states, and in June 1832 Masons attending a special session of the grand lodge at Cincinnati felt sufficiently secure to advertise a public celebration of St. John the Baptist's Day. Masonic activity, especially the chartering of new lodges and initiation of new members, increased rapidly after 1842. By 1850, there were 161 chartered lodges in Ohio; by 1860, 175; and by the mid-twentieth century, Ohio led the fifty states in number of Masons.[20]

Among those states in which Antimasonry existed but did not

flourish, Connecticut ranked behind Ohio in political activity. Masonry had come to the colony in 1750 with the chartering of a lodge at New Haven, and there were nine lodges by the outbreak of the Revolution. By 1800, Connecticut had forty-five lodges; by 1827, sixty-nine, with a total membership of about 5,000. Antimasonry arrived in the Nutmeg State through establishment of a newspaper, the *Hartford Intelligencer,* founded in 1828. An Antimasonic meeting took place at Norwich that year with more than 700 in attendance; and following the pattern, "missionaries" arrived to promote the cause, including a native son, Avery Allyn of Washington, notorious as a seceding Mason, expositor, lecturer, and author.[21]

Connecticut's first Antimasonic convention took place at Hartford in February 1829, where delegates appointed correspondence committees for the counties and a state executive committee. Actual organization of the party, however, did not commence until the second convention of February 1830 at "Allyn's Hall" in Hartford, with 140 delegates representing forty-four "towns." The delegates elected Hartford mayor Nathaniel Terry, a well-known businessman, as presiding officer and, with one exception, nominated the entire National Republican slate for state offices, including Gideon Tomlinson for governor. They refused to support the Nationals' nominee for lieutenant governor, John S. Peters, a prominent Mason, and nominated William T. Williams for that office. All of the National candidates won election, Tomlinson, being unopposed, received 12,980 votes. The obviously strong cooperation between the Antimasons and National Republicans in this 1830 election created an identity problem for the Antis that they were never able to resolve, which in part explains their relative lack of success and limited longevity in Connecticut.[22]

Whether Connecticut Antimasons held another state convention or caucus toward the end of 1830 or in 1831 is a matter of conjecture; nevertheless, an independent ticket emerged for 1831, headed by the obscure Zalmon Storrs (1779-1869) of Mansfield for governor and Dr. Eli Ives of the Yale medical faculty for lieutenant governor. Storrs, a Yale graduate who was a country store manager and later a silk thread manufacturer, received the nomination only after declinations from three other men. In the 1831 election, both Nationals and Democrats supported Peters for governor, and he achieved victory over Storrs by a vote of 12,819 to 4,778 (65 percent to 24 percent).[23]

The Antimasons held a convention in 1832, of which no record survives. Although the delegates nominated an electoral ticket pledged to Wirt and Ellmaker, whether they made a separate nomination for governor is unclear, but Calvin Willey, a Democrat and former U.S. senator, was supported by both the Democrats and most Antimasons; he lost, nevertheless, to the National Republican incumbent, Peters, 11,971 to 4,463 (70 percent to 26 percent). Having just combined with the Democrats in the governor's race, Connecticut Antimasons revealed a dexterity superior even to that of their compatriots in Rhode Island, now fusing with the Nationals to elect Nathan Smith to the U.S. Senate. Smith, a National-Whig with Antimasonic inclinations, served from 1833 until his sudden death in March 1835. In addition, Antis and Nationals joined forces to elect sixty-seven men to the state house of representatives and eight to the senate. Only in the presidential election of 1832 were the Antimasons able to maintain their identity, and the Wirt-Ellmaker ticket polled 3,409 votes (10 percent), compared with 18,155 (55 percent) for Clay and 11,269 (34 percent) for Jackson. Wirt's heaviest vote was in the northeastern part of the state in Windham and Tolland counties. The only immediate effect of Wirt's candidacy in Connecticut was to reduce the percentage of Clay's vote as compared with the 71 percent won by John Quincy Adams in 1828.[24]

By 1833, the Antimasons had returned to the tactic of a separate candidate for governor and once again nominated Storrs. In the April election, he faced Governor Peters and Democrat Henry W. Edwards, son of Pierpont Edwards, one of the founders of the Connecticut Grand Lodge. Edwards conducted a vigorous campaign, emphasizing tax reforms, universal manhood suffrage, and rotation in office in this once heavily National Republican state. He almost won, receiving 9,030 votes (41 percent), as compared with 9,212 for Peters (41.5 percent) and 3,250 votes (15 percent) for Storrs. There being no majority, the election moved to the General Assembly, where on May 11, 1833, the Antimasons, in an act of political suicide, decided to vote with the Democrats, and Edwards became Connecticut's first Jacksonian governor.[25]

Among the peripheral Antimasonic states, Connecticut was the only one to experience an attack on Freemasonry in the legislature. In 1832 four Antimasons who had served as delegates to the 1830 national convention memorialized the General Assembly, requesting repeal of an 1821 act incorporating Hiram Lodge No. 18 at Stonington. The petitioners argued that retaining these laws implied governmental approval of Masonry. They also urged the assembly to examine the nature of Masonic oaths and penalties. Yet the memorialists wavered as to whether a civil government had the power to abolish a voluntary association, stating that the force of public opinion would ultimately accomplish this goal. The memorial was referred to a select committee that lacked subpoena power, and therefore a thorough investigation of Masonry was impossible. The committee eventually produced a report that was a patchwork of compromises. Although committee members determined that the oaths (obligations) of the first two Masonic degrees displayed an "evil tendency" and were illegally administered, they did not find sufficient reason for abolishing the fraternity. They recommended a resolution requiring the assembly to place Masonic corporations on the same basis as other chartered charitable corporations, ordering them to report statistics on funds, receipts, and disbursements. The assembly quickly rejected the resolution. The following year, 1833, a petition signed by 1,400 Antimasons was presented to the legislature requesting passage of a law abolishing extrajudicial oaths. It was referred to a committee *with* full subpoena powers, but unlike the investigations in Rhode Island and Pennsylvania, only two seceding Masons testified. One, a cohort of Henry Dana Ward, was from New York; the other was Calvin Hatch, a leading seceder from Farmington. The testimony was far-ranging but indecisive; and the committee concluded that Masonic oaths were "highly improper" and ought to be prohibited by law. Antimasonic representatives now introduced a bill embodying this suggestion to the 1834 session of the General Assembly, only to have both houses vote to postpone consideration "indefinitely." This was the end of the matter.[26]

In 1834 Antimasons again attempted to elect Storrs as governor, with less success than ever before. He only received 2,398 votes (6.5 percent), compared with 15,834 (42 percent) for the National-Whig candidate, Samuel A. Foote. Once again, no candidate had a majority, and the decision fell to the legislature, which in May 1834 selected Foote, a former U.S. senator from Cheshire. Antimasons in 1835 were about to present another slate headed by Storrs, but shortly before the election the state committee adopted a resolution recommending support of the entire Whig ticket. Even with this recommendation, 757 Antis still voted for Storrs, and although the majority of the party probably supported Foote, the Democrat Edwards won, 22,129 to 20,335 for Foote. Political Antimasonry in Connecticut was finished, the only concrete result having been the two-time election of a Democratic governor who was the son of the state's most prominent Masons.[27]

Masonry in the Nutmeg State suffered trials, tribulations, and probable losses in membership (not published) comparable to those of the fraternity in Vermont and New York. A crisis occurred at the grand lodge in May 1831, when all of the officers except grand treasurer and grand secretary declined to give further service. Finally, Dr. Thomas Hubbard, of the Yale medical faculty permitted the brethren to elect him grand master "from the floor." Others then also agreed to serve in various offices, and the continuity of the grand lodge was preserved. The number of men initiated in Connecticut dropped from 138 in 1828 to "not published" for 1829-1832 but was recorded as 26 for 1833. Only twelve men were initiated throughout the entire state in 1835 and again in 1836, but this figure increased to forty-five in 1837. The number of active working lodges declined from sixty-two in 1827 to three in 1835 and 1836. The number rose to nine in 1837 but decreased to six in 1830. A Masonic revival did not take place until the 1840s. Some lodges, such as St. Paul's at Litchfield, had to hide furniture and records in members' barns and attics, and for several years after 1829, the time and place of these meetings was kept a secret. Morning Star Lodge No. 28 near Warehouse Point survived by meeting in the woods two to three times a year. In Connecticut, as in Vermont, Masonry was sometimes forced to go underground in order to survive. The best "counterattack" the Masons had was the accusation that Antimasonry was a thinly disguised attempt to revive the unity of church and state and to restore the tax-supported status of the Congregational church, which had ended in 1818. "The association of political Antimasonry with a desire for religious reestablishment was *not* an advantage at the polls in Connecticut."[28]

In the remainder of New England, Antimasonry was not an important part of the political matrix. Although the party never made much headway in New Hampshire, one of the nation's most heavily Democratic states, twenty-six of forty-eight lodges ceased to exist. Only in the old Federalist strongholds of Rockingham and Cheshire counties, the latter bordering on Vermont, did the Antimasons accumulate any strength. Isaac Hill, vitriolic editor of the *New Hampshire Patriot* and staunch Jacksonian, linked Antimasonry with Federalism and predicted a dire future for the state if Antis were elected to office. Unable to establish a newspaper or even to nominate a slate of electors by 1832, Antimasons could not function in the presidential election of that year. Jackson swept the state with 24,855 votes to 18,938 for Clay —57 percent to 43 percent. No popular votes were recorded for Wirt. The Antimasons were alleged to have held a state convention in 1833 and to have nominated candidates for governor and Congress, but the name of the gubernatorial nominee remains a mystery. Democrat Samuel Dinsmore won the election unopposed with 28,270 votes. As observed, the Antimasonic party flourished in those states where the structure and organization of one or both of the major parties was in chaos, and this was not the situation in New Hampshire.[29]

Political Antimasonry was only slightly stronger in Maine than in New Hampshire, and although neither state sent delegates to the 1830 national convention at Philadelphia, both were nominally represented at the Baltimore convention (Maine, two delegates; New Hampshire, one). Most of the Antimasonic activity in Maine prior to 1831 was on the local level. On July 4, 1832, Antimasons held their only recorded state convention at Augusta, with 150 delegates representing fifty "towns." They nominated Thomas A. Hill for governor and an electoral ticket pledged to Wirt and Ellmaker. Two of these electoral candidates, however, together with sixty other Antimasons, issued a circular advising the party faithful in Maine to vote for Clay. Other Antimasons issued their own statement urging full support of Wirt. All of the rhetoric meant little, for Jackson swept the state, winning 33,978 votes (55 percent) to 27,331 for Clay (44 percent) and 844 votes (1 percent) for Wirt. Hill may have polled about 870 votes. He ran again in 1833 and 1834, receiving 2,384 votes in 1833 and 1,076 in the latter year, according to *Niles' Register.* As in Connecticut, the Antimasons had difficulty in maintaining an identity separate from that of National Republicans, whence most had come. Presumably, the majority of Antis in Maine, as in Connecticut and New Hampshire, merged with the Whig party upon its organization. Although political Antimasonry was weak, Freemasonry in Maine suffered a noticeable decline after 1831, and the grand lodge had many problems during these years. In 1837, only one lodge was represented at the grand lodge communication; in 1842, no subordinate lodges sent delegates, nor was the grand master present, and all grand lodge offices had to be filled with pro-tems. By 1844, Freemasonry began a slow but steady revival, and by 1979 Maine, in number of Masons, was second only to Massachusetts among the New England states.[30]

New Jersey citizens expressed numerous Antimasonic sentiments but did not form an active Antimasonic party, and the Blessed Spirit remained "feeble because of the state's early formation of balanced parties." Antimasonry first appeared in the north central county of Morris, which became the site of the *Palladium of Liberty,* New Jersey's first Antimasonic press. In 1827 Morris County Antis won four seats in the General Assembly, only to lose them to the Jacksonians during the following year. Antimasonry also became prevalent in Essex County (Newark) in 1829, and in 1830 Joseph W. Moulton and Joseph Farrand founded the only New Jersey paper established for the singular purpose of promoting Antimasonry—the *Newark Monitor,*

which survived until 1834. The Democrats were weak in Essex
County, and this factor, together with a split in National Republican
ranks, provided an opening for a third party.[31]

Morris and Essex County Antimasons held a joint meeting at Newark on June 24, 1830, and proposed a state convention for New
Brunswick in August. This convention selected eight delegates to
attend the national convention at Philadelphia and established a state
corresponding committee, of which *Palladium* editor Jacob Mann
was a key member. It also nominated five pro-Clay men for the U.S.
House of Representatives, making a slate identical to that of the
National Republicans. A second state convention, held at Trenton on
June 1, 1831, selected eight delegates to the national convention at
Baltimore.[32]

National Republican strategy in the Garden State concerning the
Antimasons was characterized by "a non-committal attitude that
sought to give Anti-Masonic votes proper direction, while not ex-
pressly claiming adherence to their program." Samuel Southard, New
Jersey's most prominent National, typified this viewpoint, declaring
in 1829 that although he was not a Mason, he believed the lodge had
abused its power for political purposes; nevertheless, he never
proposed any statutory restrictions on the fraternity. His lack of
support notwithstanding, the 1831 New Jersey Antimasonic convention nominated Southard for vice president of the United States. The
National press, led by the *New Jersey Journal,* faithfully reflected the
party's continuing conciliatory attitude toward the Antimasons. Such
attitudes were necessary to elect a governor, for under New Jersey's
constitution of 1776 (and until 1844), the state's chief executive was
chosen on an annual basis by the legislative council (senate) and
General Assembly. After winning control of the assembly in 1832
with Antimasonic assistance, the Nationals elected Southard as governor.[33]

The Antimasons held their third convention at Trenton on August
22, 1832. Refraining from nominating candidates for state office, the
delegates selected an electoral ticket pledged to Wirt and Ellmaker.
Their choice had serious consequences in the November election, for
although Wirt received only 468 votes (1 percent of the total), it
contributed to Clay's defeat, and the Kentuckian lost New Jersey to
Jackson by 360 votes, 23,466 to 23,826 (49.1 percent to 49.9 percent).
In the congressional election, three of the six men elected to the House
had Antimasonic inclinations and support from the party. With this
brief flurry of activity, the Antimasonic party in New Jersey disappeared almost overnight, for return of the Nationals to power on the

state level had deprived the Antis of one of the major reasons for their existence, that is, to help the Clay party win elections. Although political Antimasonry may have been of short duration, the Antimasonic crusade had a devastating effect on New Jersey Freemasonry. Thirty-one lodges sent representatives to the 1826 communication of the grand lodge, but by 1834 that number had been reduced to four, only one more than the original number of lodges that had established the grand lodge. One act of violence against a lodge was reported during this period; in April 1830 a mob attacked the lodge in Newark at night, causing considerable damage to the premises.[34]

Michigan was the only territory to attract political Antimasonry, which evolved into the first political party since territorial organization in 1805. For most of the territorial period (1805-1837), Michigan had no political parties, but by 1819 tax-paying adult males could elect a delegate to Congress every two years, and after 1823 they elected a nine-member legislative council. This opportunity produced "spirited" election battles among rival factions but no party politics until 1829, when the Antimasons organized the first party, with the others quickly following. During its brief existence, Michigan Antimasonry was characterized by an "evangelical and moralizing style." Two Antimasonic presses, the *Detroit Courier* and Ann Arbor *Western Emigrant,* were "oriented toward moral reform," and their pages were filled with sermons and reports of progress in various causes. In addition, many leading Antimasons served on the boards of directors of numerous Christian benevolent societies. These evangelicals condemned Masonry, Catholicism, and political parties (especially the Democratic) for "submission of individual reason and conscience to a central authority." In an interesting move, Antimasons quickly associated Masonry with Catholicism and the Democratic party, claiming that Catholics usually voted for their Democratic enemies, many of whom were Masons. The evangelical quality of Michigan Antimasonry is best exemplified by a declaration made at the party's first meeting in 1829, when delegates condemned Freemasonry as a "perpetual conspiracy against morality, Christianity and republicanism." Masonry, they said, was a definite threat to Protestantism, for the lodge often served as a surrogate church for many men.[35]

Michigan Antimasonry was strong in a cluster of eastern townships near the juncture of Wayne, Oakland, and Washtenaw counties, a "miniature Burned-over District," where other reforms flourished as well, including antislavery and temperance. Many of the settlers in this area had come from New England and western New York and had friends and relatives active in the crusade. The first Antimasonic meeting in Michigan was held on January 1, 1829, at Farmington, where delegates issued a call for a territorial convention to assemble the following month. They also issued the usual address to the people, which listed familiar grievances against the lodge and praised the courage of seceding Masons. The territorial convention met at Detroit in February, with four counties represented. Delegates endorsed "Major" John Biddle for territorial delegate to Congress. Biddle, scion of the prominente Philadelphia family and younger brother of Nicholas, after serving in the U.S. Army (1813-1821) had accepted an appointment at Detroit as register of the U.S. Land Office. Described as an Antimasonic fellow traveler, he received more than 2,000 votes, some 800 more than his nearest competitor, Father Gabriel Richard, a French-born priest. Biddle served from March 4, 1829, until February 21, 1831, when he resigned.[36]

In 1831, the Antimasons, dissatisfied with Biddle's views on political Antimasonry, nominated Samuel W. Dexter, one of the editors of the *Western Emigrant* and the son of John Adams's secretary of war. One wing of Jackson's supporters, calling themselves "Democratic-Republicans," nominated John R. Williams, a former mayor of Detroit and judge. Another faction now organized as the National Republicans (although they were known to opponents as "Junto-crats") and nominated a Mason, Austin Wing, who was supported by the *Detroit Journal.* Wing won the July election with 2,039 votes, compared with 1,328 for the Antimason, Dexter, and 1,063 for Williams. This tally gives an indication of the Antimasons' relative strength in Michigan in 1831. Two years later, however, Antimasonic candidate William Woodbridge ran poor third against a Whig and the victorious Jacksonian and prominent Mason Lucius Lyon.[37]

Woodbridge's defeat led to the rapid demise of political Antimasonry and to the formation of a Whig party by 1834, incorporating the equally dormant National Republicans and Antimasons. After 1834-1835, the militant, anti-Catholic spirit of the Antimasonic evangelicals, many of whom were Presbyterians, found a welcome reception in the evangelical wing of the Whig party. It is obviously no happenstance that the Whig candidate for governor (of the state) in 1841 was Philo C. Fuller, former Antimasonic leader from western New York, and that the early strongholds of Whiggery included the previously Antimasonic eastern counties.[38]

During the Antimasonic Crusade, only two grand lodges folded (Vermont's went underground), those of Illinois and the Michigan Territory. Organized in 1826 with six lodges and Lewis Cass as grand master (he was also a past grand master of Ohio), the Grand Lodge of Michigan had expanded to nine lodges when the Antimasonic excitement began in 1827-1828. In 1829 Cass, under great public pressure, used his enormous influence as grand master and territorial governor to bring about a suspension of the grand lodge, recommending similar action to the subordinate bodies. Of nine lodges, only one, Stoney Creek Lodge (now Rochester No. 5) continued to work during the remainder of the period.[39]

Illinois had been a state (1818) less than a decade when the Morgan affair took place and political Antimasonry became a reality. Although there is no evidence of an organized effort against Freemasonry in this state, the weak and struggling grand lodge, chartered in 1822, collapsed in 1828, probably more from internal problems than as a result of outside pressures. After the demise of the Grand Lodge of Illinois, the Grand Lodges of Kentucky and Missouri chartered nine lodges in this state between 1835 and 1839, indicating that the atmosphere was not unduly hostile to Masonry. The Grand Lodge of Illinois was reestablished in 1840 and by 1856 had jurisdiction over 185 subordinate lodges. In the presidential election of 1832, ninety-seven votes were cast for Wirt and Ellmaker (0.5 percent of total), but these were individual expressions of will rather than the product of any party activity. Jackson easily carried the state over Clay, 68 percent to 31 percent. In neighboring Indiana, also a relatively new state (1816), twenty-seven votes (0.1 percent) were reported for Wirt in an election won by Jackson, 31,652 to 25,473 for Clay. Although a few state legislators had Antimasonic inclinations and the crusade was reported to have had some influence in eleven counties, Antimasonry in the Hoosier State had an ephemeral existence.[40]

Missouri, then considered more a western than a southern state, experienced Antimasonic influence and propaganda but no organized political activity. Most of the pressure was felt in the St. Louis area, and because of this localization and events in other states, at the Missouri grand lodge communication of October 1831 the officers proposed a dissolution of the grand lodge and all subordinate bodies. The delegates defeated the resolution; in 1833, however, the grand lodge moved its headquarters from St. Louis to Columbia, some 130 miles to the west, where it remained until 1837, then returning to St. Louis. When the crusade began, there were eighteen lodges in Missouri (1839); by 1833 that number had decreased to five. Among the lodges surrendering their charters was St. Louis No. 1, which had been unable to meet for more than six months, allegedly because of a combination of pressure from local ministers imbued with Antimasonic fervor and a cholera epidemic that was raging in the city at the time.[41]

The southern states were no more receptive to Antimasonry than to antislavery or to other reform movements of the Age of Jackson. A preoccupation with the defense of slavery, the nullification crisis, and the general feeling in the South that Antimasonry was another Yankee invention gave it little credence in the region. Calhoun was the only southern politician of any note who showed the slightest interest in Antimasonry and then only as a means of obtaining the presidential nomination for 1832. As Clement Eaton has observed, Southerners of the pre-Civil War South "listened to the admonition of Calhoun to meet the pernicious ideas [of reform movements] 'on the frontier.' The dynamics of Southern thought moved, after the death of Jefferson, in the direction of defense, a trend which explains much of the cultural history of the Old South."[42]

In Alabama, some Antimasonic meetings were alleged to have taken place in Dallas, Marengo, and Tuscaloosa counties, but a true party structure never evolved. Reports from other southern and border states are equally fragmentary, for example, that Antimasons held a convention in Mecklenburg County (Charlotte), North Carolina, on July 4, 1833, that was "largely attended" and resulted in the establishment of an Antimasonic tract society. In Delaware, Antimasons sent a token delegation to the 1831 national convention at Baltimore and allegedly made plans for a state convention that year, but whether it actually met is unclear. Although the national party did hold its nominating convention at Baltimore and selected William Wirt of Maryland as the standard-bearer, there was no genuine Antimasonic political activity in the Old Line State. Maryland was represented by a nominal delegation of one (John S. Shriver) at that Baltimore convention; nevertheless, no popular votes were recorded for Wirt in the state during the 1832 election. Antimasonic political activity was likewise nil in the neighboring District of Columbia.[43]

In another border state, Kentucky, considerable Antimasonic sentiment hurt the fraternity, but there is no evidence of a structured party. A convention is reported to have taken place at Carthage on January 22, 1829, but verification is not possible. On the contrary, considerable opposition to Antimasonry is apparent from comments of the press in 1829. The (Lexington) Kentucky Gazette referred to the Antimasonic excitement as "foolish," while the Louisville Public Advertiser seemed pleased that Antimasonry had made little progress in Kentucky. It commented that such a movement "cannot flourish among people who choose to deal fairly with their neighbors, and who may be sufficiently intelligent to think and act for themselves." One observer, writing seventy years later, reported that Avery Allyn had given several Antimasonic lectures and demonstrations in the Lexington area during the early 1830s. The primary effect of Antimasonry in Kentucky related to the lodges themselves. Attendance at grand lodge dropped from fifty lodges (of the original sixty-six) in 1828 to eleven in 1836, and the number of chartered lodges declined from sixty-six to thirty-seven between 1828 and 1840. The trying times that arrived with the panic of 1837 certainly contributed, as did Antimasonry, to the falling off of Kentucky Masonry during this period.[44]

# 12. The Elections of 1836 and 1840

With the rapid decline after 1832 of Antimasonry on the national level as a viable political organization, it became increasingly clear that the party's principal role in future presidential elections would be to give impetus and added strength to the candidacies of major party nominees, especially those of the Whigs. The promoters of both Daniel Webster and William Henry Harrison deemed Antimasonic endorsement of their favorites sufficiently important to produce a concerted effort to see which contender could garner the most Antimasonic support, first for the election of 1836 and thereafter for 1840.

Politicians of both major parties had often regarded Webster and Harrison as sympathetic to Antimasonry prior to 1836, especially Webster. "God-like Daniel," truly popular only among certain conservative, business-oriented Whigs of his adopted state of Massachusetts, needed every vote he could muster in the approaching struggle with the Democrat, Van Buren, and with other Whigs as well. The Whig "strategy" for 1836, motivated by a lack of unity on everything from candidates to conventions, decried the idea of holding a national convention and nominating a single candidate and called for several favorite son nominees, chosen by the state legislatures. The Whigs hoped that Van Buren would be denied a majority in the electoral college, thus transferring the decision to the House of Representatives, where one of the Whigs, perhaps Harrison, might emerge victorious. The Democrat-controlled legislature of Tennessee produced a candidate for the southern Whigs when it nominated Sen. Hugh Lawson White, formerly a friend, but now an enemy, of Jackson. White was soon selected by the Alabama legislature as well, and although he was technically not yet a Whig, this moderate states' rights advocate was endorsed by anti-Van Buren Democrats and Whigs in many southern and border states. Harrison was now gaining popularity in Pennsylvania, New York, and some of the border states, but Webster created little enthusiasm outside New England.[1]

Webster's success in soliciting Antimasonic support initially centered on efforts in Massachusetts, where he and his National Republican-Whig friends labored without success from 1833 to 1835 in an attempt to reconcile their party with the Antimasons, especially those in the legislature. The refusal of the Nationals to support John Quincy Adams for governor in 1833 and their insistence on running and ultimately electing John Davis greatly hindered this effort. Unfortunately, Webster had a long-standing dislike of Adams (dating to Adams's desertion of the Federalist party prior to the War of 1812), a feeling that Adams reciprocated. This mutual disaffection increased in 1835 when Webster backed Davis rather than Adams for the U.S. Senate, an action that infuriated the Antimasons. The majority now transferred to the Democratic party under the leadership of Hallett and his *Boston Advocate* and ultimately voted for Van Buren in 1836.[2]

Webster had taken notice of the "steadily increasing power" of Antimasonry in New York and Pennsylvania as early as 1830 and was briefly considered by a few Antis, mainly in western Pennsylvania, for their 1832 presidential nomination. Unlike Clay or Wirt, he had never been initiated into Masonry and claimed that his father had always been suspicious of the lodge. Daniel Webster had little to say on Masonry or Antimasonry before becoming a presidential candidate in 1835, his remarks prior to that time being confined to statements such as his comment to Davis in 1834 that a great majority of the people agreed with the governor: the Masons ought to relinquish their lodges "in order to bring the great body of Whigs and Antimasons, in this state, into harmonious action." Before Pennsylvania's Antimasonic convention assembled in 1835, several delegates, including Thaddeus Stevens, wrote to Webster inquiring about his opinions on Freemasonry. Replying through Antimasonic straddler Edward Everett, Webster declared that he was ready to reaffirm the the political principles and sentiments of Antimasonry, which declared that secret societies of any sort were inconsistent with a republican form of government. He also noted his approval of the recent Massachusetts law prohibiting extrajudicial oaths, but he admitted that if he were elected president, he would not promise a general proscription of Masonic officeholders.[3]

By 1834 Webster saw few problems in attracting the support of most Antimasons for his 1836 campaign, relying on his reputation as a "patriot" and a friend to the Antimasonic cause to win them over. The Antimasonic leadership, or what was left of it, was badly fragmented, but in general the party hierarchy was reluctant to support Webster. His aristocratic tastes and habits did not appeal to the masses in an age that paid at least lip service to the common man, and his former attachment to Federalism and continued ties with the Bank of the United States were political liabilities that characterized Webster as a loser, or in the phraseology of the day, as "unavailable." Although it was obvious to all but the most naive political observers that Webster's cause was hopeless, 315 Whig members of the Massachusetts legislature, following the advice of the *Boston Atlas,* met in January 17, 1835, and nominated him for the presidency. No names were then presented for the vice presidency, but some months later, Webster, perhaps with a fine sense of irony, suggested that Harrison be nominated for the nation's second highest office.[4]

Twelve days after the Whigs nominated Webster, the Hallett faction of Antimasons met in convention at Boston and nominated Van Buren for president. This action did not reflect the opinions of all Bay State Antis, for a Franklin County meeting had already defied Hallett and had declared for Webster. On March 9, the pro-Webster faction of Antimasons met at the statehouse and nominated their hero. At this point, Charles Francis Adams joined the struggle in support of Van Buren, primarily as a means of hurting Webster and the Massachusetts Whigs, whom he blamed for his father's gubernatorial and senatorial defeats. Charles Francis's aim was to persuade the Antis to support a separate organization, not to effect a merger, as Hallett desired. Charles Francis also did everything possible to discourage the Webster Whigs from joining the Antimasonic-Democratic alliance, perhaps from interest more in defeating Whigs than in aiding Van Buren. As if Webster's presidential prospects in Massachusetts were not sufficiently precarious, the senator now learned that the Antimasonic remnant in Vermont was hopelessly divided over his candidacy. His cause, therefore, appeared doomed, even before the crucial Pennsylvania Antimasonic convention of December 1835.[5]

Gen. William Henry Harrison, Virginia-born hero of the War of 1812, now of North Bend, Ohio, was, like Webster, generally regarded as an Antimasonic sympathizer by 1835. After a long career of territorial, state, and national officeholding, as well as a term as U.S. minister to Columbia (from which position he was removed by Jackson), Harrison at sixty-two became clerk of the Court of Common Pleas of Hamilton County, Ohio, in 1834. At this time Whig leaders such as Seward and Weed came to view him as the most available candidate for 1836. The term "available" then implied a willingness to support a candidate for office that related to his alleged popularity with the average voter and to his ability to be elected rather than to any qualifications for office or to positions taken on the leading issues of the day. A substantial number of Whigs and Antimasons in Ohio quickly entered the Harrison camp and by mid-1835 regarded the Hero of Tippecanoe as their "Northern Savior." Harrison's official quest for Pennsylvania's thirty electoral votes began in December 1834, when the *Pennsylvania Intelligencer* of Harrisburg, a Whig journal, proposed the general's name for the presidency. On January 29, 1835, a "Democratic-Republican" meeting of Dauphin County citizens assembled at Harrisburg and nominated Harrison "without regard to former differences of opinion." In September, more than 1,000 "Whig-Antimasons" gathered at Albany, New York, and with the "greatest enthusiasm" adopted resolutions recommending Harrison for president and Granger for vice president. Harrison's campaign thus far had progressed satisfactorily, but it fell to the Antimasons of Pennsylvania to determine whether "Old Tip" or Webster would be the Northern Whig nominee for 1836.[6]

In mid-summer of 1835, Henry Clay knowingly declared that the selection of Pennsylvania's Antimasonic convention would also be the choice of the Northern Whigs. By this point, Webster was hoping to win the endorsement of that convention through negotiations with Stevens, using Everett as an intermediary. Stevens, in turn, asked both Harrison and Webster for their views on Masonry. Harrison in an earlier letter of May 6 to the Pennsylvania Antimasonic state committee had made a poor impression when he seemed to assert that it was unconstitutional to use the ballot box to destroy Masonry. By early November, in a letter to William Ayres of the Pennsylvania legislature, the general had attempted to modify his earlier position and gave a lukewarm response, one that angered the Exclusives but pleased the Coalitionists. "Old Tip" now responded that although the federal government had no right to interfere with the "principles" or "movements" of the people, if no law had been violated, nevertheless it was the duty of the executive, through the appointing power, to inquire into the principles of those applying for office, and he would never appoint anyone who placed any "engagement or combination" above the Constitution and laws of the United States. In a letter to Stevens, written at the same time and widely circulated through the press, Harrison asserted that although he believed in the ideals of Antimasonry and thought the "evils" arising from Masonry might "form a proper subject for the deliberations and actions of some constituted authorities," the federal government lacked regulatory power over Masonry, and any attempt to exercise such power would be *"infinitely more fatal than those* [evils] *which it was intended to remedy."* After receiving this letter, Stevens wrote Harrison that he was no longer considering the general for the nomination.[7]

Webster was working diligently to secure Pennsylvania's Antimasonic nomination and visited Lancaster and Harrisburg in mid-March

1835 to encourage support for his cause. In addition, he corresponded with Stevens and Rep. Harmar Denny. Stevens made inquiries of Webster similar to those made of Harrison concerning Antimasonry, and Webster, pathetically eager to say whatever would please the Pennsylvanian, responded through Everett. Everett wrote to Stevens that Webster was ready to reaffirm the "sentiments" concerning political Antimasonry that he had already pronounced in the Senate and that on the subject of "secret societies barred by secret oaths," he was entirely in agreement with the Antimasons of Pennsylvania. Three days later, on November 5, 1835, Denny wrote Webster an extremely misleading letter, informing him that his popularity was increasing daily in the Keystone State and that Harrison could never obtain the Antimasonic nomination there, but to ensure this, Webster must make Antimasonic statements at least as strong as those uttered by Wirt in 1831, for "anything short of this would not probably be satisfactory." The following week, the Antimasons of Allegheny County (Pittsburgh) met and selected five delegates, including Denny, to the state convention. All pledged themselves to support Webster, but they immediately sought further clarification of his views on secret societies, asking whether he believed Freemasonry to be a "moral and political evil" and whether the "elective franchise" seemed an effective means of removing such an evil. In addition, the delegates asked, if a president were elected on the basis of Antimasonic principles, "do you believe it to be his duty to sustain those principles in his appointments to office?"[8]

Between November 20 and 30, 1835, Webster wrote the Antimasons of Allegheny County as well as to several of the delegates nominated at Pittsburgh, including Denny and William W. Irwin. Far exceeding Harrison in his condemnation of Masonry, Webster declared that it "is an institution, which, in my judgment, is essentially wrong in the principles of its formation; that from its very nature it is liable to abuses." He added that Masonic obligations or oaths were incompatible with the "duty" of good citizens, for all secret societies were "sources of jealousy and just alarm to others" as well as being dangerous to "civil liberty and good Government." The senator concluded that he was thrilled with the Pennsylvania Antimasons' adoption of the "supremacy of the Laws" as "their leading sentiment," for this was the foundation of all republican sentiments. He also indicated full approval of the recent Massachusetts statute prohibiting the administration of extrajudicial oaths. Irwin replied to Webster, suggesting a modification of one of his statements before it was given to the press, and the senator "humbly" complied. Unfortunately for the state of his political fortunes, if not his state of mind, the Allegheny County "nomination" and subsequent correspondence temporarily led Webster to believe he would be the choice of the forthcoming state convention.[9]

Harrison's route to nomination by Pennsylvania's Whigs and Antimasons and to eventual success in winning the state's thirty electoral votes had begun in January 1835 with the Dauphin County nomination. By December, the time of the state convention, which also met at Harrisburg in Dauphin County, "Old Tip" had the support not only of out-of-state leaders such as Seward and Weed but also of Pennsylvania's governor, Ritner. Ritner resented Stevens's attempts to dominate his administration and refused to support Webster, Stevens's apparent choice for president. The state convention assembled on Monday, December 14, and chose Denny as presiding officer. This seemed a pro-Webster action on the surface until December 16, when after a heated debate the delegates by a vote of ninety-eight to thirty-six defeated a proposal to defer the nominations until the national convention in May. When this motion failed, nine delegates, led by Stevens and also including Denny, Ellmaker, and Hiester, drew up a resolution of protest and seceded from the convention. On December 17, the remaining delegates nominated Harrison for president over Webster, eighty-nine to twenty-nine. Granger, who had received three votes on that ballot, was then unanimously selected for vice president. A number of Antimasons in Pennsylvania did not accept the convention's decision, one declaring that Harrison was no more an Antimason than Clay. Webster received the bad news from Charles Miner, editor of the Westchester *Village Record,* who referred to the recent convention as a "farce," relating that the old bogeys of Federalism and opposition to the War of 1812 had been revived and had been used against Webster before the voting. One week after the Harrisburg convention, Maryland Whigs assembled at Baltimore and nominated a slate consisting of Harrison and John Tyler. Pennsylvania provided the crucial test of Webster's candidacy, however, and after his defeat at Harrisburg, the senator's campaign collapsed outside Massachusetts.[10]

The call for a "national" Antimasonic convention by the Harrisburg seceders brought negative responses from pro-Harrison Antis, of course, but also from the pro-Van Buren faction, as in Massachusetts, where Hallett asserted that since it was impossible for Antimasons to agree on a single candidate, they must act "for themselves." Despite Hallett's warning, the convention did assemble at Philadelphia in the mayor's courtroom on May 4, 1836. Although an official list of those present was never published, it was a "slender affair," with some thirty-five to forty delegates from four states. Of these, about thirty were from Pennsylvania, four or five from Ohio, and one each from Rhode Island and New York. Reflecting the wishes of the Pennsylvania Exclusives, led by Stevens, who naturally dominated the meeting, the delegates passed a resolution asserting the inexpediency of nominating Antimasonic presidential and vice presidential candidates "under existing circumstances." Another declared that the "sole object of political Antimasonry is the entire and lasting destruction of the Institution of Free Masonry and other secret oath-bound societies." The convention appointed a new national committee of fifteen to supervise party affairs. Its members included Henry Dana Ward of New York, William A. Palmer of Vermont, John Quincy Adams of Massachusetts, Edward S. Williams of Rhode Island, Darius Lyman of Ohio, Zalmon Storrs of Connecticut, and Amos Ellmaker and Harmar Denny of Pennsylvania. In addition, delegates also selected a new six-man committee (including Stevens) to correspond with presidential nominees Harrison and Van Buren (only) and to inquire whether, if elected president, they would appoint "adhering Masons" to office.[11]

One of the few favorable editorial comments about the "National" convention of May 1836 appeared in Stevens's *Gettysburg Star*, which lauded the resolution condemning Masonry, "rebuking, in decided terms, the 'base compound' [Whiggery] disorganizing Harrisburg and other similar conventions." Weed's *Journal* predictably described the convention as an "irregular and irresponsible gathering," while Hallett's *Advocate* bluntly called the meeting a "failure as a National Convention." The Philadelphia convention was of little consequence, except for the Stevens committee's efforts to inquire about the appointment of Masons to office. Harrison gave his usual equivocal statement, declaring he would refuse to appoint any man to office "who held the opinion that his obligations to any secret society were superior to . . . the laws and Constitution of his country." Van Buren flatly declared that he would not inquire of potential officeholders if they were Masons or Antimasons, and being a Mason would neither advance nor disqualify a prospect for public office. Even after this response, Hallett could still assert that Van Buren was "decidedly" more Antimasonic than Harrison.[12]

In terms of national politics, the Antimasonic remnant entered the election of 1836 hopelessly divided. Antis in Pennsylvania and one faction in Vermont had nominated Harrison, while other factions in Massachusetts, Rhode Island, and Vermont supported Van Buren.

The majority of "1832" Antimasons were, of course, now in the Whig party, and most of them probably voted for Harrison. In Lancaster County, Pennsylvania, once the most Antimasonic jurisdiction in the United States, the Harrison-Granger electors won over the Democratic ticket by a 2,115 vote majority (6,250 to 4,145), although Van Buren carried the Keystone State by 4,200 votes. "God-like Daniel" won only Massachusetts, which he carried over Van Buren, 55 percent to 45 percent. White won Tennessee and Georgia; and Harrison carried Vermont, Delaware, New Jersey, Maryland, Kentucky, Ohio, and Indiana. Van Buren was successful in the remainder of the states, including crucial Pennsylvania and New York. Antimasonic votes helped the New Yorker carry Rhode Island by a narrow vote. The electoral and popular vote tallies were Van Buren, 170 (764,176); Harrison, 73 (550,816); White, 26 (146,107); and Webster, 14 (41,-201). Following the election, Burrowes, the Antimasonic secretary of Pennsylvania, who had Democratic inclinations, unrealistically rejoiced that his party was now "clear of Harrison, and tho crippled we are still in sufficient strength to renew the contest on the good old proscriptive ground."[13]

Burrowes was incorrect on three counts: the weakened Antimasons of 1836 were nearly extinct by 1840; proscription of Freemasonry was no longer an issue by that year; and Harrison was definitely the most "available" Whig candidate for the 1840 presidential election. Even Burrowes briefly changed his mind, and by the end of 1836 he was telling friends that he believed the Antimasons could use Harrison to their own "advantage." Stevens organized a "Democratic Antimasonic" state convention that met at Harrisburg on May 22, 1837. The delegates issued a call for a national convention to assemble in Washington, D.C., in September to nominate presidential and vice presidential candidates. They also picked a slate of delegates to attend this convention, including Stevens and Ellmaker, and urged other states to send delegates as well. The Washington convention met on September 11 as scheduled, at Brown's Hotel, but it was poorly attended, with only fifty-three delegates present, twenty-seven from Pennsylvania. The remainder came from Ohio, Massachusetts, New York, and Rhode Island. Because of the low representation, the delegates declined to make nominations at this time, preferring to adjourn, pending a convention in Philadelphia in November 1838, with the stipulation that no candidate be nominated from an unrepresented state. They also appointed a new national committee similar in composition to its predecessor, with four of the ten members being Pennsylvanians. The influence of Stevens can be seen in a resolution passed by this convention that on the surface did not appear to be the statement of a dying party: "That we will persevere in our national and state democratic-antimasonic organizations until secret oath-bound societies shall be prostrated throughout the union; and we invite all who have heretofore acted with us to reorganize and unite with us regardless of past differences of opinion with respect to men."[14]

The "last gasp" of the national Antimasonic party took place at Philadelphia on November 13, 1838, with a final "national" convention, although to many outside observers the gathering appeared little more than a meeting of New York and Pennsylvania Whigs. It was appropriate, although evidently not premeditated, that this assemblage take place in Philadelphia, site of the party's first national convention in 1830. Information about this 1838 meeting is sparse and existing accounts vary considerably in content. Unfortunately for posterity, convention officials never published any official proceedings. According to the usually reliable *Niles' Register,* about 119 delegates, representing six states, displayed a strong pro-Harrison, pro-Whig bias, nominating Harrison and Webster for president and vice-president. *Niles'* reported that 101 votes had been cast: Pennsylvania, 30; Ohio, 21; New York (which had not really had an Antimasonic party since 1834), 42; Rhode Island, 4; and Massachusetts, 14.[15]

The pro-Clay *Washington National Intelligencer,* hostile to Harrison, published an extremely negative account of this convention, contradicting much of the information in *Niles' Register.* According to the *Intelligencer,* the delegates did not meet in Philadelphia because of its sentiments for Clay but instead assembled at Temperance Hall in the Northern Liberties of Philadelphia County. They met for three short periods on two different days, with as few as fifty in attendance, forty from Pennsylvania. This report also indicates that Webster received the vice presidential nomination by only a two-vote margin over Ritner of Pennsylvania. The *Intelligencer* dismissed this final Antimasonic convention as "a feeble and uncalled-for attempt to forestall and control the decision of the Whig Convention." Other reports indicate that the true "tone" of the convention was set by delegate Ebenezer Clough, a Whig from Massachusetts, who gave a "eulogy" on Whig principles, declaring them to be those of the American Revolution and hoping that Harrison and Webster would win the election "in order that the country might get into the good old Whig times again."[16]

With his nomination by the Antimasons at Philadelphia in 1838 and by the Whigs at Harrisburg the following year, William Henry

Harrison was really the nominee of both parties in 1840, although the former had virtually ceased to exist as a separate entity by the time the "log cabin and hard cider" campaign took place. One month prior to receiving the nomination of the Antimasons, Harrison indicated that if it were proferred, it would be a mixed blessing. He did not wish to run unless he had the united support of the Whig party, and he certainly did not wish to be viewed as the leader of a nearly defunct third party. In addition, Harrison feared that this nomination would identify him more fully in the public mind with the Antimasons and would revive the hostility between Masons and Antimasons that still lingered in several states, especially Pennsylvania and New York. When, on December 2, 1838, the general replied to Denny, accepting the recent nomination of the Antimasonic convention, he did so in his usual noncommittal manner, stating: "This is the second time that I have received from the patriotic party, of which you yourself are a distinguished member, the highest evidence of confidence that can be given to a citizen of our republic." Harrison also promised to limit himself to one term, to restrict the presidential veto to unconstitutional measures only, and not to allow the executive branch to become the inspiration for legislation. Although not one word was spoken about Masonry or Antimasonry, the committee was satisfied.[17]

Harrison's candidacy received two additional boosts prior to the national Whig convention of December 1839. On May 22 of that year, nearly 100 "Friends of Harrison" assembled at Harrisburg. Directed by Stevens, the delegates passed a series of motions endorsing a Harrison-Webster ticket and three resolutions denouncing Masonry. The latter action, combined with the delegates' failure to make any reference to "Whig principles," indicates that this was really another Antimasonic meeting, and it was so reported by *Niles' Register.* On September 4, a "Unity and Harmony Anti-Van Buren Convention" also met at Harrisburg and was composed of pro-Harrison Antimasons and Whigs, including the seventeen men who had seceded from Whig state convention at Chambersburg on June 13, when that body insisted on nominating Clay. The Unity and Harmony delegates endorsed Harrison as the only available Whig contender for 1840. When the national Whig convention did assemble at Harrisburg on December 2, two rival Pennsylvania delegations appeared, the pro-Clay group selected at Chambersburg and the pro-Harrison men chosen at Harrisburg on September 4. A compromise gave control of a unified delegation to the Antimasons, under the leadership of Charles Boies Penrose, grandfather of Boies Penrose, later the Republican boss of Pennsylvania.[18]

The Whig convention of 1839 was an exciting affair that saw Henry Clay lose the nomination to Harrison, largely over the issue of availability. The general's strong support from the Antimasonic wing of the northeastern state delegations was also an important factor in his success. Clay was the frontrunner, but Weed and Seward, "privately friendly" to Harrison, had also promoted the candidacy of Gen. Winfield Scott, and his delegates from New York and New Jersey held the balance of power. It was later charged that Scott's delegates were really for Harrison, and his candidacy was intended to head off Clay. "The adoption of the unit rule by the Scott-Harrison majority makes this plausible, for it suppressed a Clay minority in several states." After numerous ballots, Harrison received the nomination with 148 votes, compared with 90 for Clay and 16 for Scott. In an effort to placate Clay's furious supporters, the convention nominated the Kentuckian's friend, former senator John Tyler, a strong states' rights advocate and former Democrat from Virginia, who seemed an ideal choice to balance the ticket. Any claims Webster might have had to the vice presidential nomination were quickly forgotten in the rush to select Tyler.[19]

The subsequent campaign was dull until a disparaging remark about Harrison's alleged senility and proclivity for log cabins and hard cider from the *Baltimore Republican* motivated two Pennsylvanians, banker Thomas Elder and editor Richard S. Elliott, to devise the most intriguing campaign in U.S. history. In a programmed concoction of ballyhoo, the aristocratic Harrison, son of a signer of the Declaration of Independence, was portrayed as the "simple soldier-farmer of North Bend who would restore government to the people." With the aid of journalists such as Weed and Horace Greeley, a plethora of songs, slogans, poems, rallies, and parades emerged, drowning whatever issues might have been raised (at least in the North) in a tidal wave of log cabins and hard cider. Harrison won a stunning victory over Van Buren (although neither carried the state of his birth), receiving 234 electoral votes to the New Yorker's 60. The popular vote showed less disparity: Harrison, 1,275,390 (52.8 percent); Van Buren, 1,128,854 (46.8 percent). Almost unnoticed amid the Harrison landslide were the 6,797 votes polled by James G. Birney of the antislavery Liberty party, most of them cast in former Antimasonic strongholds of Massachusetts and New York. Harrison carried Pennsylvania by only 351 popular votes, with Antimasonic support for "Old Tip" being a major factor in his narrow victory; voter participation in the Keystone State reached a then all-time high of 76 percent. Of the thirty Harrison electors chosen in Pennsylvania, twenty-three were former Antimasons, including Ritner. The Antimasonic faction of the Whig party had high hopes for patronage and influence in the Harrison administration, but these went unfulfilled except for the appointment of Granger as postmaster general. Harrison's death one month after his inauguration and Tyler's accession to the presidency and subsequent feud with Clay and the congressional Whigs ended whatever real influence the Antimasons might have exercised in that administration. Not until after the Civil War did Antimasonry again assume a political role, and then it had little notoriety or visible success.[20]

# 13. The Blessed Spirit

The initial outrage in western New York that resulted from William Morgan's abduction and probable murder in 1826, following publication of his Masonic exposé, produced a crusade of evangelistic fervor that was at first centered in the small-town and rural churches, especially certain Baptist and Presbyterian congregations. Although the movement was once considered to have appealed primarily to the economically disadvantaged, recent research indicates that Antimasonry, at least in western New York, had a much broader base, attracting prosperous farmers and small-town merchants who were as angry about the Morgan affair as their poorer neighbors. Antimasonry, whether moral crusade or political party, never held much interest for the inhabitants of the large and more sophisticated cities of the Northeast, especially Boston, New York, and Philadelphia, where Masonry was the strongest. Less appreciative of the sometimes paranoid, conspiracy-oriented propaganda of the Antimasons and less influenced by the revivalistic fervor of the early crusade, big-city voters remained largely untouched by the "Blessed Spirit" and immune to its pronouncements.

When in 1827 the general public realized that Masonic influence and "stonewalling" techniques were preventing or delaying a proper exercise of the legal and judicial processes concerning the Morgan investigations, Antimasonry ceased to be a church-oriented movement and quickly evolved into a political party that aimed at barring Masons from holding office and serving on juries, ultimately seeking to destroy the fraternity altogether. A group of young, efficient anti-Jackson politicians and journalists, led by William H. Seward and Thurlow Weed, directed this transition. By 1830 the party had spread rapidly into Pennsylvania, Massachusetts, Vermont, Rhode Island, Connecticut, New Jersey, Ohio, and the Michigan Territory. Political Antimasonry flourished wherever the two-party system was weak or fractured, as in New York, Vermont, and Pennsylvania, but it developed slowly in those states with a strong two-party structure (such as Ohio) or in states such as New Hampshire and New Jersey, where one party usually dominated most elections.

Following the organizational phase of 1827-1830, the Antimasonic party entered a second stage: from 1830 to 1833 it acted as an independent force in national politics. The Antimasons held a national administrative convention in 1830, the first such meeting of any party, and sponsored the first national nominating convention at Baltimore in 1831. This exciting and innovative period of party development culminated with William Wirt's ill-fated presidential campaign of 1832 against Past Grand Masters Henry Clay and Andrew Jackson. The Wirt campaign quickly became a futile effort, not only because of its inherent inability to win a national election against ever-popular Jackson but also because of the strenuous infighting between Antimasonic purists and pragmatists (or coalitionists), who had arranged for joint electoral tickets with pro-Clay National Republicans in New York, Pennsylvania, and Ohio. All three coalitions failed miserably, producing only bitter recriminations between the two factions and helping to hasten Antimasonry's demise in New York and Ohio. Wirt carried Vermont with its seven electoral votes, winning the Green Mountain State with only a plurality of popular votes.

The third stage of political Antimasonry, 1833 to 1843, witnessed the rapid decline of the party as a national entity, although it actually achieved its major electoral and legislative triumphs on the state level in Pennsylvania, Rhode Island, and Vermont during this period. In New York, the cradle of Antimasonry, Weed and his circle could hardly wait for the dust to settle on the 1832 election before merging with the Nationals to form the Whig party in 1833-1834. Except in Pennsylvania, Antimasonry was a little more than memory by 1837, although three sham "national" conventions in 1836, 1837, and 1838 attempted to present the illusion of a national party. In the Keystone State, Thaddeus Stevens kept the cause alive as late as 1843 through his forceful personality, organizational ability, and the publicity generated by his infamous but nonproductive legislative investigation of Masonry in 1835-1836.[1]

In the aftermath of Wirt's 1832 presidential debacle, the political accomplishments of Antimasonry on the state and local levels are often ignored. The party briefly became dominant in Vermont, a state where the Democrats were extremely weak and voters were frequently attracted to moralistic causes and crusades. Vermont Antimasons, in addition to carrying the state for Wirt in 1832, were able to elect William A. Palmer as governor for four consecutive terms, 1831-1835. In Pennsylvania, which among the Middle Atlantic states had the weakest National Republican organization, the Antis fused with National Republicans-Whigs to elect Joseph Ritner to one three-year term as governor. Ritner's victory in 1835 was made possible by an open split among Pennsylvania Democrats, who offered two candidates for governor, George Wolf and Henry Muhlenberg, only to see both defeated by the "Old Dutch Farmer." In Pennsylvania as well as in Massachusetts, Antimasonry briefly became the second, although not the dominant, party.

Rhode Island Antimasons, who held the balance of power between the long-dominant Nationals and weak but power-hungry Jacksonians, became the masters of coalition politics, aligning first briefly with the Nationals and then with the Democrats to elect John Brown Francis as governor to five one-year terms, 1833-1838. Although Rhode Island journalist Benjamin F. Hallett (who moved to Massachusetts in 1831) had once described the Antimasons as an "inflexible minority," the dexterity of party leaders in arranging coalitions, not only in Rhode Island, but in New York, Pennsylvania, and Ohio as well, proves that political Antimasons were, in the main, an extremely *flexible minority.*[2]

In New York, Pennsylvania, Massachusetts, Vermont, and Ohio, the Antimasons after 1834 became an influential, anti-Clay faction of the Whig party, probably providing the majority of initial Whig votes in the first two states as well as in the Michigan Territory. In those states where the Antis helped organize the Whig coalition, Antimasonry left the new party a heritage of "egalitarianism and evangelism." Northern Whigs often voiced the familiar Antimasonic principle that government and legislation should be used to improve society, "morally and economically." The Seward-Weed faction of Empire State Whiggery remained that party's most progressive element, turning to antislavery in the 1840s, becoming known first as Conscience Whigs in the 1850s and as the radical core of Republicans by 1856. The Republicans' moralistic opposition to slavery appealed to many former Antis as Antimasonry's moralistic antagonism to secret societies had once invoked their enthusiasm.[3]

The Whigs were not the only party to gain adherents and ideology from Antimasonry. The bulk of Massachusetts Antis, led by Hallett, joined the "Democracy" along with remnants in Vermont and Rhode Island. Some Antimasons were attracted by the Democrats' advocacy of the protection of individual rights from the coercive power of special interests and monopolies; others resented the long-standing dominance of the Nationals-Whigs in their respective states. Fears about the corrupting, conspiratorial influence of Freemasonry gave way to apprehensions about the Bank of the United States and other Jacksonian bogies.

In addition to supplying the Northern Whigs (and later the Republicans) with a certain ideology and moral fervor, Antimasons, especially in Pennsylvania and New York, were influential in promoting Harrison's presidential candidacy in 1836 and 1840, eliminating Webster as a serious contender in 1836 and denying Clay the Whig nomination in 1839. Although Harrison was more equivocal on Masonry than Webster, he, unlike Clay, had never joined the fraternity. For this reason and others, "Old Tip" was the Whigs' most "available" nominee for 1840. By that year, Stevens, the leader of the Pennsylvania purists, or Exclusives, had become just as much as a pragmatist as Seward or Weed and saw Harrison as a means to a great Whig-Antimasonic victory. The old general was swept into office on a tidal wave of log cabins and hard cider, but unfortunately for the Antimasonic wing of Whiggery, the fruits of victory were few and bitter.

Both the Antimasonic and later the Know-Nothing (or American) parties "singled out targets which could plausibly be blamed for disorienting social and economic developments." For the Know-Nothings, the "Great Beast" or Satan was the Roman Catholic Church; for the Antimasons, the "monster" was undemocratic, unchristian Freemasonry. The most obvious, albeit temporary, accomplishment of Antimasonry, both as a crusade and party, was the near-total destruction of the fraternity in Vermont, New York, Pennsylvania, Massachusetts, Rhode Island, Connecticut, and Ohio. Although reliable statistics are scarce and estimates vary, total Masonic membership in the United States may have declined as much as two-thirds, from more than 100,000 in the mid-1820s to some 40,000 a decade later. In Vermont, the grand lodge went underground for ten years, and the fraternity virtually ceased to exist. Losses of two-thirds and more in terms of members and the number of active lodges were recorded in Pennsylvania, Rhode Island, and New York. In the latter state, the tally of Masons dropped from 20,000 to 3,000 and the number of working lodges from 480 to 82. Even in the West, Antimasonry was a factor in the demise of the Grand Lodges of Illinois (1828) and Michigan Territory (1829). The Blessed Spirit's ruinous effect on American Masonry was only temporary, however, and a Masonic revival was under way by the 1850s, although it was not until after the Civil War that the losses of the 1827-1840 period were fully recouped. As the influential evangelist and dedicated Antimason Charles G. Finney wrote in 1869: "Forty years ago, we supposed that it was dead, and had no idea that it could ever revive. But, strange to tell, while we were busy getting rid of slavery, Freemasonry was revived, and extended its bounds most alarmingly."[4]

Among the Antimasons' most touted achievements were the legislative investigations of Freemasonry, conducted with the intentions of producing statutes that would, in effect, outlaw the fraternity. Connecticut led the way with the first such inquiry (1833), followed by Massachusetts (1834), and Pennsylvania (1835-1836). Although Vermont held no inquiry, the Antimasons' election of Palmer as governor in 1831 and domination of the assembly ultimately produced the first legislation (1833) prohibiting extrajudicial oaths, that is, Masonic obligations, which were the most vital portion of the initiatory or degree work. Had such a law been enforced in any of the three states that enacted it, it would have completely killed Masonry within its jurisdiction. Passage was often by a near-unanimous vote of the legislature, perhaps indicating the extent to which the major parties were willing to curry Antimasonic favor or perhaps simply attesting to fear of retaliation. Passage was one matter, enforcement another, and there is no recorded instance of the law's application in Vermont or in any other state.

Connecticut's 1833 legislative investigation of Masonry was a feeble affair, producing some vague recommendations but no proscriptions. In Rhode Island, an inquiry of the General Assembly in 1831 was characterized by great diversity of opinion and animosity between the Antimasonic and National Republican committee members and ultimately produced three varying reports. Both the dominant Nationals and the weak but ambitious Democrats were eager for Antimasonic votes on other matters, including patronage, and helped the Antis pass a series of extremely vindictive, proscriptive laws. Extrajudicial oaths were prohibited in 1833. The following year, the legislature repealed the civil charters of six local Masonic corporations, in reality a meaningless gesture, but it also passed an annual returns statute, requiring the remaining sixteen Masonic corporations to submit yearly lists of members and officials, the dates and times of meetings and, most important, a written copy of the highly secret oath or obligation taken by candidates during each of the three Blue Lodge degrees. Failure to comply was made punishable by the substantial fine of $100. In 1835, this law was applied to all Masonic bodies, whether incorporated or not. Failure of a lodge to make the annual returns could lead to a fine of $1,000. Again, had these laws been enforced, Masonry and all other secret societies would have disappeared in Rhode Island, but there is no documentary evidence to indicate that application was ever attempted, much less accomplished.

Massachusetts held a legislative investigation of Freemasonry in 1834, forcing the surrender of the grand lodge's civil charter of incorporation (meaningless from a Masonic standpoint) and passage of the familiar statute outlawing extrajudicial oaths. As elsewhere, application or enforcement was never undertaken.

Pennsylvania had the dubious distinction of having the most publicized inquiry into the "evils" of Freemasonry. Although it established Stevens's reputation for vindictiveness and vituperation and attracted national attention with the summoning of twenty-five high-ranking Masonic witnesses, including former governor Wolf, this vendetta accomplished nothing in terms of legislation or Masonic charter repeal. Stevens became known as the high priest of Antimasonry and made it clear that he was the undisputed leader of the party in Pennsylvania, remaining so until the last vestige had disappeared in Lancaster County in 1843. Antimasonry was, for Stevens, unlike with Seward and Weed, a matter of principle as well as a political vehicle, and he remained violently opposed to all secret societies until his death in 1868. In the 1840s, however, he began to transfer his crusading zeal from Antimasonry to antislavery, and abolitionism became his major interest and passion.

Although Antimasonry nearly destroyed Masonry in those states in which the Blessed Spirit was a political or moral-ethical factor and achieved a certain amount of political success on the state level, the party was a dismal failure on the national scene. At least twenty to twenty-four Antimasons served at one time or another in the U.S. House of Representatives and one in the U.S. Senate; these men, nevertheless, lost their political identity upon entering Congress, most of them being classified with the National Republicans-Whigs, with whom they were in general agreement on all issues except Masonry. The only instance in which Antimasonry was even discussed in Congress came in 1828 with presentation of a memorial concerning the use of abandoned Fort Niagara in the Morgan abduction. The petition was referred to a committee and was quickly forgotten. The leading Antimason in Congress was, of course, John Quincy Adams, who in 1834 attempted without success to organize his colleagues with respect to programs, goals, and tactics. Failing in this task, Adams abandoned Antimasonry as a lost cause.

In terms of winning presidential elections, Antimasonry was doomed in the absence of a consensus in 1831-1832 favoring amalgamation with the Nationals and support of Clay, something much desired by Weed and Seward but unpopular with many of the rank-and-file members. Weed, nevertheless, must have taken perverse satisfaction in seeing his New York Antimasons absorb the Nationals to form the Whig party in 1833-1834, a pattern copied, although usually in reverse, in other northeastern states. As an independent national political entity, Antimasonry could never change its image of an extremist, paranoid, one-idea party whose adherents, in terms of economic and political views on all subjects but Masonry, were almost undistinguishable from the two major anti-Jackson parties of that era.

As with many crusades, the fires of Antimasonry burned too brightly at first, only to wane suddenly before the party could firmly establish itself on the national level. Wirt's overwhelming defeat in 1832 convinced Weed and other pragmatists of the futility of maintaining the party as a national or regional organization, hence the almost breathtaking swiftness of the transition to Whiggery in New York. Perhaps Antimasonry's brief existence as a national organization was "itself a reflection of the fact that the Masonic Order was not a plausible enemy and was at best an unlikely cause of America's troubles." In the eyes of most Americans of that day, a genuine Masonic *conspiracy* to cover up the Morgan affair or to infiltrate and subvert the government was never proven.[5]

The Antimasonic crusade of 1827-1843 was ultimately beneficial to Freemasonry in the United States, although few brethren would have agreed with this assessment at the time. The Blessed Spirit frequently caused the defection of those who had little interest in the fraternity or who had joined from "unworthy motives," such as promoting business or professional careers. The crusade forced those lodges that did survive to heal internal divisions and to become less "public." The Masonic practice of marching in procession wearing aprons, badges of office, and other regalia to celebrate the two St. John's Days, cornerstone levelings, and other dedications virtually disappeared after 1830, not to resume, if at all, until the 1850s. The disappearance of these customs removed a major source of irritation to the non-Masonic populace, who viewed such ceremonies as threatening displays of the Masonic power and exclusiveness that had so accentuated the isolation of the lodge from the rest of the community. A less positive feature of the restoration period was the diminished role that Freemasonry played after 1850 as a nonsectarian moral tradition. "It had ceased its appeal to the intellectual and socio-cultural leader, and had much less of an impact on the mind of the nation." To regain public acceptance after the devastation of the Antimasonic era, Masonry became more fraternal and less intellectual, aligning more with "Protestant values and insofar as it was political, with conservation partisanship."[6]

Antimasonry as a crusade against all secret societies in general and against Freemasonry in particular did not end with the 1840s. A revival of Antimasonic sentiment occurred after 1867 under the aegis of the National Christian Association and its Chicago-based publication, the *Christian Cynosure*. This "American party" ultimately ran a Vermonter, Gen. John Wolcott Phelps, for president in 1880, but he polled only 700 votes. Organized opposition to Masonry has continued to the present day, with a number of religious denominations actively discouraging their communicants from seeking Masonic membership, among them the Lutheran Church Missouri Synod (LCMS), the Church of Jesus Christ of Latter Day Saints (Mormons), and the Assemblies of God. These denominations regard Masonry as unchristian, and a "substitute church." As one LCMS publication, *Masonry in the Light of the Bible*, has declared: "The religion of Masonry is the general religion of nature. The result is necessarily an anemic, watered-down religious philosophy which has lost its force and meaning in vague generalizations." Other, less vocal objections come from those who dislike the mere existence of any secret society in the United States, believing it undemocratic and anti-American to permit the continuation of an organization that does not accept all elements of the population, including women, to membership. The Blessed Spirit has obviously survived to the present day, albeit reduced in capacity and influence, and continues to coexist with its "insidious enemy," Freemasonry. Both appear likely to persist into the twenty-first century, with the specter of William Morgan lurking in the background.[7]

# Notes

The following institutions have been designated throughout the notes by the abbreviations that appear in parentheses: Library of Congress (LC), Maryland Historical Society (MdHS), Massachusetts Historical Society (MaHS), Rhode Island Historical Society (RIHS), and Vermont Historical Society (VHS).

## CHAPTER 1

1. Alice Felt Tyler, *Freedom's Ferment: Phases of American Social History from the Colonial Period to the Outbreak of the Civil War* (1944; reprint ed., New York: Harper and Row, 1962), pp. 351-52; Whitney R. Cross, *The Burned-over District: The Social and Intellectual History of Enthusiastic Religion in Western New York, 1800-1850* (Ithaca: Cornell University Press, 1950), pp. 3-5. Cross defines the Burned-over District geographically as "that portion of New York State laying west of the Catskill and Adirondack Mountains." See also Herbert Ershkowitz, "Anti-Masonry and the Formation of the Second Party System" (Paper delivered at the annual meeting of the Society of Historians for the Early American Republic, Annapolis, August, 1979), pp. 2-3; Leland M. Griffin, "The Antimasonic Persuasion: A Study of Public Address in the American Antimasonic Movement, 1826-1838" (Ph.D. diss., Cornell University, 1950), p. 245.

2. Charles McCarthy, "The Antimasonic Party: A Study of Political Antimasonry in the United States, 1827-1840," in *Annual Report of the American Historical Association, 1902,* 2 vols. (Washington, D.C.: U.S. Government Printing Office), 1:369-71, 538-50; Ronald P. Formisano and Kathleen Smith Kutolowski, "Antimasonry and Masonry: The Genesis of Protest, 1826-1827," *American Quarterly* 29 (1977): 140-46 and notes; John Bach McMaster, *A History of the People of the United States from the Revolution to the Civil War,* 8 vols. (New York: D. Appleton, 1891-1913), 5:109-20; William Gribbin, "Antimasonry, Religious Radicalism, and the Paranoid Style of the 1820's," *History Teacher* 7 (1974): 241; Rob Morris, *William Morgan; or, Political Anti-Masonry, Its Rise, Growth and Decadence* (New York: Robert McCoy, 1883).

3. Formisano and Kutolowski, "Antimasonry and Masonry," pp. 153, 162-63.

4. The best narrative account of the Morgan affair, although it contains some factual errors and a pro-Masonic bias, is Clarence O. Lewis, "The Morgan Affair," manuscript, in the possession of the Lockport Public Library, Lockport, New York. Lewis, a former Niagara County (New York) historian, based his unannotated résumé on sixty years of research.

5. Lewis, "Morgan Affair," pp. 1-2; Robert D. Burns, "The Abduction of William Morgan," *Rochester Historical Society, Publication Fund Series* 6 (1972): 220-21; Glyn-

don G. Van Deusen, *Thurlow Weed: Wizard of the Lobby* (Boston: Little, Brown, 1947), p. 38.

6. Lewis, "Morgan Affair," p. 2; Formisano and Kutolowski, "Antimasonry and Masonry," p. 147; Harold V. B. Voorhis, "The 'Morgan Affair' of 1826 in the U.S.A.," *Transactions of the Quatuor Coronati Lodge No. 2076, London* 76 (1963): 198; Donovan D. Tidwell, "Rev. David Bernard—Antimason," *Transactions, Texas Lodge of Research* 9 (1973-74): 204; *Report on the Abduction and Murder of William Morgan, Made to the Senate, Feb. 14, 1829* (Albany: n.p., 1829), p. 3 [in the Seward Pamphlet Collection, Rhees Library, University of Rochester]; Griffin, "Antimasonic Persuasion," p. 146.

7. Lewis, "Morgan Affair," p. 2; Burns, "Abduction," p. 221; Alphonse Cerza, *Anti-Masonry* (Fulton, Mo.: Ovid Bell Press, 1962), p. 36; Cross, *Burned-over District*, p. 114; Van Deusen, *Weed*, p. 37.

8. Formisano and Kutolowski, "Antimasonry and Masonry," pp. 147-48; Lewis, "Morgan Affair," pp. 2-4; William Morgan, *Illustrations of Masonry: By One of the Fraternity Who has Devoted Thirty Years to the Subject* (1827; reprint ed., Chicago: Ezra A. Cook Publications, n.d.), pp. v-vi.

9. Lewis, "Morgan Affair," p. 3; Van Deusen, *Weed*, pp. 38-39; Thurlow Weed, *Autobiography of Thurlow Weed*, ed. Harriet A. Weed (Boston: Houghton Mifflin, 1883), p. 321.

10. Lewis, "Morgan Affair," pp. 7-12, 32; George H. Blakeslee, "A History of the Antimasonic Party" (Ph.D. diss., Harvard University, 1903), chap. 2, pp. 23-24; Samuel Flagg Bemis, *John Quincy Adams and the Union* (New York: Alfred A. Knopf, 1956), pp. 276-77; Jabez D. Hammond, *The History of Political Parties in the State of New York From the Ratification of the Federal Constitutions to December, 1840,* 2 vols. (Cooperstown, N.Y.: H. & E. Phinney, 1844), 2:370; Van Deusen, *Weed*, p. 39; Cross, *Burned-over District*, p. 115; Burns, "Abduction," p. 219; Griffin, "Antimasonic Persuasion," p. 127; Delmar D. Darrah, *The Evolution of Freemasonry* (Bloomington, Ill.: Masonic Publishing, 1920): p. 247; Formisano and Kutolowski, "Antimasonry and Masonry," pp. 152-53.

11. Formisano and Kutolowski, "Antimasonry and Masonry," pp. 141-46, 151-55, 161; Lee Benson, *The Concept of Jacksonian Democracy: New York as a Test Case* (1961; reprint ed., New York: Atheneum, 1969): p. 17; Van Deusen, *Weed*, p. 39; Cross, *Burned-over District*, p. 115; Hammond, *Political Parties*, 2:377.

12 Formisano and Kutolowski, "Antimasonry and Masonry," p. 149; Henry Brown, *Narrative of the Anti-Masonic Excitement, in the Western Part of the State of New York During the Years 1826-7, 8 and part of 1829* (Batavia, N.Y.: Adams and McCleary, 1829), pp. 40, 61, 120-47, 217, 236.

13. Clinton was then grand high priest of the general (national) grand Royal Arch chapter. Lewis, "Morgan Affair," pp. 13-14; Formisano and Kutolowski, "Antimasonry and Masonry," p. 156.

14. Weed, *Autobiography*, pp. 283-84; Griffin, "Antimasonic Persuasion," pp. 101, 118; De Alva Stanwood Alexander, *A Political History of the State of New York*, 2 vols. (New York: Henry Holt, 1906), 1:336.

15. Lewis, "Morgan Affair," pp. 22-23, 27.

16. Lewis, "Morgan Affair," pp. 15, 29; Formisano and Kutolowski, "Antimasonry and Masonry," pp. 156-57; New York, General Assembly, *Journal of the Assembly, Fiftieth Session,* 1827, p. 587.

17. *Laws of the State of New York, Fiftieth Session, First Meeting* (Albany: 1827), pp. 312-13, 348-49; McCarthy, "Antimasonic Party," pp. 372-73; *Albany Argus,* April 5 and 12, 1827.

18. McCarthy, "Antimasonic Party," p. 371; Formisano and Kutolowski, "Antimasonry and Masonry," pp. 140, 142, 157, 159; Martin Van Buren to Churchill C.Cambreleng, October 23, 1827, Martin Van Buren Papers, LC.

19. Lewis, "Morgan Affair," pp. 15, 17-19; Brown, *Narrative,* p. 207; *Rochester Anti-Masonic Enquirer,* April 8 and 15, 1828.

20. Van Deusen, *Weed,* p. 41.

21. Lewis, "Morgan Affair," pp. 21, 30.

22. Lorman A. Ratner, "Antimasonry in New York State, A Study in Pre-Civil War Reform" (M.A. thesis, Cornell University, 1958), pp. 31-32.

CHAPTER 2

1. *Encyclopedia Americana,* 37th ed., s. v. "Masonic Fraternity"; George H. T. French, "Freemasonry: Unique, Separate and Cooperative," *Philalethes* 32 (June 1979): 13; Douglas Knoop and G. P. Jones, "Masonic History Old and New," *Transactions of the Quatuor Coronati Lodge No. 2076, London* 55 (1944): 293.

2. Robert Freke Gould, *History of Freemasonry, Its Antiquities, Symbols, Constitutions, Customs, etc. . . . ,* 6 vols. (New York: John Beacham, 1884-87); Henry Carr, "Six Hundred Years of Craft Masonry" (Paper delivered before the Victoria, British Columbia, Lodge of Education and Research, Victoria, May, 1976), pp. 1-2; Knoop and Jones, "Masonic History," pp. 294-98; Dorothy Ann Lipson, *Freemasonry in Federalist Connecticut* (Princeton, N.J.: Princeton University Press, 1977), pp. 5, 20-22.

3. Lipson, *Freemasonry in Connecticut,* pp. 7, 48-49; Norris S. Barratt and Julius F. Sachse, *Freemasonry in Pennsylvania, 1727-1907, As Shown By the Records of Lodge No. 2 of Philadelphia,* 3 vols. (Philadelphia: n.p., 1908), 1:1-2, 4; James R. Case, "Henry Price," *Knight Templar* 22 (April 1976): 11; *Encyclopedia Americana,* s.v. "Masonic Fraternity"; Darrah, *Evolution of Freemasonry,* pp. 320-21.

4. Ratner, "Antimasonry in New York," pp. 7-8; idem, *Antimasonry: The Crusade and the Party* (Englewood Cliffs, N.J.: Prentice-Hall, 1970), p. 8; Alphonse Cerza, "Effects of the War of Independence on American Freemasonry," *Transactions, Texas Lodge of Research* 13 (1977-78): 31-32; Lipson, *Freemasonry in Connecticut,* pp. 61, 71, 228; Robert Freke Gould, *The Concise History of Freemasonry,* rev. ed. (New York: McCoy Publishing and Masonic Supply, 1924), pp. 449-50.

5. Lipson, *Freemasonry in Connecticut,* pp. 7, 143-45, 148-49, 238, 354.

6. Kathleen Smith Kutolowski, "The Antimasonic Impulse: Social Sources of Electorate and Elite in Genesee County, New York" (Paper delivered at the annual meeting of the American Historical Association, San Francisco, December, 1978), p. 10; idem, "The Janus Face of New York's Local Parties: Genesee County, 1821-1827," *New York History* 59 (1978): 159-64.

7. Douglas Knoop and G. P. Jones, eds., "An Antimasonic Leaflet of 1698," *Transactions of the Quatuor Coronati Lodge No. 2076, London* 54 (1942): 152-54; "Early Exposés of Freemasonry," Miscellaneous Manuscripts, VHS; Carr, "Six Hundred Years," pp. 8-15; Alphonse Cerza, "Masonic Literature," *Dallas Scottish Rite Herald* 58 (May 1978): 4; Samuel Prichard, *Masonry Dissected* ... (London: J. Wilford, 1730): passim; "An Eighteenth Century Attack upon Freemasonry," (London) *Freemason* 47 (1907-8): 746; Lewis, "Morgan Affair," p. 1; Voorhis, "Morgan Affair," p. 198; William L. Cummings, comp., *A Bibliography of Anti-Masonry* (New York: Press of Henry Emerson, 1963), p. 43; *Jachin and Boaz; or, An Authentic Key to the Door of Free-Masonry* (London: W. Nicoll, 1762); *"Three Distinct Knocks" and "Jachin and Boaz,"* introd. Harry Carr (Bloomington, Ill.: Masonic Book Club, 1981).

8. Ratner, "Antimasonry in New York," pp. 5, 7, 38; idem, *Antimasonry,* p. 4.

9. Seymour Martin Lipset and Earl Raab, *The Politics of Unreason: Right Wing Extremism in America, 1790-1970* (New York: Harper and Row, 1970), p. 35; Vernon Stauffer, *New England and the Bavarian Illuminati* (New York: Columbia University Press, 1918), pp. 10-11, 150-53, 157-64, 169-218, 229-30, 246-51, 287-93, 319-26, 340-45.

10. Arthur B. Darling, *Political Changes in Massachusetts, 1824-1848: A Study of Liberal Movements in Politics* (New Haven: Yale University Press, 1925), pp. 85-86.

11. Sydney Nathans, *Daniel Webster and Jacksonian Democracy* (Baltimore: Johns Hopkins University Press, 1973), p. 83; Ratner, "Antimasonry in New York," pp. 20-22, 38; Lipset and Raab, *Politics of Unreason,* pp. 42-43; Griffin, "Antimasonic Persuasion," pp. 4-5; Tyler, *Freedom's Ferment,* pp. 358, 310; and Edward Pessen, *Jacksonian America: Society, Personality, and Politics* (Homewood, Ill.: Dorsey Press, 1969), p. 278; David Brion Davis, "Somes Themes of Counter-Subversion: An Analysis of Anti-Masonic, Anti-Catholic and Anti-Mormon Literature," *Mississippi Valley Historical Review* 47 (1960): 223-34.

12. Ershkowitz, "Anti-Masonry," p. 2.

13. Formisano and Kutolowski, "Antimasonry and Masonry," p. 142; John G. Stearns, *An Inquiry Into the Nature and Tendency of Speculative Free-masonry,* 3d ed. (Utica: Northway and Bennett, 1827), p. 130; Ratner, "Antimasonry in New York," pp. 39-40; Moses Thatcher, *An Address Delivered Before the Antimasonic Convention ... For Plymouth County ... Dec. 9, 1829* (Boston: John Marsh, 1830), pp. 4-7.

14. Ratner, "Antimasonry in New York," p. 32; Davis, "Some Themes of Counter-Subversion," pp. 206, 208, 211-12, 215; *Anti-Masonic Review and Magazine* 1 (December 1828): 3-4; Hammond, *Political Parties,* 2: 385; *An Abstract of the Proceedings of the (First) Anti-Masonic State Convention of Massachusetts ... Boston, Dec. 30 and 31, 1829, and Jan. 1, 1830* (Boston: John Marsh, 1830), pp. 8-10; Warren G. French, "Lebbeus Armstrong: Godfather of Temperance," *New York History* 36 (1955): 291-96; Lebbeus Armstrong, *Masonry Proved to be a Work of Darkness, Repugnant to the Christian Religion and Inimical to a Republican Government* (New York: By the author, 1830), pp. 23-34; William Henry Brackney, "Religious Antimasonry: the Genesis of a Political Party" (Ph.D. diss., Temple University, 1976), pp. 273-94.

15. Ershkowitz, "Anti-Masonry," pp. 5-6; Davis, "Some Themes of Counter-Subversion," p. 215; *Lancaster* (Pa.) *Anti-Masonic Herald,* September 4, 1829; Solomon

Southwick, *An Oration: Delivered by Appointment, on the Fourth Day of July, A.D., 1828, in the Presence of the Convention of Seceding Free Masons* (Albany: Webster and Wood, 1828), p. 48. A peculiar aspect of some Antimasonic propaganda, considering the papal bull of 1738, which forbade Catholics to affiliate with Freemasonry, was the warning that the "secret power" of Masonry was similar to the secret, "insidious power" of the Jesuits. See David Bernard, ed., *Light on Masonry: A Collection of all the Most Important Documents on the Subject of Speculative Freemasonry* . . . (Utica: William Williams, 1829), p. 336.

16. Lipson, *Freemasonry in Connecticut,* pp. 8, 81, 120-21; Michael F. Holt, "The Antimasonic and Know-Nothing Parties," in *History of U.S. Political Parties,* ed. Arthur M. Schlesinger, Jr., 4 vols. (New York: Chelsea House, 1973), 1: 538; Ershkowitz, "Anti-Masonry," p. 3; Ratner, "Antimasonry in New York," pp. 28-29, 44, 48-51; Ronald P. Formisano, *The Birth of Mass Political Parties: Michigan, 1827-1861* (Princeton, N.J.: Princeton University Press, 1971), 63-64.

17. Brackney, "Religious Anti-Masonry," pp. 293, 336-37; Cross, *Burned-over District,* pp. 117-18; Southwick, *An Oration,* p. 24; Armstrong, *Masonry Proved to be a Work of Darkness,* pp. 3-4, 7, 14, 17-20; Seth Hunt to William H. Seward, September 19, 1831, William H. Seward Papers, Rhees Library, University of Rochester; [Lebbeus Armstrong], *An Appeal to Christian Ministers in Connection with Speculative Free Masonry* (n.p., 1829), pp. 1-8; James C. Odiorne, comp., *Opinions on Speculative Free Masonry* . . . (Boston: Perkins and Marvin, 1830), pp. 150-54.

18. French, "Masonic Penalties," *Texas Freemason* 11 (August 1973): 22; L. L. Walker, Jr., "Of Oaths, Vows, and Obligations," *Transactions, Texas Lodge of Research* 15 (1979-80): 43, 52-54.

19. Thatcher, *An Address* . . ., p. 18; *Proceedings, Antimasonic State Convention, Massachusetts, 1829-30,* p. 8; Stearns, *An Inquiry,* pp. 111-12.

20. Seth Hunt to William H. Seward, September 19, 1831, Seward Papers: Lipson, *Freemasonry in Connecticut,* pp. 260-61; *New England Anti-Masonic Almanac, For 1829* (Boston: J. Marsh, 1829), p. 12; *Lancaster Anti-Masonic Herald,* June 26 and July 18, 1828; John Gest, *A. Brief Defense of John the Baptist, Against Foul Slander and Wicked Libel of Freemasons* (Philadelphia: William K. Boden, 1834), pp. 10-11; Charles P. Sumner, *A Letter on Speculative Free Masonry* (Boston: John Marsh, 1829), pp. 13-14.

21. William R. Taylor and Christopher Lasch, "Two 'Kindred Spirits': Sorority and Family in New England, 1839-1846," *New England Quarterly* 36 (1963): 34-35; Lipson, *Freemasonry in Connecticut,* pp. 9, 186-87, 329-31, 333-36; *Ravenna* (Ohio) *Star,* June 23, 1830; Warren M. Durkee, "Anti-Masonic Movement in Ohio" (M.A. thesis, Ohio State University, 1935), p. 59.

22. Richard Hofstadter, *The Paranoid Style in American Politics and Other Essays* (New York: Alfred A. Knopf, 1965), p. 35; *Anti-Masonic Review* 5 (1830): 131; Davis, "Some Themes of Counter-Subversion," pp. 221-22; Gustavus Myers, *History of Bigotry in the United States* (New York: Random House, 1943), pp. 134-35.

23. Tidwell, "Bernard," pp. 204-10; Cross, *Burned-over District,* pp. 122-23; Brackney, "Religious Antimasonry," pp. 255-61, 296-99; Lipson, *Freemasonry in Connecticut,* pp. 282-83; Bernard, ed., *Light on Masonry,* iii-ix, passim; John Quincy Adams, *Letters on the Masonic Institution* (Boston: T. R. Marvin, 1847), p. 229.

24. Griffin, "Antimasonic Persuasion," p. 179; Brackney, "Religious Antimasonry," pp. 182-90, 269-75; Stearns, *An Inquiry,* passim.

25. "A Foul Vocabulary," *American Freemasonry: A Monthly Masonic Magazine* 1 (1858): 377.


CHAPTER 3

1. Brackney, "Religious Antimasonry," pp. 1, 4, 125, 131-32; Ratner, "Antimasonry in New York," pp. 55-57; Formisano, *Birth of Mass Parties,* p. 61; Dixon Ryan Fox, *The Decline of Aristocracy in the Politics of New York, 1801-1819* (1919; reprint ed., New York: Harper and Row, 1965), p. 340.

2. Cross, *Burned-over District,* pp. 3, 76, 116-17; Brackney, "Religious Antimasonry," pp. 3-4, 95-96, 267-68, 322.

3. Cross, *Burned-over District,* p. 123; Ratner, "Antimasonry in New York," p. 45; Brackney, "Religious Antimasonry," p. 96.

4. Paul E. Johnson, *A Shopkeeper's Millennium: Society and Revivals in Rochester, New York, 1815-1837* (New York: Hill and Wang, 1978), p. 90; Thurlow Weed, *Memoir of Thurlow Weed,* ed. Thurlow Weed Barnes (Boston: Houghton Mifflin, 1883), pp. 30-31; Cross, *Burned-over District,* pp. 121-23; Brackney, "Religious Antimasonry," pp. 132-33, 137, 140-42.

5. Weed, *Autobiography,* pp. 302-03; Brackney, "Religious Antimasonry," pp. 132-33, 143-48, 153-55, 166-67, 176; idem, "Experience versus Conviction: The Baptist Response to the Antimasonic Impulse, 1826-1830," *Foundations* 21 (1978): 167-80.

6. Brackney, "Religious Antimasonry," pp. 181, 303-4, 331-33, 339; Johnson, *Shopkeeper's Millennium,* pp. 75-77; Susan Porter Benson, " 'A Union of Men, and Not of Principles': The Rhode Island Antimasonic Party" (M.A. thesis, Brown University, 1971), p. 92; Benjamin Cowell, *An Address Delivered Before the Antimasonic Convention, Holden at Providence, November 2, 1832* (Providence: Edward and J. W. Cory, 1832), pp. 1, 7; Ratner, "Antimasonry in New York," pp. 64-65; Odiorne, *Opinions on Speculative Freemasonry,* pp. 214-15;

7. *Proceedings of the Antimasonic Republican Convention of the County of Cayuga, Held at Auburn, Jan. 1, 1830...* (Auburn, N.Y.: n.p., 1830), p. 6, Ratner, *Antimasonry,* p. 14; Griffin, "Antimasonic Persuasion," pp. 35, 236; Kutolowski, "Janus Face," pp. 157-64; Alvin Kass, *Politics in New York State, 1800-1830* (Syracuse: Syracuse University Press, 1965), p. 207; Edward Pessen, *Jacksonian America: Society, Personality, and Politics,* rev. ed. (Homewood, Ill.: Dorsey Press, 1978), p. 262.

8. Johnson, *Shopkeeper's Millennium,* pp. 29, 66-69; *Rochester Daily Telegraph,* October 13, 1828.

9. Van Deusen, *Weed,* pp. 43-44; Hammond, *Political Parties,* pp. 2, 380, 383; David M. Ellis and others, *A Short History of New York State* (Ithaca: Cornell University Press, 1957), pp. 143-44, 212; Richard P. McCormick, *The Second American Party System: Party Formation in the Jacksonian Era* (Chapel Hill: University of North Carolina Press, 1966), pp. 107-19; Ershkowitz, "Anti-Masonry," p. 4.

10. Erik McKinley Eriksson, "The Anti-Masonic Party," *Builder* 7 (1921): 72; Pessen, *Jacksonian America,* rev. ed., pp. 278-79; Cross, *Burned-over District,* pp. 116-17; Blakeslee, "Antimasonic Party," chap. 6, pp. 43-44; Glyndon G. Van Deusen,

*William Henry Seward* (New York: Oxford University Press, 1967), p. 12; *Proceedings of the Anti-Masonic Convention in the State of New York, Held at Utica, August 11, 1830* (Utica: William Williams, 1830), p. 5; Holt, "Antimasonic and Know-Nothing Parties," pp. 583-84.

11. Kutolowski, "Antimasonic Impulse," pp. 4-7, 11-12; idem, "Antimasonry Revisited: An Historiographic Overview" (paper delivered to the Albany [N.Y.] Seminar, May, 1981), pp. 9-13; Ronald P. Formisano, "Antimasons and Masons: Massachusetts and New York" (Paper delivered at the annual meeting of the America Historical Association, 1978).

12. Kutolowski, "Janus Face," p. 165; James S. Chase, *Emergence of the Presidential Nominating Convention, 1789-1832* (Urbana: University of Illinois Press, 1972), pp. 96, 135-38; Eriksson, "Anti-Masonic Party," p. 73.

13. Van Deusen, *Weed,* pp. 39-40; idem, "Thurlow Weed in Rochester," *Rochester History* 2 (1940): 3-4, 8-9; *Rochester Daily Telegraph,* November 21 and 28, 1826; Weed, *Autobiography,* pp. 212-13.

14. Van Deusen, *Weed,* pp. 40-50; idem, "Weed in Rochester," pp. 14-15; *Rochester Daily Telegraph,* August 30 and September 15, 1827; Johnson, *Shopkeeper's Millennium,* p. 68; William B. Rochester to Josiah Gates, November 29, 1827, Weed Papers, Rhees Library, University of Rochester; Albert H. Tracy to Weed, December 17, 1827, ibid.

15. James S. Chase, "Genesis of the First National Political Convention: A Case Study in the Development of An American Institution," *Social Science Quarterly* 50 (1969): 95-97; Weed, *Autobiography,* pp. 242-43, 299-301; Brackney, "Religious Anti-Masonry," pp. 304-5; Johnson *Shopkeeper's Millenium,* pp. 16-20.

16. Hammond, *Political Parties,* 2: 378; Van Deusen, *Weed,* p. 40; McCarthy, "Antimasonic Party," pp. 302, 373-74; Brackney, "Religious Antimasonry," p. 306; Chase, "First National Convention," p. 96; Ratner, *Antimasonry,* pp. 8-11; Ershkowitz, "Anti-Masonry," pp. 6-7; Samuel R. Gammon, *The Presidential Campaign of 1832,* Johns Hopkins University Studies in History and Political Science 40 (Baltimore: Johns Hopkins University Press, 1922), p. 33.

17. McCarthy, "Antimasonic Party," pp. 373-74; Formisano and Kutolowski, "Antimasonry and Masonry," p. 100; Van Deusen, *Weed,* pp. 41-43; Hammond, *Political Parties,* 2:382-83; *Albans Argus,* November 14, 21, 1827; Kutolowski, "Antimasonic Impulse," p. 1.

18. Brackney, "Religious Antimasonry," pp. 306-7; Chase, "First National Convention," p. 98; *Albany Argus,* May 17, 1828; U.S., Congress, House, *Register of Debates,* 20th Cong., 1st sess., May 12, 1828, cols. 2644-48.

19. Brackney, "Religious Antimasonry," pp. 308-11; *Proceedings of the Adjourned Convention of Masons, Held at LeRoy* (New York), *July 4th 1828;* n.p., n.d.; Bernard, ed., *Light on Masonry,* pp. 445-51; McCarthy, "Antimasonic Party," p. 378; *Albany Argus,* July 14, 1828; Southwick, *An Oration . . .,* pp. 4, 25.

20. McCarthy, "Antimasonic Party," p. 379; *Albany Argus,* July 28, 1828; Kass, *Politics,* pp. 126-27; Fox, *Decline of Aristocracy in New York,* pp. 342-43.

21. Brackney, "Religious Antimasonry," pp. 314-19; *Albany Argus,* August 21, 23, 26, and 30, September 3, 6, 10, and 12, 1828; Chase, "First National Convention," pp. 99-101; Alexander, *Political History of New York,* 1:361-64; Erik McKinley Erickson,

"Minor Prophets of Anti-Masonry," *Grand Lodge Bulletin, Grand Lodge of Iowa* 27 (1926): 156; *Proceedings... Utica Convention... August 4, 1828...*, in Bernard, ed., *Light on Masonry,* pp. 464, 565.

22. McCarthy, "Antimasonic Party," pp. 379-80; *Albany Argus,* September 11 and 15, 1828; Brackney, "Religious Antimasonry," pp. 226-32, 239, and 316; Eriksson, "Minor Prophets," pp. 155-56; William H. Seward, *An Autobiography from 1831 to 1834...*, ed. Frederick W. Seward (New York: D. Appleton, 1877), p. 71.

23. Hammond, *Political Parties,* 2:389; Brackney, "Religious Antimasonry," pp. 317-23; Bates Cook to Weed, February 28, 1828, Weed Papers; Philo C. Fuller to Weed, September 18, 1828, ibid.; Nathan Sargent to Weed, October 26, 1828, ibid.; *Albany Argus,* September 30 and October 11, 1828; Weed, *Autobiography,* pp. 307-09; *Rochester Anti-Masonic Enquirer,* September 23, October 7 and 14, 1828.

24. Van Deusen, *Weed,* p. 49; Chase, "First National Convention," p. 102; Brackney, "Religious Antimasonry," p. 323; *Albany Argus,* November 18 and 24, 1828; Robert A. Diamond, ed., *Congressional Quarterly's Guide to U.S. Elections* (Washington, D.C.: Congressional Quarterly, 1975), p. 422.

25. Eriksson, "Minor Prophets," pp. 155-56; Fuller to Weed, August 20, 1830, Weed Papers; Erik McKinley Eriksson, "Millard Fillmore: Anti-Mason," *Grand Lodge Bulletin, Grand Lodge of Iowa* 27 (1926): 5-8; Robert J. Rayback, *Millard Fillmore: Biography of a President* (Buffalo: H. Stewart, Buffalo Historical Society, 1959), pp. 32-39, 67-68.

26. Van Deusen, *Weed,* pp. 47-48; Chase, *Emergence,* pp. 134-35; Kass, *Politics,* p. 126; McCarthy, "Antimasonic Party," pp. 377-78; *Albany Argus,* April 9 and July 14, 1828; Benson, *Jacksonian Democracy,* pp. 28-29; Albert H. Tracy to Weed, June 19, 1828, Weed Papers; Weed, *Autobiography,* p. 302; Seward, *Autobiography,* p. 71.

27. Robert V. Remini, *The Election of Andrew Jackson* (Philadelphia: J. B. Lippincott, 1963), p. 187; Hammond, *Political Parties,* 2:391-93; Van Deusen, *Weed,* p. 49; *Albany Argus,* November 15, 18, 24, and 27, 1828; Seward, *Autobiography,* p. 74; Diamond, ed., *Guide to U.S. Elections,* p. 265.

28. Van Deusen, *Weed,* pp. 49-50; *Albany Argus,* February 23, 1829; Brackney, "Religious Antimasonry," pp. 325-27; *Proceedings of a Convention of Delegates From the Different Counties... Opposed to Free-Masonry... Albany, February 19-21, 1829* (Rochester: Weed and Sprague, 1829), pp. 12, 17-19, 38-39; Chase, "First National Convention," pp. 102-3.

29. *Albany Argus,* February 26, 1829; Richard R. Lansing to Weed, February 27, 1829, Weed Papers; Fuller to Weed, September 8, 1829, ibid.

30. McCarthy, "Antimasonic Party," pp. 386-89; *Albany Argus,* March 2, 1829; *Rochester Daily Advertiser and Telegraph,* October 12, 1829; Van Deusen, *Weed,* pp. 50-51; *Rochester Anti-Masonic Enquirer,* November 17 and 24, 1829.

CHAPTER 4

1. Seward, *Autobiography,* pp. 74-83; 179, 182; William Kent to Seward, November 27, 1829, Seward Papers; Van Deusen, *Seward,* pp. 13-18; *Proceedings, Antimasonic Convention, Cayuga, 1830...*, passim; William H. Seward, *The Works of William H. Seward,* ed. George E. Baker, 3 vols. (New York: Redfield., 1853), 1:xxvii-xxxv, 3:1-9.

2. McCarthy "Antimasonic Party," pp. 391-94; *Albany Argus,* March 1 and 9, 1830.

3. *Rochester Anti-Masonic Enquirer,* January 5, March 10 and 30, 1830; Boughton to Weed, March 24 and 26, 1829, Weed Papers; B. D. Packard & Co. to Weed, July 1, 1829, ibid.; Weed, *Autobiography,* pp. 350-62; *Albany Evening Journal,* March 22, 1830.

4. Joseph R. Swan to Weed, January 23, 1830, Weed Papers; Whittlesey to Weed, January 26, March (n.d.), April 11, and July 30, 1830, ibid.; Glyndon G. Van Deusen, "Thurlow Weed: A Character Study," *American Historical Review* 49 (1943-44): 437; idem, *Weed,* pp. 54, 57; McCarthy "Antimasonic Party," pp. 390-91, 398-400; *Albany Argus,* March 27, 1830; *Albany Evening Journal,* handbill, n.d. [November 1830].

5. Brackney, "Religious Antimasonry," pp. 327-31, *Proceedings, Antimasonic Convention, Utica, 1830,* pp. 4-16; *Albany Evening Journal,* August 18, 1830.

6. James A. Woods to Seward, April 27, 1830, Seward Papers; John C. Spencer to Weed, August 1, 1830, Weed Papers; Philo C. Fuller to Weed, August 20, 1830, ibid.; *Albany Argus,* July 22, August 16 and 21, 1830; Seward, *Autobiography,* pp. 78-79; *Albany Evening Journal,* August 21, 1830.

7. Seward, *Autobiography,* p. 180; *Albany Evening Journal,* handbill, n.d. [November 1830]; (New York) *Working Man's Advocate,* November 14, 1829; Walter Hugins, *Jacksonian Democracy and the Working Class: A Study of the New York Workingmen's Movement, 1829-1827* (Stanford, Calif.: Stanford University Press, 1960), pp. 12-15, 136-37, 207n.

8. Benson, *The Concept of Jacksonian Democracy,* pp. 35-38; Hugins, *Jacksonian Democracy and the Working Class,* pp. 16, 18, 21; Stevens to Weed, August 16, 1830, Weed Papers.

9. Weed, *Autobiobraphy,* pp. 367-68; *Working Man's Advocate,* October 1, 9, 22, 23, and 29, November 6 and 9, 1830; Stevens to Weed, August 31, 1830, Weed Papers.

10. Whittlesey to Weed, January 29, 1830, Weed Papers; Granger to Weed, October 5, 1830, ibid.; Weed to Granger, September 15, 1830, ibid.; Van Deusen, *Weed,* pp. 56-57; *Albany Evening Journal,* October 11 and 25, 1830.

11. Van Deusen, *Weed,* p. 57; McCarthy, "Antimasonic Party," pp. 403-4; *Albany Argus,* November 11, 1830; Weed, *Autobiography,* 1:368; Blakeslee, "Antimasonic Party," chap. 6, pp. 51-52; *Albany Evening Journal,* November 2, 12, 23, and 26, December 7 and 17, 1830; Granger to Weed, December 8, 1830, Weed Papers.

12. McCarthy, "Antimasonic Party," pp. 404-5.

13. Ibid., pp. 408-10; *Albany Argus,* February 21 and 22, 1831.

14. McCarthy, "Antimasonic Party," pp. 406-7; *Albany Argus,* March 21, 1831; *Working Man's Advocate,* April 4, 1831; *Albany Evening Journal,* March 15 and 25, April 5, 8, 22, and 29, 1831; Seward, *Works,* 3:338-49.

15. Seward to Weed, October 19, 1831, Weed Papers; Seward to Weed, November 14, 1831, ibid.; Weed to Seward, October 31, 1831, Seward Papers; *Albany Argus,* November 15 and 18, 1831.

16. Van Deusen, *Seward,* p. 19; Holley to Seward, January 2, 1832, Seward Papers; Albert H. Tracy to Seward, November 25 and December 2, 1831, ibid.; Seward to Weed, November 14, 1831, Weed Papers.

17. Van Deusen, *Weed,* pp. 59-61; Ershkowitz, "Anti-Masonry," p. 8; *Albany Argus,* February 4, 1832; Seward, *Autobiography,* pp. 213-14; Anonymous to Seward April 6,

1832, Seward Papers; John C. Spencer to Seward, March 5, 1832, ibid.; Boughton to Seward, May 4, 1832, ibid.; Granger to Weed, February 21, 1832, Weed Papers.

18. Van Deusen, *Weed,* pp. 61-62; Orville L. Holley to Seward, May 8, 1832, Seward Papers; Tracy to Seward, May 30 and June 12, 1832, ibid.; Spencer to Weed, June 1 and 7, 1832, ibid.; William H. Maynard to Weed, May 22 and June 8, 1832, Weed Papers; Childs to Weed, June 1, 1832, ibid.; Seward to Weed, June 9, 1832, ibid.; Weed to Oran Follett, May 10, 1832, ibid.; Weed to Seward, May 27, 1832, Seward Papers.

19. *Albany Argus,* June 23 and October 26, 1832; *Albany Evening Journal,* June 23 and 28, October 29, 1832; *Niles' Register* 42 (June 30, 1832); 322; Weed, *Autobiography,* pp. 413-14; Weed to Spencer, June 7 and July 13, 1832, Weed Papers.

20. Van Deusen, *Weed,* p. 62; John C. Spencer to Weed, July 13 and September 18, 1832, Weed Papers; George H. Boughton to Weed, September 7, 1832, ibid.; Albert H. Tracy to Weed, September 11, 1832, ibid.; Barber to Weed, September 18, 1832, ibid.; *Albany Argus,* August 14, September 18, October 4 and 11, 1832; *Albany Evening Journal,* November 3, 1832.

21. McCarthy, "Antimasonic Party," p. 413; *Albany Evening Journal,* August 24 and September 14, 1832; Samuel N. Sweet to Seward, August 20, 1832, Seward Papers; Tracy to Seward, August 24, 1832, ibid.; Seward to Weed, July 16 and August 19, 1832, Weed Papers; Granger to Weed, August 10, 1832, ibid.

22. Weed, *Autobiography,* pp. 413-14; *Albany Evening Journal,* November 1 and 6, 1832; Samuel E. Lyman to Weed, September 5, 1832, Weed Papers; Davis to Weed, September 23, 1832, ibid.; Granger to Weed, November 2, 1832, ibid.

23. Van Deusen, *Weed,* p. 64; Blakeslee, "Antimasonic Party," chap. 8, pp. 55-56; *Albany Argus,* November 12 and 21, 1832; *Niles' Register* 43 (December 1, 1832): 213; Diamond, ed., *Guide to U.S. Elections,* pp. 266, 422.

24. Granger to Weed, November 13, 1832, Weed Papers; *Albany Evening Journal,* November 9 and 21, 1832; Weed to Granger, November 11, 1832, in Weed, *Memoir,* 2:45-46; Patterson to Weed, November 15, 1832, in ibid., pp. 47-48; Seward, *Autobiography,* pp. 218-20.

25. Van Deusen, *Weed,* p. 65; Seward *Autobiography,* p. 101; Childs to Weed, November 27, 1832, Weed Papers; Holley to Seward, December 1, 1832, Seward Papers.

26. Van Deusen, *Weed,* p. 66; Eriksson, "Minor Prophets," p. 161; *Biographical Directory of the American Congress, 1774-1971,* 4th ed. s.v. "Tracy, Albert Haller"; Clark to Patterson, November 29, 1832, and January 6, 1833, George W. Patterson Papers, University of Rochester; Tracy to Seward, May 17 and June 18, 1833, Seward Papers.

27. Ebenezer Baldwin to Weed, August 11, 1833, Weed Papers; Weed to Patterson, May 21 and October 8, 1833, Patterson Papers; Weed to Seward, July 20, 1833, Seward Papers; *Albany Evening Journal,* July 6, August 10, and November 1, 1833; Childs to Weed, October 4, 1833, Weed Papers.

28. McCarthy, "Antimasonic Party," pp. 424-25; *Albany Argus,* November 16, 1833; *Albany Evening Journal,* November 8, 1833; Patterson to Weed, December 4, 1833, Weed Papers; Weed to Patterson, December 11, 1833, Patterson Papers.

29. Seward, *Works,* 3:349-55; Hallett to Weed, January 12, 1833, Weed Papers; Fuller to Hallet, December 30, 1833, ibid.; Hallet to Seward, May 12, 1834, Seward

Papers; Weed to Seward, May 20 and 26, 1834, ibid.; *Boston Advocate*, March 6 and 7, 1834.

30. Ershkowitz, "Anti-Masonry," pp. 15-16; John Vollmer Mering, *The Whig Party in Missouri* (Columbia, Mo.: University of Missouri Press, 1967), p. 4; Johnson, *Shopkeeper's Millennium*, pp. 128-30; Samuel N. Sweet to Seward, March 11, 1834, Seward Papers; Albert H. Tracy to Seward, June 9 and July 5, ibid.; Patterson to Weed, May 26, 1834, Weed Papers; *Albany Evening Journal*, April 8, 1834.

31. Ershkowitz, "Anti-Masonry," pp. 8-9; Cross, *Burned-over District*, p. 116; Diamond, ed., *Guide to U.S. Elections*, p. 422; Weed, *Autobiography*, pp. 423, 430-31; Seward, *Autobiography*, p. 147; *Albany Argus*, September 13, 1834; *Boston Advocate*, December 9, 1834; Clark to Patterson, July 21, 1834, Patterson Papers.

32. Ratner, "Antimasonry in New York," pp. 33-34; Van Deusen, *Seward*, pp. 25-26; Weed to Seward, March 8, 1835, Seward Papers; Thurlow Weed, *The Facts Stated—Hon. Thurlow Weed on the Morgan Abduction* (Chicago: National Christian Association, 1882), p. 14.

33. Peter Ross, *A Standard History of Freemasonry in New York*, 2 vols. (New York: Lewis Publishing, 1901), 1:353-54; Ossian Lang, *History of Freemasonry in the State of New York* (New York: Grand Lodge of New York, 1922), pp. 123-34; "Incidents of Anti-Masonry—How Political Anti-Masonry Began" *Ashlar* 11 (1855-56): 147-49.

34. Charles T. McClenachan, *History of the Most Ancient and Honorable Fraternity of Free and Accepted Masons of New York . . .*, 4 vols. (New York: Grand Lodge of New York, 1892), 2:458, 595, 600-5; Ross, *Freemasonry in New York*, 1:359-60.

35. Ross, Freemasonry in New York, 1:361, 365-66; McClenachan, *History of Masons of New York*, 3:1.

36. McClenachan, *History of Masons of New York*, 3:2-3, 10-11; Ross, *Freemasonry in New York*, 1:366, 368.

37. "Minutes," *Transactions of the American Lodge of Research* 6 (1952-56): 295; Erik McKinley Eriksson, "Effects of Anti-Masonry on the Masonic Fraternity, 1826-1856," *Builder* 13 (1927): 33-36; Lang, *Freemasonry in New York*, pp. 126, 134-35; Ross, *Freemasonry in New York*, 1:367; Jesse B. Anthony, comp., *Review of the Grand Lodge Transactions of the State of New York, 1781 to 1852* (Troy, N.Y.: H. W. Scribner, 1869), pp. 107-8.

38. Eriksson, "Effects of Anti-Masonry," pp. 35-36; Anthony, *Review of the Grand Lodge Transactions*, pp. 107-8.

## CHAPTER 5

1. Eriksson, "Minor Prophets," p. 157; Gammon, *Presidential Campaign of 1832*, pp. 36-39; Chase, *Emergence*, pp. 136-38, 145, 148-49; *Harrisburg* (Pa.) *Republican and Anti-Masonic Inquirer*, September 18, 1830; *Proceedings of the United States Anti-Masonic Convention, Held at Philadelphia, September 11, 1830* (Philadelphia: I. P. Trimble, 1830), pp. 1, 7, 69-72, 106.

2. Chase, *Emergence*, pp. 146-53; *Proceedings, U.S. Antimasonic Convention, Philadelphia, 1830*, pp. 12-13, 73-75, 85-135; *Albany Evening Journal*, June 1 and 3, September 15, 1830; *Niles' Register* 39 (October 2, 1830): 91; Seward, *Autobiography*, p. 78; Philo C. Fuller to Thurlow Weed, August 30, 1830, Weed Papers.

3. *Proceedings, U.S. Antimasonic Convention, Philadelphia, 1830,* pp. 6, 9, 13, 74, 84, 96, 131-33; *Harrisburg Republican and Anti-Masonic Inquirer,* September 25, 1830; Chase, *Emergence,* pp. 153-55.

4. Chase, *Emergence,* pp. 157-59; Ellmaker to Seward, May 5, 1831, Seward Papers; Holley to Seward, August 9, 1831, ibid.; Maynard to Seward, May 31, 1831, ibid.

5. Chase, *Emergence,* p. 159; *Boston Advocate,* January 14, 1832; *Niles' Register* 41 (January 7, 1832): 346; Glyndon G. Van Deusen, *The Life of Henry Clay* (Boston: Little, Brown, 1937), p. 241; *Ravenna Star,* January 13, 1832; Weed, *Autobiography,* p. 350; James Clark to Weed, January 22, 1831, Weed Papers.

6. Van Deusen, *Clay,* pp. 241-43; Daniel Webster to Albert H. Tracy, January 15, 1831, in Daniel Webster, *The Papers of Daniel Webster,* ed. Charles M. Wiltse, 3 vols. to date (Hanover, N.H.: University Press of New England, 1973-77), 3:97-99; Weed, *Autobiography,* pp. 350-54; *Albany Evening Journal,* December 6-8, 1830, January 10, February 5, and June 1, 1831; Chase, *Emergence,* pp. 159-61; Clay to Brooke, June 23, 1831, in Henry Clay, *The Works of Henry Clay, Comprising His Life, Correspondence and Speeches,* ed. Calvin Colton, 10 vols. (New York: G. P. Putnam's, 1904), 4:304; Clay to J. S. Johnston, July 23, 1831, in ibid., pp. 308-9; Clay to John Bailhache, November 24, 1830, in ibid., pp. 289-90; Clay to Brooke, October 4, 1830, in ibid., p. 316.

7. Chase, *Emergence,* pp. 163-65; *Niles' Register* 40 (August 27, 1831): 453; Richard Rush, *A Letter on Freemasonry to the Committee of the Citizens of York County, Pennsylvania* (Boston: Kimball and Johnson, 1831), passim; John Harvey Powell, *Richard Rush: Republican Diplomat* (Philadelphia: Univesity of Pennsylvania Press, 1942), pp. 232-33; Albert H. Tracy to Seward, June 2, 1831, Seward Papers; William H. Maynard to Seward, August 12, 1831, ibid.; Ellmaker to Seward, August 1, 1831, ibid.; Seward to Weed, June 22 and July 17, 1831, Weed Papers.

8. Bemis, *John Quincy Adams and the Union,* pp. 288-92; John Quincy Adams, *Memoirs of John Quincy Adams, Comprising Portions of his Diary from 1795 to 1848,* ed. Charles Francis Adams, 12 vols. (1847-77; reprint ed., Freeport, N.Y.: Books for Libraries Press, 1969), 8:403-4 (entry of August 27, 1831), 8:412-13 (entry of September 14, 1831); Seward to Weed, September 14, 1831, Weed Papers.

9. Chase, *Emergence,* p. 159; Seward to Weed, August 2, 1831, Weed Papers; Eriksson, "Minor Prophets," p. 210; Charles M. Wiltse, *John C. Calhoun: Nullifier 1829-1839* (Indianapolis: Bobbs-Merrill, 1949), pp. 121-22; Duff Green to Richard Crallé, September 11 and October 4, 1831, Duff Green Papers, LC; Calhoun to Christopher Vandeventer, May 25, 1831, in John C. Calhoun, *The Papers of John C. Calhoun,* 14 vols, to date, ed. Robert L. Meriwether, W. Edwin Hemphill and Clyde N. Wilson, 11 (Columbia, S.C.: University of South Carolina Press, 1978), 11:395; Calhoun to Vandeventer, August 5, 1831, in ibid., p. 450, and August 17, 1831, in ibid., p. 457; Calhoun to Samuel D. Ingham, May 25, 1831, in ibid., pp. 392-93.

10. Chase, *Emergence,* p. 167; Seth Hunt to William H. Seward, September 14, 1831, Seward Papers; William Wallace Irwin to Webster, August 25, September 17, 1830, in *Webster Papers,* ed. Wiltse, 3:84, 410.

11. Francis P. Weisenburger, *The Life of John McLean: A Politician on the United States Supreme Court* (Columbus: Ohio State University Press, 1937), pp. vii, 2-4, 77; Chase, *Emergence,* pp. 162-63; Frederick Whittlesey to Weed, July 6, 1830, Weed

Papers; Whittlesey to McLean, June 9, 1839, John McLean Papers, LC; McLean to Harris, May 24, 1830, ibid.; McLean to Robert Hanna, November 1, 1830, ibid.

12. Warren Jenkins to McLean, July 17, 1831, McLean Papers; Albert H. Tracy to McLean, August 20, 1831, ibid.; Chase, *Emergence,* pp. 169-70; *Gettysburg* (Pa.) *Anti-Masonic Star and Republican Banner,* September 20, 1831; Maynard to Seward, May 31, 1831, Seward Papers; Weed to Seward, July 24, 1830, ibid.; Tracy to Seward, July 25, 1831, ibid.; Weed to McLean, August 23, 1831, McLean Papers; Boughton to Weed, March 15, 1831, Weed Papers; Seward to Weed, August 8, 1831, ibid.; Hunt to Seward, June 30, August 6 and 31, 1831, Seward Papers; Webster to Charles Miner, August 28, 1831, in *Webster Papers,* ed. Wiltse, 3:119-20; Webster to Nathan Hale, September 5, 1831, ibid., pp. 120-21.

13. Chase, *Emergence,* pp. 158-59, 171-72; *Niles' Register* 41 (December 3, 1831); 259-60; Weisenburger, *McLean,* pp. 78-79; Wiltse, *Calhoun, Nullifier,* p. 129; B. W. Richards to McLean, September 8 and 10, 1831, McLean Papers; Richard Rush to McLean, September 27, 1831, ibid.

14. Albert J. Beveridge, *The Life of John Marshall,* 4 vols. (Boston: Houghton Mifflin, 1916-19), 1:187, 2:176, 4:522-24; Marshall to Edward Everett, July 22, 1833, Edward Everett Papers, MaHS; Joseph Ritner, *Vindication of General Washington from the Stigma of Adherence to Secret Societies* (Boston: Ezra Lincoln, 1841) pp. 2-4; John Marshall, "Opinions of the Late Chief Justice of the United States, John Marshall, Concerning Freemasonry," *Antimasonic Pamphlets* (n.p.: VHS, n.d.).

15. Gammon, *Presidential Campaign of 1832,* pp. 45-52; Seward, *Autobiography,* p. 89; Chase, *Emergence,* pp. 173-74; idem, "First National Convention," pp. 92 and 92n; Thomas F. Woodley, *Thaddeus Stevens* (Harrisburg: Telegraph Press, 1934), p. 62; *Proceedings of the Second United States Anti-Masonic Convention, Held at Baltimore, September, 1831* (Boston: Boston Type & Foundry, 1832), pp. 85-87.

16. Van Deusen, *Seward,* p. 19; Chase, *Emergence,* p. 175; Weed, *Autobiography,* p. 389; Wirt to Salmon P. Chase, November 11, 1831 (copy), William Wirt Papers, MdHS; Wirt to Phelps, October 28, 1831, William Wirt Papers, LC.

17. William Wirt, *Memoirs of the Life of William Wirt,* ed. John P. Kennedy, 2 vols. (Philadelphia: Lea and Blanchard, 1850), 2:300-3; Van Deusen, *Weed,* pp. 58-59; Chase, *Emergence,* pp. 175-78, 181, 294; *Proceedings, U.S. Antimasonic Convention, Baltimore, 1831,* pp. 59-61; *Washington National Intelligencer,* October 19, 1831.

18. Seward to Weed, July 17, 1831, Weed Papers; Chase, *Emergence,* p. 179; *Washington National Intelligencer,* October 17, 1831; Rush to Spencer, November 8, 1831, in *A Collection of Letters on Freemasonry in Chronological Order* (Boston: T. R. Marvin, 1849), pp. 63-64; F. R. Diffenderiffer, ed., "Politics Seventy-five Years Ago: Letters of Hon. Amos Ellmaker to Thaddeus Stevens," *Historical Papers and Addresses of the Lancaster County Historical Society* 8 (1904): 36-47; *Harrisburg* (Pa.) *Telegraph,* October 5, 1831.

19. *Dictionary of American Biography,* 1st ed., s.v. "Wirt, William"; Erik McKinley Eriksson, "William Wirt: Antimasonic Presidential Candidate," *Grand Lodge Bulletin, Grand Lodge of Iowa* 27 (1926): 120-21; John B. Boles, *A Guide to the Microfilm Edition of the William Wirt Papers* (Baltimore: Maryland Historical Society, 1971), pp. 3-6.

20. Marvin R. Cain, "William Wirt against Andrew Jackson: Reflection on an Era," *Mid-America* 47 (1965): 113-14; William R. Taylor, "William Wirt and the Legend of the Old South," *William and Mary Quarterly*, 3rd ser., 14 (1957): 482-84.

21. Leonard D. White, *The Jeffersonians: A Study in Administrative History, 1801-1829* (New York: Macmillan, 1951), pp. 344-46; Cain, "Wirt against Jackson," pp. 113-14, 120-21; Boles, *A Guide*, pp. 6-9; Eriksson, "Wirt," pp. 121-22; Taylor, "Wirt," pp. 477-78.

22. *Proceedings, U.S. Antimasonic Convention, Baltimore, 1831*, p. 59; Cain, "Wirt against Jackson," p. 132; Wirt to Salmon P. Chase, November 11, 1831, Wirt Papers, MdHS.

23. Griffin, "Antimasonic Persuasion," pp. 258-61; Cain, "Wirt against Jackson," p. 131; *Proceedings, U.S. Antimasonic Convention, Baltimore, 1831*, pp. 63-64.

24. Wirt to Robert Walsh, October 14, 1831, Wirt Papers, LC; *Proceedings, U.S. Antimasonic Convention, Baltimore, 1831*, pp. 63-67.

25. *Proceedings, U.S. Antimasonic Convention, Baltimore, 1831*, p. 67; Spencer to Wirt, September 28, 1831, Wirt papers, MdHS.

26. Wirt to Luke Tiernan, September 28, 1831, Wirt Papers, MdHS; Wirt to Carr, October 5, November 27, 1831, ibid.

27. *Washington Globe*, September 30, October 6 and 11, 1831; *Washington National Intelligencer*, October 5 and 13, 1831.

28. Seward to Weed, October 19, 1831, Weed Papers; Hunt to Seward, October 3, 1831, Seward Papers; Whittlesey to Seward, October 17, 1831, ibid.; Tracy to Seward, October 6, 1831, ibid.

29. Wirt to Carr, September 30, 1831, Wirt Papers, LC.

30. Wirt, *Memoirs*, 2:309, 314; Wirt to Richard Rush, October 6, 1831, Wirt Papers, LC; Wirt to William Cabell, October 3, 1831, ibid.; Wirt to John Glenn, March 27 and April 16, 1832, Wirt Papers, MdHS; Wirt to Ambrose Spencer, April 16, 1832, Wirt Papers, LC; Wirt to Samuel Southard, November 29, 1832, ibid.; Wirt to Carr, May 23 and October 25, 1832 (copies), Wirt Papers, MdHS.

31. Gammon, *Presidential Campaign of 1832*, pp. 142-43; Wirt to John McLean, April 17, 1832, McLean Papers; Wirt, *Memoirs*, 2:330-31; Wirt to John T. Lomax, November 15, 1832, Wirt Papers, LC; Wirt to Joseph White, October 10 and November 14, 1831, ibid.; Green to Wirt, August 7, 1832 (copy), Wirt Papers, MdHS; *Boston Advocate*, December 6, 1832; Wirt to Dabney Carr, September 6 and October 20, 1832, Wirt Papers, MdHS; to William Cabell, October 3, 1831, Wirt Letterbook, Wirt Papers, LC.

32. Cain, "Wirt against Jackson," p. 133; Wirt to William Cabell, October 3, 1831, Wirt Papers, LC; Paul DeWitt, *Andrew Jackson and Freemasonry* (Paper delivered at the Tennessee Historical Society, n.p., n.d. [1947]), pp. 2-6; Jackson to Col. James A. Hamilton, April 29, 1828, in Andrew Jackson, *Correspondence of Andrew Jackson*, ed. John Spencer Bassett, 7 vols. (1929; reprint ed., New York: Kraus Reprints, 1969), 3:399. Note the misinterpretation of this letter in Robert V. Remini, *Andrew Jackson and the Course of American Freedom, 1822-1832* (New York: Harper and Row, 1981), p. 140. See also Jackson to Gen. W. R. Swift, June 2, 1828, *Jackson Correspondence*, 3:408; Jackson to Van Buren, December 6, 1831, ibid., 4:379.

33. Cain, "Wirt against Jackson," pp. 135-37; Wirt to Mrs. Elizabeth Wirt, October 10, 1831, and November 5, 1832, Wirt Papers, MdHS; Wirt to Catherine Wirt, November 8, 1832, ibid.; Wirt to Carr, February 10 and October 20, 1832 (copies), ibid.

34. Wirt to Ambrose Spencer, April 16, 1832, Wirt Papers, LC; Samuel T. Lyman to Wirt, October 7, 1832, Wirt Papers, MdHS; Ambrose Spencer to Daniel Webster, March 14 and September 27, 1832, *Webster Papers,* ed. Wiltse, 3:158, 455; Webster to Abraham Van Vechten, July 2, 1832, in ibid., p. 184; Orville L. Holley to Seward, April 18, 1832, Seward Papers; Frederick Whittlesey to "Men of Influence in the Several States," October 30, 1832, Weed Papers; Amos Ellmaker to Thaddeus Stevens, August 16, 1832, in Diffenderiffer, ed., "Politics Seventy-five Years Ago," pp. 42-43. In New York, the fusion ticket lost to Jackson, 154,896 to 168,497; in Pennsylvania, 66,706 to 90,973; and and in Ohio 76,566 to 81,246—with a separate Antimasonic ticket receiving 538 votes ( 0.3 percent). See Diamond, ed., *Guide to U.S. Elections,* p. 266.

35. Eugene H. Roseboom, *A History of Presidential Elections: From George Washington to Richard Nixon,* 3rd ed. (New York: Macmillan, 1970), p. 105n; *Danville* (Vt.) *North Star,* October 29, 1832; (Providence) *Rhode Island American,* October 3, 1832, *Vermont Patriot and State Gazette,* December 10, 1832; Elizabeth Wirt to William Wirt, November 5, 1832, Wirt Papers, MdHS; Diamond, ed., *Guide to U.S. Elections,* p. 266.

36. Chase, *Emergence,* p. 181; Cain, "Wirt against Jackson," pp. 137-38; Wirt to Elizabeth Wirt, November 11, 1832, Wirt Papers, MdHS; Wirt to Dabney Carr, January 6 (or 8), 1833, ibid.; Wirt to John C. Spencer, November 26, 1832, Wirt Papers, LC; Wirt to John T. Lomax, November 15, 1832, ibid.; Wirt to Samuel Southard, November 29, 1832, ibid.; Southard to Henry Clay, December 1, 1832; Clay, *Works* 4:344; Wirt to Richard Rush, November 27, 1832, Wirt Papers, MdHS.

37. Wirt to editor (Daniel Mowry) of *Rhode Island American,* November 17, 1832, Wirt Papers, LC; *Rhode Island American,* November 22, 1832; *Boston Advocate,* November 24, 1832; Wirt to Dabney Carr, March 8, 1833, Wirt Papers, MdHS; Wirt to Hallett, January 9, 1834 (copy), ibid.

CHAPTER 6

1. Andrew E. Nuquist and Edith W. Nuquist, *Vermont State Government and Administration: An Historical and Descriptive Study of the Living Past* (Burlington: University of Vermont, 1966), pp. 8, 28-29; McCormick, *Second American Party System,* p. 70; Peter S. Onuf, "State-Making in Revolutionary America: Independent Vermont as a Case Study," *Journal of American History* 67 (1981): 797-815.

2. Chester R. Palmer, "A Political Biography of William Adam Palmer, 1781-1860" (M.A. thesis, University of Illinois, 1953), pp. 70, 72-74; Philip A. Grant, "The Antimasons Retain Control of the Green Mountain State," *Vermont History* 34 (1966): 169-70; Walter H. Crockett, *Vermont, The Green Mountain State,* 5 vols. (1921-23; reprint ed., Burlington: Vermont Farm Bureau, 1938), 3:162; Daniel B. Carroll, "The Unicameral Legislature of Vermont," *Proceedings of the Vermont Historical Society* 3 (1932): 40-41, 67.

3. Palmer, "Palmer," p. 74; David M. Ludlum, *Social Ferment in Vermont, 1791-1850* (New York: Columbia University Press, 1939), pp. 89-90, 114; John Spargo, *One*

*Hundred Thirty Years of Masonry in Bennington, Vermont* (Rutland, Vt.: Tuttle, 1925), p. 17; Holt, "Antimasonic and Know-Nothing Parties," pp. 583-84; Melvin A. Shore, "The Anti-Masonic Party and Anti-Masonry" (M.A. thesis, Bridgewater State University [Mass.], 1973), p. 64.

4. John Spargo, *The Rise and Progress of Freemasonry in Vermont, the Green Mountain State, 1765-1944* (Burlington: Grand Lodge of Vermont, 1944), pp. 49-52; Palmer, "Palmer," p. 75; Ludlum, *Social Ferment,* pp. 92-93, 102, 104-9; Tunbridge, [Free Will Baptist] Monthly Meeting, Record Book, 1825-76, entry for July 1830, VHS; *Proceedings of the "Montpelier [Congregational] Association." In Reply to Annexed Statements of Henry Jones ... In Relation to the Influence of Freemansonry in the Churches* (Danville, Vt.: E. Eaton, 1830), pp. 6, 21; Henry Jones, *Letters on Masonry, Addressed to the Followers of Christ ...* (Boston: Antimasonic Free Press, 1829), pp. 1-5, 7, 17, 23-30, 34-38, 47.

5. McCarthy, "Antimasonic Party," p. 505; *Danville North Star,* September 18, 1829; *Proceedings, Antimasonic Convention of 1831, Baltimore,* p. 70; "Reason in the Midst of Fanaticism," *Ashlar* 1 (1855-56): 491; Chase, *Emergence,* p. 138; *Records of the Governor and Council of the State of Vermont, 1777-1836,* ed. E. P. Walton, 8 vols. (Montpelier: J. & J. Poland, 1879), 8:216.

6. Crockett, *Vermont,* 3:227-30; Blakeslee, "Antimasonic Party," chap. 7, pp. 13-14; (Montpelier) *Vermont Watchman and State Gazette,* November 10 and 24, 1829.

7. *Bennington* (Vermont) *Gazette,* March 9 and August 25, 1829; *Vermont Watchman and State Gazette,* August 11, 1829; McCarthy, "Antimasonic Party," p. 506; Ludlum, *Social Ferment,* pp. 116-17; Palmer, "Palmer," pp. 79-82; *Records of the Governor and Council, Vermont,* 7:347; Diamond, ed., *Guide to U.S. Elections,* p. 433.

8. Blakeslee, "Antimasonic Party," chap. 7, pp. 15-16; Palmer, "Palmer," pp. 82-84; *Vermont Watchman and State Gazette,* August 10, 1830; *Proceedings of the Anti-Masonic State Convention* (Vermont), *Holden at Montpelier, June 23, 24 and 25, 1830* (Middlebury: O. & J. Miner, 1830), pp. 9-10, 34-35.

9. McCarthy, "Antimasonic Party," p. 507; *Records of the Governor and Council, Vermont,* 7:395; *Danville North Star,* September 7, 1830; Diamond, ed., *Guide to U.S. Elections,* p. 433.

10. Blakeslee, "Antimasonic Party," chap. 7, p. 18; *Albany Evening Journal,* November 13, 1830; *A Memorial to the Legislature of Vermont, For the Repeal of Acts Incorporating the Grand Lodge and Grand Chapter of Vt. Presented October 23, 1830* (n.p., n.d.), pp. 1-2; *Records of the Governor and Council, Vermont* 7:413.

11. McCormick, *Second American Party System,* p. 73; *Danville North Star,* September 8, 1829; *Montpelier State Journal,* December 26, 1831.

12. Palmer, "Palmer," pp. 27-28, 31-42, 88-90; *Proceedings of the Anti-masonic State Convention, Holden at Montpelier, June 15 and 16, 1831, With Reports, Addresses, etc.* (Montpelier: Gamaliel Small, 1831), passim; *Vermont Watchman and State Gazette,* October 17, 1831; *Records of the Governor and Council, Vermont,* 8:2, 6-7; Diamond, ed., *Guide to U.S. Elections,* p. 433.

13. Palmer, "Palmer," pp. 3-4, 88; Lee S. Tillotson, *Ancient Craft Masonry in Vermont* (Montpelier: Capital City Press, 1920), p. 142; *Records of the Governor and Council, Vermont,* 8:1-2; *Encyclopedia of Vermont Bibliography,* 1st ed., s.v. "Palmer, William Adam."

14. Palmer, "Palmer," pp. 58, 60-62; Crockett, *Vermont*, 3:262-63.

15. Palmer, "Palmer," pp. 119-22; *Vermont Watchman and State Gazette*, October 24 and November 7, 1831; *Vermont Patriot and State Gazette*, November 7, 1831.

16. Ludlum, *Social Ferment*, p. 122; Tillotson, *Ancient Craft Masonry*, p. 99; *Danville North Star*, July 19, 1831; *Records of the Governor and Council, Vermont*, 8:263.

17. Charles A. Morse, "William Slade: Congressional Career, 1831-43" (M.A. thesis, University of Vermont, 1965), pp. i, 1, 14-16, 18, 23, 31-34, 45-47, 50-53, 60-61, 66, 103; Ludlum, *Social Ferment*, p. 103; Palmer, "Palmer," p. 93; *Albany Evening Journal*, July 9, 11, and 18, November 5, 1831; Eriksson, "Minor Prophets," pt. 2, p. 216; Grant, "Antimasons Retain Control," pp. 172-73.

18. *Vermont Patriot and State Gazette*, October 1, 1832; Palmer, "Palmer," pp. 95-98; Joe W. Specht, "Andrew Jackson and the Problem of Internal Improvements" (M.A. thesis, North Texas State University, 1973), pp. 68-72; *Bennington Gazette*, February 21, 1832; Blakeslee, "Antimasonic Party," chap. 9, pp. 59-60; *Montpelier State Journal*, July 2, 1832; *Danville North Star*, September 3, 1832.

19. *Niles' Register* 43 (October 27, 1832): 133; *Records of the Governor and Council, Vermont*, 8:58-60; *Vermont Patriot and State Gazette*, October 22, 1832; *Danville North Star*, October 27, 1832; *Albany Evening Journal*, November 8, 1832; Diamond, ed., *Guide to U.S. Elections*, p. 433.

20. *Danville North Star*, October 15 and 29, November 12 and 19, December 10, 1832; *Montpelier State Journal*, November 12 and December 10, 1832; Grant, "Antimasons Retain Control," p. 170; McCarthy, "Antimasonic Party," pp. 510-11; *Albany Argus*, November 26, 1832; *Vermont Patriot and State Gazette*, November 26, 1832; *Niles' Register* 43 (December 1, 1832): 213.

21. *Danville North Star*, January 21, and May 20, 1833; *Montpelier State Journal*, January 21, March 11 and 25, July 1 and 22, 1833; *Proceedings of the Anti-Masonic State Convention, Holden at Montpelier, Vt., June 26 and 27, 1833, with Resolutions, Reports and Addresses* (Montpelier: Knapp and Jewett, 1833), pp. 1-32; *Niles' Register* 44 (July 20, 1833): 337, 348.

22. *Vermont Patriot and State Gazette*, August 5 and 19, 1833; *Niles' Register* 44 (July 27, 1833): 354; Palmer, "Palmer," pp. 103-6; *Painesville Telegraph*, July 19, 1833; *Montpelier State Journal*, September 9, 1833.

23. *Vermont Patriot and State Gazette*, October 14, 1833; *Montpelier State Journal*, October 14, 1833, January 20, 1834; *Records of the Governor and Council, Vermont*, 8:106; *Danville North Star*, September 23 and October 14, 1833; *Niles' Register* 45 (September 21, October 10 and 26, 1833): 55, 115, 131; Diamond, ed., *Guide to U.S. Elections*, p. 433.

24. *Records of the Governor and Council, Vermont*, 8:18, 58-60, 71, 142, 159, 263-70, 284; *Journal of the General Assembly of the State of Vermont, 1831*, pp. 26-28, 48; ibid., *1832*, pp. 42-46, 150-57; ibid., *1833*, p. 36; *Danville North Star*, October 22, 1832; *Vermont Patriot and State Gazette*, November 26, 1832; *Montpelier State Journal*, January 14 and December 2, 1833; *Acts Passed by the Legislature of . . . Vermont at Their October Session, 1833*, pp. 15-16.

25. *Vermont Patriot and State Gazette*, March 10 and April 14, 1834; *Montpelier State Journal*, May 26 and June 9, 1834.

26. p. 129; *Montpelier State Journal,* July 14, August 4 and 18, 1834; J. B. Hollinbeck to E. and T. Mills, August 16, 1834, Miscellaneous Correspondence, VHS.

27. Ludlum, *Social Ferment,* pp. 129-30; Palmer, "Palmer," pp. 109-10; Grant, "Antimasons Retain Control," pp. 184-87; *Montpelier State Journal,* September 15 and October 13, 1834; *Danville North Star,* October 13 and 20, 1834; *Niles' Register* 47 (September 27, 1834): 53, 117; *Records of the Governor and Council, Vermont,* 8:163-64.

28. *Danville North Star,* May 19, November 17, and December 3, 1834; *Montpelier State Journal,* September 15 and Octover 27, 1834; McCarthy, "Antimasonic Party," p. 514; *Records of the Governor and Council, Vermont,* 8:270-73; *Journal, General Assembly of Vermont, 1834,* pp. 33-35; William Slade to Hezekiah Niles, *Niles' Register* 47 (November 15, 1834): 163; ibid., December 13, 1834, p. 238.

29. Martin Flint to William Niles, February 8, 1835, Miscellaneous Correspondence, VHS; *Vermont Patriot and State Gazette,* July 6 and August 31, 1835; *Niles' Register* 49 (November 14, 1835): 173.

30. *Vermont Patriot and State Gazette,* July 20, 27, August 10, 24, and 31, 1835; Palmer, "Palmer," p. 114; *Danville North Star,* August 31, 1835.

31. McCarthy, "Antimasonic Party," p. 514; *Records of the Governor and Council, Vermont,* 8:218-19; *Danville North Star,* October 5, 12, and 19, 1835; *Vermont Patriot and State Gazette,* October 12, 1835.

32. *Vermont Patriot and State Gazette,* September 14 and 21, October 19, 1835; *Records of the Governor and Council, Vermont,* 8:215, 219-20, 245; *Journal, General Assembly of Vermont, 1835,* pp. 143-44.

33. Palmer, "Palmer," pp. 133-38, 144-45.

34. Grant, "Antimasons Retain Control," pp. 179-80; Morse, "Slade," pp. 65-66; *Montpelier State Journal,* March 1 and 8, 1836; *Vermont Watchman and State Gazette,* March 1 and June 9, 1836; *Vermont Patriot and State Gazette,* May 9, 1836; *Boston Advocate,* February 19, 1836.

35. *Vermont Watchman and State Gazette,* March 8, 1836; *Montpelier State Journal,* March 1 and 8, 1836; *Danville North Star,* February 24, March 7 and 11, May 2, 1836; *Boston Advocate,* March 1, 4, 7, and 11, 1836; C. C. Waller to Hollinbeck, March 14, 1836, John Hollinbeck Papers, VHS; Hollinbeck to N. L. Whittemore, May 20 and 25, 1836, ibid.

36. Morse, "Slade," pp. 35, 60-66; Palmer, "Palmer," pp. 117, 141-45; *Vermont Patriot and State Gazette,* May 9 and June 6, 1836; *Danville North Star,* May 9, June 6, September 5, and November 7, 1836.

37. *Vermont Patriot and State Gazette,* July 4, 18, 27, September 19, and November 21, 1836; *Vermont Watchman and State Gazette,* September 20, 1836; *Montpelier State Journal,* November 22, 1836; Diamond, ed., *Guide to U.S. Elections,* pp. 266, 433.

38. Spargo, *One Hundred and Thirty Years,* pp. 3, 15; [Anonymous], *History of Rising Sun Lodge No. 7, AF & AM, Royalton, Vt.* (n.p., n.d. [1907]), p. 4; James Whitelaw, Survey for Jonathan Taylor, June 11, 1831, Miscellaneous Correspondence, VHS; Tillotson, *Ancient Craft Masonry,* p. 100; *Woodstock American Whig,* December 10, 1831.

39. Marsh O. Perkins and Warren G. Reynolds, comps., *1794-1894: Centennial Celebration of the M. W. Free and Accepted Masons of the State of Vermont . . .* (n.p.,

1894), p. 61; Tillotson, *Ancient Craft Masonry,* pp. 98-99; *Records of the Grand Lodge of Free and Accepted Masons of the State of Vermont, From 1794 to 1846, Inclusive* (Burlington: Free Press Association, 1870), pp. 370, 381, 384.

40. Tillotson, *Ancient Craft Masonry,* pp. 100-7; *Danville North Star,* October 7, 21, and 28, 1833; *Montpelier State Journal,* October 14, November 4 and 25, 1833; William Slade to [Samuel] Elliot, July 17, 1833, in William Slade, Letters, 1815-57, Billings Library, University of Vermont; Notice of September 16, 1833, Nathan B. Haswell Papers, VHS; *Records, Grand Lodge of Vermont,* pp. 386, 390-92.

41. *Records, Grand Lodge of Vermont,* pp. 401-6, 410-17; Shore, "Anti-Masonic Party," pp. 70-71; Perkins and Reynolds, *Vermont,* pp. 63-68; Spargo, *Rise and Progress of Freemasonry,* pp. 57-62; Tillotson, *Ancient Craft Masonry,* pp. 109-13, 145; *Montpelier State Journal,* November 3, 1834; *Danville North Star,* November 10 and 24, 1834; *Vermont Patriot and State Gazette,* March 7, 1836.


CHAPTER 7

1. Philip S. Klein, *Pennsylvania Politics, 1817-1832: A Game without Rules* (Philadelphia: Historical Society of Pennsylvania, 1940), p. 279; Philip S. Klein and Ari Hoogenboom, *History of Pennsylvania* (New York: McGraw-Hill, 1973), p. 126; Ershkowitz, "Anti-Masonry," pp. 4-5; John M. Belohlavek, *George M. Dallas: Jacksonian Patrician* (University Park: Pennsylvania State University Press, 1977), pp. 17-18.

2. Holt, "Antimasonic and Know-Nothing Parties," pp. 586-87; Willia G. Shade, "Pennsylvania Politics in the Jacksonian Period: A Case Study, Northampton County, 1824-1844," *Pennsylvania History* 39 (1972): 318; J. Cutler Andrews, "The Antimasonic Movement in Western Pennsylvania," *Western Pennsylvania Historical Magazine* 18 (1935): 256-58, 260, 266; Stanley S. Zyckowski, "The Antimasonic Party in Pennsylvania" (M.A. thesis, Pennsylvania State University, 1937), pp. 6-7.

3. Milton W. Hamilton, "Anti-Masonic Newspapers, 1826-1834," *Papers of the Bibliographical Society of America* 32 (1938): 75; John E. McNeal, "The Antimasonic Party of Lancaster County: 1828-1843," *Journal of the Lancaster County Historical Society* 69 (1965): 60; Andrews, "Antimasonic Movement," p. 261; *Lancaster Anti-Masonic Herald,* June 26, September 19 and 26, October 30, and November 21, 1828; ibid., February 20 and March 6, 1829.

4. David R. Keller, "Nativism or Sectionalism: A History of the Know-Nothing Party in Lancaster County, Pennsylvania," *Journal of the Lancaster County Historical Society* 75 (1971): 43; "Anti-Masonic Days Recalled," *Lancaster County Historical County Papers* 15 (1911): 225-26; *Lancaster Anti-Masonic Herald,* July 25, 1828, February 27, and March 13, 1829.

5. Fawn M. Brodie, *Thaddeus Stevens: Scourge of the South* (New York: W. W. Norton, 1959), pp. 23-32; Erik McKinley Eriksson, "Thaddeus Stevens: 'Arch Priest of Anti-Masonry,'" *Grand Lodge Bulletin, Grand Lodge of Iowa* 27 (1926): 38-39; Thomas F. Woodley, *Great Leveler: The Life of Thaddeus Stevens* (New York: Stockpole and Sons, 1937), pp. 37-38; William H. Egle, *History of Perseverance Lodge No. 21, F. & A. M., at Harrisburg, Pennsylvania* (Harrisburg: Harrisburg Publishing, 1901), p. 166; *Philadelphia Keystone* 1 (May 9, 1868): 341; Alphonse Cerza, "Anti-Masonry," *Transactions, Quatuor Coronati Lodge No. 2076, London* 80 (1967); 247.

6. Norman B. Wilkinson, "Thaddeus Stevens: A Case of Libel," *Pennsylvania History* 18 (1951): 317-20; Alphonse B. Miller, *Thaddeus Stevens* (New York: Harper, 1939), p. 42; Woodley, *Great Leveler,* pp. 33, 61; Ralph Korngold, *Thaddeus Stevens: A Being Darkly Wise and Rudely Great* (New York: Harcourt, Brace, 1955), p. 26; Richard N. Current, *Old Thad Stevens* (Madison: University of Wisconsin Press, 1942), p. 15; Oscar J. Harvey, *A History of Lodge No. 61, F. & A.M., Wilkes-Barre, Pa.* (Wilkes-Barre: n.p., 1897), p. 86; Speech, November 1837, Article and Book File, Edward McPherson Papers, LC.

7. Woodley, *Stevens,* p. 55; *Gettysburg Anti-Masonic Star and Republican Banner,* December 23, 1834; *Proceedings, U.S. Antimasonic Convention, Philadelphia, 1830,* p. 130; Wilkinson, "A Case of Libel," pp. 319-25; *Free-Masonry Unmasked: or, Minutes of the Trial of a Suit in the Court of Adams County, wherein Thaddeus Stevens, Esq. was Plaintiff and Jacob Lefever, Defendant* (Gettysburg: R. W. Middleton, 1835), pp. iii-xiv, passim; Stevens to Sarah Stevens, April 27, 1830, Thaddeus Stevens Papers, LC.

8. *Proceedings of the General County Anti-Masonic Meeting, Held in Lancaster, Penn. April 23, 1829* (Lancaster: Fenn and Fenton, 1829), pp. 1-30; *Lancaster Anti-Masonic Herald,* April 24, May 15, and July 17, 1829; Egle, *Perseverance Lodge,* p. 163; Chase, *Emergence,* p. 143; Pessen, *Jacksonian America* (rev. ed.), p. 264; *Harrisburg Republican and Anti-Masonic Inquirer,* July 11, 1829.

9. Henry R. Mueller, *The Whig Party in Pennsylvania* (New York: Columbia University, 1922), pp. 18-19; Charles M. Snyder, *The Jacksonian Heritage: Pennsylvania Politics, 1833-1848* (Harrisburg: Pennsylvania Historical and Museum Collection, 1958), pp. 71-72.

10. McCarthy, "Antimasonic Party," p. 432; Belohlavek, *Dallas,* p. 29; Klein, *Pennsylvania Politics,* pp. 286, 331-32.

11. *Lancaster Anti-Masonic Herald,* October 2, 16, and 23, 1829; Andrews, "Antimasonic Movement," pp. 261-62; Keller, "Nativism or Sectionalism," p. 43; *Harrisburg Republican and Anti-Masonic Inquirer,* October 17 and 24, 1829; *Proceedings, U.S. Antimasonic Convention, Baltimore, 1831,* p. 70; Diamond, ed., *Guide to U.S. Elections,* p. 426.

12. Chase, *Emergence,* p. 144; Klein, *Pennsylvania Politics,* p. 327; (Harrisburg) *Pennsylvania Reporter and Democratic Herald,* February 9, 1830; *Albany Argus,* October 18, 20, 21, 25, and November 25, 1830; ibid., June 3 and 16, 1831; Zyckowski, "Antimasonic Party," pp. 14-16, 17-21; McCarthy, "Antimasonic Party," pp. 435-41; Woodley, *Stevens,* pp. 54, 61-62; *Harrisburg Chronicle,* October 6, 1831; *Albany Evening Journal,* October 25 and 29, 1831.

13. Blakeslee, "Antimasonic Party," chap. 7, p. 11; Rush to Citizens of York, Pennsylvania, May 4, 1831, in *A Collection of Letters on Freemasonry in Chronological Order,* pp. 15-16; Rush to Timothy Fuller [and others] of the Massachusetts State Antimasonic Convention, June 30, 1831, in ibid., pp. 26-30; Rush to Amos Ellmaker and others, August 13, 1831, in ibid., pp. 44-54; Rush to John C. Spencer, November 8, 1831, in ibid., pp. 55-64.

14. McCarthy, "Antimasonic Party," pp. 444-47; *Harrisburg Telegraph,* February 25, May 2, and September 5, 1832; *Albany Evening Journal,* February 29, 1832; *Journal of the . . . House of Representatives of the Commonwealth of Pennsylvania, 1831-1832,* 1:455, 458; *Journal of the Senate of the Commonwealth of Pennsylvania, 1831-32,* 1:376;

Klein and Hoogenboom, *History of Pennsylvania,* pp. 128-29; *Lancaster Anti-Masonic Herald,* August 27, 1832; *Lancaster Journal,* October 5, 1832; *Pennsylvania Reporter and Democratic Herald,* September 21, 1830.

15. Snyder, *Jacksonian Heritage,* p. 25; *Albany Argus,* October 12, 13, and 24, 1832; *Boston Advocate,* November 5, 1832; *Harrisburg Telegraph,* November 7, 1832; Diamond, ed., *Guide to U.S. Elections,* p. 426.

16. *Pennsylvania Reporter and Democratic Herald,* July 27 and October 19, 1832; *Harrisburg Telegraph,* June 6 and July 4, 1832; *Albany Evening Journal,* September 24, 1832; *Harrisburg Pennsylvania Intelligencer,* October 18, 1832; *Harrisburg Chronicle,* October 15, 1832; Mueller, *Whig Party in Pennsylvania,* pp. 12-13; "Memoirs of a Senator from Pennsylvania, Jonathan Roberts, 1771-1854," *Pennsylvania Magazine of History and Biography* 62 (1938): 512-13; *Niles' Register* 43 (October 27, 1832): 136-37.

17. *Gettysburg Anti-Masonic Star and Republican Banner,* October 23 and 30, 1832; *Harrisburg Telegraph,* October 17, 1832; McNeal, "Antimasonic Party of Lancaster County," p. 76; Ellmaker to Stevens, August 16, 1832, in Diffenderiffer, ed., "Politics Seventy-five Years Ago," pp. 40-43; (Philadelphia) *United States Gazette,* October 18, 1832.

18. *Harrisburg Telegraph,* March 28 and July 4, 1832; *Boston Advocate,* March 2, October 26, November 9 and 13, 1832; *Harrisburg Chronicle,* October 8, 1832; *Niles' Register* 43 (November 10, 1832): 171; Diamond, ed., *Guide to U.S. Elections,* p. 266; Herman Hailperin, "Pro-Jackson Sentiment in Pennsylvania, 1820-1828," *Pennsylvania Magazine of History and Biography* 50 (1926): 193-240.

19. *Harrisburg Telegraph,* November 14, 1832; *Boston Advocate,* November 23, 1832; Keller, "Nativism or Sectionalism," p. 44; Andrews, "Antimasonic Movement," p. 263; *Albany Argus,* November 27, 1832; Diamond, ed., *Guide to U.S. Elections,* pp. 266, 426.

20. Snyder, *Jacksonian Heritage,* pp. 31-33; Adams, *Memoirs,* 9:37-38 (entry of November 22-23, 1833); Mueller, *Whig Party in Pennsylvania,* p. 14.

## CHAPTER 8

1. "Masons," 1831-39, Speech and Article Book File, Edward McPherson Papers; Alfred Creigh, *Masonry and Anti-Masonry: A History of Masonry as it Has Existed in Pennsylvania Since 1792* (Philadelphia: Lippincott, Gramboard, 1854), pp. 87-94; Woodley, *Stevens,* pp. 65-69; *Pennsylvania House Journal, 1833-34,* 1:369-70; *Pennsylvania Reporter and Democratic Herald,* February 21, 1834.

2. Eriksson, "Stevens," p. 41; *Pennsylvania House Journal, 1833-34,* 1:414, 437, 454, 548-51, 605, 647; ibid., 2:734-37; *Pennsylvania Senate Journal, 1833-34,* 1:466.

3. Mueller, *Whig Party in Pennsylvania,* pp. 15-18; Snyder, *Jacksonian Heritage,* pp. 45-48; McCormick, *Second American Party System,* p. 143; *Pennsylvania Intelligencer,* May 29, 1834; *Niles' Register* 46 (July 7, 1834): 243.

4. Woodley, *Stevens,* pp. 71-74; *Pennsylvania House Journal, 1834-35,* 1:25, 45, 435-37, 484-85, 557-59, 593, 829-30.

5. Current, *Old Thad Stevens,* pp. 22-24; Snyder, *Jacksonian Heritage,* pp. 50-53;

*Pennsylvania House Journal, 1834-35,* 1:887; *Pennsylvania Senate Journal, 1834-35,* 1:387.

6. McCarthy, "Antimasonic Party," pp. 467-69; Snyder, *Jacksonian Heritage,* pp. 54-62; *Biographical Directory of the American Congress, 1774-1971,* 4th ed., s. v. "Muhlenberg, Henry Augustus Philip"; *Niles' Register* 48 (March 14, 1835): 20-21; ibid., 48 (March 28, 1835), p. 65; ibid., 48 (May 16, 1835), p. 190; ibid., 49 (November 21, 1835): 189.

7. Snyder, *Jacksonian Heritage,* pp. 65-66; Frank Gerrity, "The Masons, the Antimasons and the Pennsylvania Legislature, 1834-1836," *Pennsylvania Magazine of History and Biography* 99 (1975): 184; Mueller, *Whig Party in Pennsylvania,* pp. 18-19; *Pennsylvania Intelligencer,* March 5, 11, and 13, 1835; *United States Gazette,* August 14, 1835.

8. Belohlavek, *Dallas,* p. 58; Snyder, *Jacksonian Heritage,* pp. 67, 222; *Niles' Register* 49 (November 28 and December 5, 1835): 214, 230; Diamond, ed., *Guide to U.S. Elections,* p. 427.

9. Norman D. Brown, *Daniel Webster and the Politics of Availability* (Athens: University of Georgia Press, 1966), pp. 127-28, 135; Snyder, *Jacksonian Heritage,* pp. 68-71.

10. McCarthy, "Antimasonic Party," pp. 180-81; Mueller, *Whig Party in Pennsylvania,* pp. 29-31; *Niles' Register* 49 (December 19, 1835): 287-88; *Pennsylvania Intelligencer,* December 18 and 21, 1835; *Pennsylvania Reporter and Democratic Herald,* December 27, 1835, and January 5, 1836.

11. Gerrity, "Masons, Antimasons," pp. 186, 203; Woodley, *Stevens,* pp. 75-77; *Niles' Register* 49 (December 26, 1835): 291-92; *Harrisburg Telegraph,* February 27 and March 2, 1836; *Pennsylvania Reporter and Democratic Herald,* March 4 and 8, June 10, 1836; *Pennsylvania House Journal, 1835-36,* 1:11, 14, 39, 84-87, 524, 564-70, 628, 636, 643-44; *Pennsylvania Senate Journal, 1835-36,* 1:511, 678, 830, 842, 887.

12. Gerrity, "Masons, Antimasons," pp. 180-85; Snyder, *Jacksonian Heritage,* pp. 72, 80-81.

13. Korngold, *Stevens,* pp. 29-30; William H. Egle, "The Buckshot War," *Pennsylvania Magazine of History and Biography* 23 (1899): 138; *Niles' Register* 49 (January 23 and 30, 1836): 345, 379-81; Pennsylvania General Assembly, House of Representatives, *Report of the Committee Appointed to Investigate the Evils of Freemasonry and other Secret Societies . . .* (Harrisburg: Theo Fenn, 1836), pp. 3-8; Pennsylvania, General Assembly, House of Representatives, *Testimony Taken By the House of Representatives to Investigate the Evils of Freemasonry* (Harrisburg: Theo Fenn, 1836), pp. 33-38 (hereinafter cited as *Testimony Taken By the Committee*); *Pennsylvania Reporter and Democratic Herald,* January 22, 1836.

14. Gerrity, "Masons, Antimasons," p. 191; *Testimony Taken By the Committee,* pp. 4-29, 43-45.

15. Belohlavek, *Dallas,* pp. 58-59, 194; *Pennsylvania House Journal, 1835-36,* 2:221, 234-35, 245-46; *Pennsylvania Reporter and Democratic Herald,* January 15 and 19, 1836; *Gettysburg Anti-Masonic Star and Republican Banner,* January 18, 1836.

16. Gerrity, "Masons, and Antimasons," pp. 187, 194, 197; Belohlavek, *Dallas,* pp.

56-58; *Pennsylvania House Journal, 1835-36,* 2:247-48; *Pennsylvania Reporter and Democratic Herald,* January 29, 1836.

17. Gerrity, "Masons, Antimasons," pp. 195; Egle, *Perseverance Lodge,* pp. 182-83; *Pennsylvania Reporter and Democratic Herald,* January 22, 26, 29, February 5, 1836; *United States Gazette,* January 25, 1836; *Pennsylvania House Journal, 1835-36,* 1:230, 234, 253, 302-12, 315-17; *A Strike for Civil Liberty, the Constitution and the Rights of Man, Exhibited in the Conduct, Letters, Protests and Addresses of a Number of Citizens Summoned to Attend Before a Committee of the House of Representatives, at the City of Harrisburg, Appointed to Investigate the Evils of Freemasonry, During the Session of the General Assembly of Pennsylvania, 1835-36* (Philadelphia: Robert De Silber, 1836), pp. 1-18.

18. Gerrity, "Masons, Antimasons," pp. 199-206; Current, *Old Thad Stevens,* pp. 30-31; Zyckowski, "Antimasonic Party," pp. 38-39; *Albany Argus,* January 28, 1836; *Pennsylvania Reporter and Democratic Herald,* January 22, 1836; *Harrisburg Chronicle,* March 10, 1836; "Antimasonry in the Legislature of Pennsylvania in 1836," *Freemason's Monthly Magazine* 32 (1873): 230.

19. Snyder, *Jacksonian Heritage,* pp. 69, 75-78; Biddle to Stevens, July 3, 1838, in Nicholas Biddle, *Correspondence of Nicholas Biddle Dealing with National Affairs, 1807-1844,* ed. Reginald C. McGrane (Boston: Houghton Mifflin, 1919), p. 315.

20. McCarthy, "Antimasonic Party," pp. 482-83; Mueller, *Whig Party in Pennsylvania,* pp. 32-34; *Niles' Register* 51 (November 26, and December 10, 1836): 195, 226; *Harrisburg Chronicle,* November 23, 1836; Diamond, ed., *Guide to U.S. Elections,* p. 266.

21. Snyder, *Jacksonian Heritage,* pp. 74-75, 102-3; *Pennsylvania House Journal, 1837-38,* 2:17; *Harrisburg Telegraph,* May 27 and October 19, 1837; *Pennsylvania Intelligencer,* March 7, 1838; *United States Gazette,* September 7 and October 11, 1838.

22. Snyder, *Jacksonian Heritage,* pp. 124, 219; Mueller, *Whig Party in Pennsylvania,* 44-45; *Niles' Register* 55 (October 6, 1838): 91; *Harrisburg Telegraph,* March 9, 1838; *United States Gazette,* March 30, 1838.

23. Klein and Hoogenboom, *History of Pennsylvania,* pp. 133-34; McCarthy, "Antimasonic Party," pp. 493-95; *Harrisburg Telegraph,* August 1, September 5, 12, and 14, and October 3, 1838.

24. Klein and Hoogenboom, *History of Pennsylvania,* p. 134; [Sister] M. Theophane Geary, *History of Third Parties in Pennsylvania, 1840-1860* (Washington: Catholic University of America, 1938), p. 9; *Pennsylvania Senate Journal, 1838-39,* pp. 799-821; *Pennsylvania House Journal, 1838-39,* 2:143-44.

25. Mueller, *Whig Party in Pennsylvania,* pp. 51-55; Snyder, *Jacksonian Heritage,* pp. 134-41; Stevens to Edward [?] McPherson, May 24, 1839, Stevens Papers, LC; Citizens of Lancaster County to Stevens, June 8, 1839, ibid.; unsigned vignette, p. 6, Miscellaneous Papers, in ibid.; *Report of the Select Committee Appointed to Inquire into the Cause of an Armed Force, Being Brought to the Capital of Pennsylvania, Whether any Disturbance took Place in the Senate Chamber on the 4th of December, 1838 ...* (Harrisburg: E. Guyer, 1839), pp. 39-62.

26. Eriksson, "Stevens," p. 43; William M. Stuart, "The Antimasonic Phase of Johnson's Impeachment," *Transactions, American Lodge of Research* 2 (1934-38): 150; Stevens to McPherson, June 26, 1867, Stevens Papers, LC.

27. *Pennsylvania State Journal, 1838-39,* 1:1170; McCormick, *Second American Party System,* pp. 144-45; Snyder, *Jacksonian Heritage,* pp. 142-43; *Niles' Register* 57 (September 14, 1839): 46-47.

28. Snyder, *Jacksonian Heritage,* pp. 151-52, 178-79; McNeal, "Antimasonic Party in Lancaster County," pp. 114-17; *Niles' Register* 65 (December 16, 1843): 244; Scott to Stevens, November 13, 1841, Stevens Papers, LC.

29. Harvey, *A History of Lodge No. 61,* p. 73; Barratt and Sachse, *Freemasonry in Pennsylvania,* 3:200, 277-78; Thomas Kittera to Committee of Correspondence, September 1, 1829, in Joshua Lyte, comp., *Reprint of the Minutes of the Grand Lodge of Free and Accepted Masons of Pennsylvania* 6 (1828-39): 62; George R. Welchans and Andrew H. Hershey, *History of Lodge No. 43, F. & A.M. of Lancaster, Pennsylvania, 1785-1835 . . .* (Lancaster: By the Lodge, 1936), pp. 148-49.

30. Lyte, comp., *Reprint, Minutes of the Grand Lodge of Pennsylvania* 6 (1838-39): 6, 27, 273, passim; Eriksson, "Effects of Antimasonry," p. 75; Barratt and Sachse, *Freemasonry in Pennsylvania,* 3:278-79.

31. Lyte, comp., *Reprint, Minutes of the Grand Lodge of Pennsylvania,* 6:v, 324-44, 360; Joseph Kingsbury to Nisbet, December 14, 1839, in ibid., p. 497; Barratt and Sachse, *Freemasonry in Pennsylvania,* 3:343-44.


CHAPTER 9

1. *Proceedings, Antimasonic State Convention, Massachusetts, 1829-30,* p. 7; Darling, *Political Changes,* pp. 86-90.

2. Blakeslee, "Antimasonic Party," chap. 7, pp. 12, 22-24; *Boston Advocate,* June 8, 1835; *Abstract, Proceedings of the First State Convention,* pp. 3, 11, 13, 20-21.

3. Darling, *Political Changes,* p. 92; "Anti-Masonry in Faneuil Hall in 1830: Alleged Masonic Riot," *Freemasons Monthly Magazine* 32 (1873): 194-98.

4. McCarthy, "Antimasonic Party," p. 517; *An Abstract of the Proceedings of [the Second] State Convention of Massachusetts . . . Boston, May 19 & 20, 1831* (Boston: Office of the Boston Press, 1831), pp. 3, 61-63; Phelps to Lincoln, July 7, 1831, Levi Lincoln Papers, MaHS.

5. Darling, *Political Changes,* pp. 93-97; McCarthy, "Antimasonic Party," pp. 517-18; *Biographical Directory of the American Congress, 1777-1971,* 4th ed., s.v. "Lathrop, Samuel"; *Niles' Register* 41 (October 22, 1831): 152; *Boston Advocate,* January 6 and 26, 1832; Webster to Henry Clay, October 5, 1831, in Wiltse, ed., *Webster Papers,* 3:129; Webster to Ambrose Spencer, November 16, 1831, in ibid., pp. 134-35; Diamond, ed., *Guide to U.S. Elections,* p. 412.

6. *Dictionary of American Biography,* s.v. "Hallett, Benjamin Franklin"; *Historical Catalog of Brown University, 1864-1914* (Providence: Brown University, 1914), p. 95; Frederick Freeman, *The History of Cape Cod: Annals of the Thirteen Towns of Barnstable County,* 2 vols. (Boston: W. H. Piper, 1869), 1:706-10, 2:339-40.

7. *Boston Advocate,* December 27, 1831; Pessen, *Jacksonian American,* rev. ed., p. 209.

8. "Biographical Sketch of R. W. Charles W. Moore," *New England Freemason* 1 (January 1874): 2-3, 10-11; *Boston Advocate,* January 3 and 10, 1832.

9. Chase, *Emergence,* p. 140; [Proceedings] *Fourth Antimasonic State Convention ... of Massachusetts ... Boston, Sept. 11, 12 & 13, 1833 ...* (Boston: Jonathan Howe, 1833), p. 44; Darling, *Political Changes,* pp. 104-5; *Boston Advocate,* September 8 and 11, November 6, 8, and 23, December 6, 14, and 25, 1832; Diamond, ed., *Guide to U.S. Elections,* pp. 266, 412.

10. McCarthy, "Antimasonic Party," p. 381; Erik McKinley Eriksson, "John Quincy Adams: Anti-Masonic Letter Writer," *Grand Lodge Bulletin, Grand Lodge of Iowa* 27 (1926): 89-93; Bemis, *John Quincy Adams and the Union,* pp. 276, 281-82; Daniel Walker Howe, *The Political Culture of the American Whigs* (Chicago: University of Chicago Press, 1979), p. 55; Adams, *Letters on the Masonic Institution,* pp. 2-14; Adams, *Memoirs,* 7:345 (entry of October 25, 1827), 8:399 (entry of August 27, 1831).

11. Adams to John B. Davis, April 6, 1832, in *Niles' Register* 45 (October 5, 1833): 86; Adams, *Letters on the Masonic Institution,* pp. 203, 243; Adams, *Memoirs,* 8:364 (entry of May 31, 1831), 8:366-67 (entry of June 6, 1831), 8:379 (entry of July 7, 1831), 9:16-17 (entry of September 26, 1833).

12. Darling, *Political Changes,* pp. 16-17, 30, 105-8; Adams, *Memoirs,* 9:6 (entry of July 10, 1833), 9:11 (entry of July 30, 1833), 9:14 (entry of September 14, 1833).

13. Bemis, *John Quincy Adams and the Union,* pp. 297-98; *Proceedings, Fourth Antimasonic State Convention, Massachusetts, 1833,* pp. 3, 24-25, 28-29, 40; *Boston Advocate,* September 13 and 14, 1833; Adams, *Memoirs,* 9:14 (entry of September 14, 1833), 9:14-15 (entry of September 20, 1833).

14. Darling, *Political Changes,* pp. 108-14; Adams, *Letters on the Masonic Institution,* pp. 256-58; *Boston Advocate,* September 17 and 19, 1833.

15. Adams, *Memoirs,* 9:16 (entry of September 23, 1833); *Boston Advocate,* September 18, October 25, and November 11, 1833; Adams to Levi Lincoln, December 5, 1833, Lincoln Papers; *Boston Post,* November 5 and 26, 1833; *Adams and Lathrop,* Antimasonic Broadsides, MaHS; *New England Antimasonic Almanac, 1833,* p. 27.

16. Bemis, *John Quincy Adams and the Union,* pp. 299-300; *Boston Post,* November 18, 1833, and January 6, 1834; *Boston Advocate,* November 22, 1833; Diamond, ed., *Guide to U.S. Elections,* p. 412.

17. Adams, *Memoirs,* 9:39 (entry of November 26, 1833), 9:58-59 (entry of December 22, 1833), 9:59 (entry of December 24, 1833), 9:62-63 (entry of December 31, 1833), 9:64-67 (entry of January 2, 1834); *Boston Advocate,* January 2, 9, and 10, 1834.

18. Bemis, *John Quincy Adams and the Union,* pp. 299-304; Adams, *Memoirs,* 9:114-15 (entry of March 27, 1834); Adams, *Letters on the Masonic Institution,* pp. 204-18.

19. "Sketch of Charles W. Moore," p. 4; *Boston Advocate,* March 1, 1831, *Proceedings, Grand Lodge of Massachusetts, 1826-1844* (Boston: Clafflin, n.d.), p. 241.

20. "Sketch of Charles W. Moore," pp. 5-9; *Proceedings, Grand Lodge of Massachusetts, 1826-1844,* pp. 241, 319-21, 385; *Boston Advocate,* March 1, 1833 and January 3, 1834; *Boston Post,* January 25 and 29, 1834.

21. Darling, *Political Changes,* pp. 119-20; Nathans, *Webster and Jacksonian Democracy,* p. 87; *Boston Advocate,* February 20 and March 9, 1834; *Boston Post,* January 1 and 10, 1834; Webster to Levi Lincoln, January 8, 1834, in Wiltse, ed., *Webster Papers,* 3:300; Webster to White, January 10, 1834, in ibid., pp. 305-6.

22. Ershkowitz, "Anti-Masonry," p. 12; Adams, *Memoirs,* 9:75 (entry of January 13, 1834); Nathans, *Webster and Jacksonian Democracy,* p. 88.

23. McCarthy, "Antimasonic Party," p. 522; Adams, *Memoirs,* 9:104 (entry of February 27, 1834); *An Investigation into Freemasonry by a Joint Committee of the Legislature of Massachusetts* (Boston: Dutton and Wentworth, 1834), pp. 1, 11, 49, 63-64, 71-76; *Boston Post,* January 31, and February 1, 1834.

24. [E. H. Cobb], "A Reminiscence of the Dark Days of Anti-Masonry," *Philadelphia Keystone* 11 (July 21, 1877): 21; *Boston Post,* January 28, 29, 30, 31, February 14 and 24, and March 13, 1834; *Laws of the Commonwealth of Massachusetts, Passed at the Several Sessions of the General Court, Beginning Jan. 1834 and Ending April 1836* 13 (Boston: Dutton and Wentworth, 1836): 88-89.

25. *Boston Advocate,* July 1, 1834, and January 31, 1835; [Cobb], "A Reminiscence of the Dark Days of Anti-Masonry," p. 21.

26. Nathans, *Webster and Jacksonian Democracy,* p. 87; Adams, *Memoirs,* 9:63-66 (entry of January 2, 1834), 9:70-71 (entry of January 7, 1834), 9:74-75 (entry of January 13, 1834), 9:103-4 (entry of February 28, 1834); *Boston Post,* January 6, 1834.

27. Nathans, *Webster and Jacksonian Democracy,* pp. 84-85; Morton to Simpson, February 17, 1834, Marcus Morton Letterbook, vol. 1, MaHS; *Boston Advocate,* July 1, 1834; *Resolutions Adopted by the Antimasonic Members of the Legislature of Massachusetts, opposed to the Nomination of Martin Van Buren and Richard M. Johnson, for President and Vice President of the U.S. At a Meeting held in the Chamber of the House of Representatives, March 1, 1836* (Boston: P. Horton, 1836), p. 16.

28. Nathans, *Webster and Jacksonian Democracy,* p. 89; *Boston Advocate,* March 21, and October 17, 1834; Adams, *Memoirs,* 9:184 (entry of September 6, 1834); [Proceedings], *Fifth Antimasonic State Convention, for 1834 . . . for Massachusetts, Held at Boston, September 10, and 11, 1834 . . .* (Boston: Leonard W. Kimball, 1834), pp. 8-12, 31, 34-36.

29. Darling, *Political Changes,* pp. 126-28; *Boston Advocate,* October 11 and 17, November 11, 13, and 18, 1834; Hallett to Bancroft, November 2, 1834, George Bancroft Papers, MaHS; Diamond, ed., *Guide to U.S. Elections,* pp. 412, 562.

30. Darling, *Political Changes,* pp. 185-87; Bemis, *John Quincy Adams and the Union,* pp. 311, 313-14; *Boston Advocate,* February 26, March 2 and 6, 1835.

31. Ershkowitz, "Anti-Masonry," p. 13; *Boston Advocate,* June 25 and November 1, 1835.

32. Darling, *Political Changes,* pp. 191-93n; *Niles' Register* 49 (November 21, 1835): 190; *Boston Advocate,* November 1, 6, and 8, 1835.

33. *Boston Advocate,* December 23, 1835, January 25 and 30, February 1, March 22, and May 4, 1836; *Resolutions Adopted by the Antimasonic Members of the Legislature of Massachusetts,* pp. 3-4, 6, 10, 14, 17-18; Diamond, ed., *Guide to U.S. Elections,* p. 266.

34. Ershkowitz, "Anti-Masonry," p. 14; Martin B. Duberman, "Charles Francis Adams, Antimasonry and the Presidential Election of 1836," *Mid-America* 43 (1961): 123-24; Morton to Hallett, August 3, 1836; Morton Letterbook, vol. 1; Adams, *Memoirs,* 9:313 (entry of November 18, 1836); *Boston Advocate,* September 1 and 30, October 3, 13, and 19, November 1 and 21, 1836; *Albany Evening Journal,* May 7, 1836; Diamond, ed., *Guide to U.S. Elections,* p. 266.

35. *Boston Advocate,* June 8 and 16, 1835; *Proceedings of the Grand Lodge of Massachusetts, 1826-1844,* pp. 59, 189-90, 345-46; Eriksson, "Effects of Anti-Masonry," p. 73.

## CHAPTER 10

1. *Boston Advocate,* February, 3, 1834, and January 30, 1835; Blakeslee, "Antimasonic Party," chap. 7, p. 36; Benson, "A Union of Men," pp. 45-47. Benson observes that it would be "unrewarding" to analyze the distribution of Antimasonic votes "geographically," but she does note that Antimasonry was not a "country party," as historians previously believed.

2. McCormick, *Second American Party System,* pp. 77-78.

3. McCormick, *Second American Party System,* pp. 78, 85; Benson, "A Union of Men," pp. 2-5.

4. Eriksson, "Effects of Anti-Masonry," p. 73; Edward Field, ed., *State of Rhode Island and Providence Plantation at the End of the Century: A History,* 3 vols. (Boston and Syracuse: Mason Publishing, 1902), 3:496-500, 507.

5. Benson, "A Union of Men," pp. 13-17; *Pawtucket* (Mass.) *Herald and Independent Inquirer,* November 12 and 26, December 3, 1828; (Newport) *Anti-Masonick Rhode Islander* April 25, November 18 and 25, 1829; (Providence) *Rhode Island American,* August 31, 1827.

6. Chase, *Emergence,* p. 141; Benson, "A Union of Men," pp. 9, 18-23, 25, 27-28, 37; *Providence Free Press and Pawtucket Herald,* March 25, April 1 and 15, and May 13, 1830; *Rhode Island American,* April 6 and 23, May 7 and 11, September 17 and 21, October 8 and 12, November 16, 1830.

7. Blakeslee, "Antimasonic Party," chap. 7, pp. 36-38; Benson, "A Union of Men," pp. 30, 37-38; *Rhode Island American,* December 31, 1830.

8. Benson, "A Union of Men," pp. 37-44; *Rhode Island American,* January 28, February 10, March 11, April 12, and May 6, 1831; Francis to J. R. Waterman, February 10, 1831, John R. Waterman-Warwick Papers, RIHS; Diamond, ed., *Guide to U.S. Elections,* p. 427.

9. Henry W. Rugg, *History of Freemasonry in Rhode Island* (Providence: E. L. Freeman, 1893), p. 97; Benson, "A Union of Men," pp. 52-56; *Proceedings of the Rhode Island Anti-Masonic State Convention, September 14, 1831* (Providence: Office of the *Daily Advertiser,* 1831), pp. 3-8; *Providence Republican Herald,* October 15, 1831; *Providence Journal,* September 15, 1831.

10. Benson, "A Union of Men," pp. 46-49; *Rhode Island American,* January 14 and June 7, 1831.

11. Blakeslee, "Antimasonic Party," chap. 7, p. 38; *Rhode Island American,* November 8 and 29, 1831; *Providence Journal,* January 23 and 27, 1832.

12. Field, *Rhode Island,* 1:322; ibid., 3:509-10; *Rhode Island American,* December 9, 13, and 20, 1831; *Providence Journal,* December 10 and 12, 1831.

13. Benson, "A Union of Men," pp. 59, 63; *Report of the Committee Appointed by the General Assembly of Rhode Island to Investigate the Charges Against Freemasonry & Masons in the Said State ...* (Providence: William Marshall, 1832), pp. 7, 11-12; Benjamin F. Hallett et al., *Legislative Investigation into Masonry ...* (Boston: Office

of the *Daily Advocate,* 1832), p. 31; *Providence Republican Herald,* December 3, 1831.

14. Benson, "A Union of Men," pp. 59-61; *Rhode Island American,* January 24, 1832; *Report of the Committee,* pp. 5-20, 35, 43-57, 68-72.

15. Benson, "A Union of Men," pp. 61-63, 142; Field, *Rhode Island,* 1:322; ibid., 3:510-11; *Rhode Island American,* December 20, 1831, January 24 and 31, February 3 and 10, 1832; William Sprague, Jr., *An Official Report, by William Sprague, Jr., One of the Committee of the House of Representatives of Rhode Island, Upon the Subject of Masonry* (Providence: Office of the *Daily Advertiser,* 1832), pp. 4, 16.

16. Rugg, *Freemasonry in Rhode Island,* pp. 101-5; *Declaration of the Freemasons of Rhode Island* (n.p., 1833), p. 12; *Providence Journal,* January 2, 1832.

17. Benson, "A Union of Men," pp. 65, 71-75; Benjamin Knight, Sr., *History of the Sprague Families of Rhode Island, Cotton Manufacturers and Calico Printers from William I to William IV* (Santa Cruz, Calif.: H. Coffin, 1881), pp. 11-16, 19, 21-25.

18. Benson, "A Union of Men," pp. 76-79; Philip A. Grant, Jr., "Party Chaos Embroils Rhode Island," *Rhode Island History* 26 (1967): 114; *Providence Journal,* February 24, March 30, April 12 and 19, and May 3, 1832; *Rhode Island American,* April 20, May 1 and 4, 1832; Diamond, ed., *Guide to U.S. Elections,* p. 427.

19. Benson, "A Union of Men," pp. 80-93; *Providence Journal,* May 4, 19, and 25, June 9 and 26, July 4 and 21, August 30, and November 24, 1832; *Rhode Island American,* August 14 and 31, 1832; Patrick T. Conley, *Democracy in Decline: Rhode Island's Constitutional Development, 1796-1841* (Providence: Rhode Island Historical Association, 1977), p. 266.

20. Benson, "A Union of Men," pp. 88-94; *Rhode Island American,* August 3, November 20, 23, and 29, 1832; *Providence Journal,* November 28, 1832; Diamond, ed., *Guide to U.S. Elections,* p. 266.

21. Benson, "A Union of Free Men," pp. 94, 102-5; Allen to Francis, January 5, 1833, John Brown Francis Collection, RIHS; *Rhode Island American,* December 18, 1832; ibid., January 22 and 25, 1833; *Boston Advocate,* January 24, 1833; Journal [unpublished], Rhode Island House of Representatives, 1831-33, p. 602 (State Archives, Providence); Journal [unpublished], Rhode Island Senate, entry for January 22, 1833 (State Archives); Acts and Resolves [unpublished], General Assembly of Rhode Island 38 (1830-33): 133 (State Archives).

22. *Rhode Island American,* January 11 and 22, 1833; *Providence Rebublican Herald,* January 19, 1833; Christopher Allen to John Brown Francis, January 5, 1833, Francis Collection.

23. Benson, "A Union of Men," pp. 107-8; Cowell to Francis, February 7, 1833, Francis Collection; Pearce to Potter, February 3, 1833, Elisha R. Potter Papers, RIHS; *Biographical Cyclopedia of Rhode Island,* 1st ed., s.v. "Francis, John Brown."

24. Benson, "A Union of Men," pp. 108-10; Benjamin Hazard to Francis, March 10, 1833, Francis Collection; Hazard to Nicholas Brown, March 10, 1833, ibid.; Moses Brown Ives to Francis, March 14, 1833, ibid.; Thomas P. Ives to Francis, March 20, 1833, ibid.; Sprague, Jr., to Francis, April 1, 1833, ibid.; Benjamin Cowell to Elisha R. Potter, March 15, 1833, Potter Papers; Allen to Potter, March 27, 1833, ibid.; Dutee J. Pearce to Potter, April 4, 1833, Ibid.; *Providence Republican Herald,* March 20 and April 3, 1833.

25. Benson, "A Union of Men," pp. 110-12; *Providence Republican Herald,* March 23, April 3, 6, 13, and 17, and July 6, 1833; *Providence Microcosm,* March 23, 1833; *Boston Advocate,* April 25, 1833; Francis to Hallett, April 16, 1833, Francis Collection.

26. McCarthy, "Antimasonic Party," pp. 552-53; Benson, "A Union of Men," pp. 113-15; *Providence Republican Herald,* May 4, 1833; Diamond, ed., *Guide to U.S. Elections,* p. 427.

27. Benson, "A Union of Men," pp. 118-19; Pearce to Daniel Webster, August 11, 1833, Daniel Webster Papers, Dartmouth College; Francis to Christopher G. Champlin, August 10, 1833, Francis Collection; Francis to Pearce, August 5, 1833, ibid.

28. McCarthy, "Antimasonic Party," pp. 552-53; Benson, "A Union of Men," pp. 120-21; *Providence Microcosm,* August 24, 1833, Nathan B. Sprague to Potter, August 22, 1833, Potter Papers; Sprague Jr., to John Brown Francis, August 17, 1833, Francis Collection.

29. Benson, "A Union of Men," pp. 121-24; *Providence Microcosm,* August 24, 1833; *Providence Republican Herald,* August 31, October 2 and 5, November 9, 20, and 23, 1833; Diamond, ed., *Guide to U.S. Elections,* p. 560; Pearce to Potter, August 2, 1833, Potter Papers; Allen to Potter, August 19, 1833; ibid.; George Church to E. R. Potter, Jr., December 6, 1833, ibid.

30. Field, *Rhode Island,* 1:324-25, 3:513; *Providence Republican Herald,* July 6 and November 6, 1833, January 22 and 25, 1834; *Boston Advocate,* September 16, 1833.

31. Benson, "A Union of Men," pp. 126-27; *Providence Republican Herald,* January 25 and 29, 1834.

32. *Boston Advocate,* February 3 and 19, 1834; *Painesville* (Ohio) *Telegraph,* February 21, 1834; *Providence Republican Herald,* February 5, 1834; *Proceedings... of the Grand Lodge of Rhode Island..., 1834* (Providence: Cranston and Hammond, 1834), p. 8; Journal, Rhode Island House of Representatives, 1833-34, pp. 788-89; Journal, Rhode Island Senate, entry for February 1, 1834, Acts and Resolves ... of Rhode Island, 39 (1833-35): 44.

33. Benson, "A Union of Men," pp. 142-46; Rugg, *Freemasonry in Rhode Island,* pp. 106-8; *Proceedings, Grand Lodge of Rhode Island, 1834,* pp. 6-8; W. M. Cunningham, *History of Freemasonry in Ohio From 1791 ... to 1844, Inclusive* (Cincinnati: J. H. Bromwell, 1909), pp. 334-37; *Providence Republican Herald,* May 14, 1834.

34. *Providence Republican Herald,* November 1 and 5, December 27, 1834; *Boston Advocate,* January 30, 1835; Journal, Rhode Island House of Representatives, entry for January 21, 1835.

35. *Providence Republican Herald,* July 15, 1835.

36. *Providence Republican Herald,* March 1, 15, 26, and 29, April 2, 1834; *Providence Journal,* March 15, 18, 19, 24, 27, and 31, April 2 and 3, 1834.

37. Ershkowitz, "Anti-Masonry," p. 15; *Providence Republican Herald,* April 5, 12, and 19, May 10, 1834; *Providence Journal,* April 7, 11, and 14, 1834; *Niles' Register* 46 (April 26, 1834): 132; Francis to Byron Diman, April 4, 1834, Francis Collection; Diamond, ed., *Guide to U.S. Elections,* p. 427.

38. Benson, "A Union of Men," pp. 143-46; *Providence Republican Herald,* August 30, September and October 25, 1834; ibid., January 28, February 21, March 7 and 28, 1835.

39. *Proceedings of the Antimasonic State Convention, held Jan. 16, 1835: And the*

*Proceedings of their Nominating Committee, Held at the State House in Providence; February 22, 1835* (Providence: n.p., 1835), p. 5; *Providence Journal,* February 28, March 6 and 11, April 6, 1835; *Providence Republican Herald,* March 28, April 11 and 14, 1835.

40. Benson, "A Union of Men," pp. 151-56; Grant, "Party Chaos Embroils Rhode Island," pp. 29-31; *Providence Republican Herald,* May 13 and 16, July 15 and 22, August 1, 22, and 29, 1835; Diamond, ed., *Guide to U.S. Elections,* pp. 427, 564.

41. *Providence Republican Herald,* December 9, 1835; Allen to Francis, February 5, 1835, and July 2, 1837, Francis Collection.

42. *Niles' Register* 50 (April 30, 1836): 145; *Providence Republican Herald,* March 5 and 9, April 15, May 7, and October 5, 1836; Diamond, ed., *Guide to U.S. Elections,* pp. 266, 467.

43. Benson, "A Union of Men," pp. 161-67; *Providence Republican Herald,* February 1, March 15, May 6, June 24, July 1, 8, 12, 22, August 19, 23, and 29, September 2, 1837; Allen to Francis, July 2 and August 8, Francis Collection.

44. Diamond, ed., *Guide to U.S. Elections,* p. 427; *Providence Journal,* August 31, 1837, January 12 and 15, February, 7, 12, 16, 22, 23, and 27, April 2, 10, and 18, and May 5, 1838; *Biographical Cyclopedia of Rhode Island,* 1st ed., s.v., "Sprague, William, Jr."; Allen to Francis, December 22, 1837, Francis Collection; E. R. Potter, Jr., to Francis, April 15, 1838, ibid.

45. Benson, "A Union of Men," pp. 172-75.

46. Rugg, *Freemasonry in Rhode Island,* pp. 88-89; 111, 108-9; *Proceedings, Grand Lodge of Rhode Island, 1834,* pp. 8, 12.

CHAPTER 11

1. Carl Witke, ed., *History of Ohio,* 6 vols. (Columbus: Ohio State Archeological and Historical Society, 1941), vol. 3, *The Passing of the Frontier,* by Francis P. Weisenburger, p. 264; Durkee, "Anti-Masonic Movement," pp. 10-14; *Painesville Telegraph,* March 7, 1828, and March 27, 1829.

2. Durkee, "Anti-Masonic Movement," pp. 12-21; *Painesville Telegraph,* September 22 and October 20, 1829, February 25, March 2 and 9, April 23, 1830.

3. Durkee, "Anti-Masonic Movement," pp. 18-25, 31; *Proceedings of the Ohio Antimasonic Convention, Held at Canton Ohio, July 21-22, 1830* (n.p., n.d.), pp. 1-16; *Painesville Telegraph,* July 13 and 27, 1830.

4. McCarthy, "Antimasonic Party," pp. 526-27; Weisenburger, *Passing of the Frontier,* p. 265; *Painesville Telegraph,* September 21, October 5, 19, and 26, 1830.

5. Weisenburger, *Passing of the Frontier,* pp. 265-66; *Journal of Proceedings, Ohio Antimasonic Convention, Columbus, January 11, 1831* (Milan, Ohio: *Milan Free Press,* 1831), pp. 3, 15-17; *Painesville Telegraph,* November 2, 1830, February 8 and October 18, 1831; (Columbus) *Ohio State Journal,* January 12, October 27, 1831.

6. Willis Thornton, "Gentile and Saint at Kirtland," *Ohio State Archaeological and Historical Quarterly* 63 (1954): 13-14; *Painesville Telegraph,* February 15, 1831.

7. Durkee, "Anti-Masonic Movement," pp. 34-36; *Painsville Telegraph,* June 21, 1832; *Ohio State Journal,* June 23, 1832; *Ravenna Star,* March 22, June 21 and 28, July 3, 1832.

8. Weisenburger, *Passing of the Frontier,* pp. 268-69; Durkee, "Anti-Masonic Movement," pp. 36-37; *Ohio State Journal,* September 15, 1832; *Ravenna Star,* September 13 and 20, 1832; *Sandusky Clarion,* September 19, 1832,

9. *Painesville Telegraph,* June 21, 1832, citing *Ohio Register,* n.d.; *Ravenna Star,* June 28, August 30, September 13, 20, and 23, October 4, 1832; *Ohio State Journal,* September 19, 1832.

10. Blakeslee, "Antimasonic Party," chap. 8, pp. 54, 58; *Painesville Telegraph,* October 5 and 12, 1832; *Ravenna Star,* October 11 and 18, 1832; *Ohio State Journal,* October 20, 1832; Diamond, ed., *Guide to U.S. Elections,* p. 424.

11. McCormick, *Second American Party System,* p. 266; Blakeslee, "Antimasonic Party," chap. 8, pp. 41-44; *Niles' Register* 43 (October 20, 1832): 118; ibid., 43 (October 27, 1832), p. 138; *Painesville Telegraph,* October 27, 1832; *Ohio State Journal,* October 19, 1832, *Ravenna Star,* November 1, 1832.

12. Durkee, "Anti-Masonic Movement," pp. 40-41; citing *Xenia Free Press,* October 28, and November 3, 1832; *Ravenna Star,* November 1, 1832.

13. Durkee, "Anti-Masonic Movement," p. 42; *Painesville Telegraph,* October 25, and November 1, 1832; *Ravenna Star,* November 1, 1832; *Ohio State Journal,* October 27, 1832.

14. Weisenburger, *Passing of the Frontier,* pp. 270-71; Diamond, ed., *Guide to U.S. Elections,* p. 266; *Ravenna Star,* November 8, 15, and 29, 1832; *Ohio State Journal,* November 10 and 17, 1832.

15. Durkee, "Anti-Masonic Movement," pp. 44-45; *Ravenna Star,* January 17 and March 24, 1832; *Painesville Telegraph,* March 1 and 29, 1833.

16. *Ravenna Star,* March 24, April 11 (citing *Ohio Register,* n.d.), June 27, August 15 and 22, and September 19, 1833; *Painesville Telegraph,* May 10, September 13 and 27, 1833.

17. *Painesville Telegraph,* October 4, 7, 11, 18, November 29, December 6, 1833; *Ravenna Star,* October 10 and December 12, 1833.

18. Weisenburger, *Passing of the Frontier,* p. 320; Durkee, "Anti-Masonic Movement," pp. 44-45; *Painesville Telegraph,* January 10, February 17, April 19, May 2, September 5, and October 18, 1834.

19. Weisenburger, *Passing of the Frontier,* p. 320; Durkee, "Anti-Masonic Movement," pp. 45-46, 51; *Ravenna Star,* March 27, 1835.

20. Cunningham, *History of Freemasonry in Ohio,* pp. 327-52; Eriksson, "Effects of Antimasonry," pp. 75-76, 104; *Proceedings of the Grand Lodge ... of Ohio ... From 1808 to 1842, Inclusive* (Columbus: Follett, Foster, 1857), pp. 221-340; *Ohio State Journal,* June 9, 1832.

21. Lipson, *Freemasonry in Connecticut,* pp. 1, 271, 277, 280-82; Jarvis Means Morse, *A Neglected Period of Connecticut History, 1818-1850* (New Haven: Yale University Press, 1933), p. 106; James R. Case, "Avery Allyn—Recreant Knight," *Knight Templar* 26 (1980): 21-22.

22. Blakeslee, "Antimasonic Party," chap. 7, p. 33; Chase, *Emergence,* p. 141; Lipson, *Freemasonry in Connecticut,* pp. 296-97, 301; Diamond, ed., *Guide to U.S. Elections,* p. 401.

23. Morse, *A Neglected Period,* pp. 106, 108-9; Diamond, ed., *Guide to U.S. Elections,* p. 401.

24. Morse, *A Neglected Period,* pp. 112, 114; Diamond, ed., *Guide to U.S. Elections,* pp. 265-66, 401; Lipson, *Freemasonry in Connecticut,* p. 303; *Biographical Directory of the American Congress, 1774-1791,* 4th ed., s.v. "Smith, Nathan" and "Willey, Calvin"; *Boston Advocate,* November 10, 1832.

25. Morse, *A Neglected Period,* pp. 115-16; Lipson, *Freemasonry in Connecticut,* pp. 307-8; *Niles' Register* 44 (April 27, 1833): 131; Diamond, ed., *Guide to U.S. Elections,* p. 401.

26 Lipson, *Freemasonry in Connecticut,* pp. 304-10; ibid., citing *Memorial Against the Masonic Incorporation of Connecticut: Together with the Report and Some of the Debates in the General Assembly, May, 1832* (n.p., n.d.), pp. 1-4; [Alexander Ogle, Jr.], *Truth's Proofs that Masonic Oaths Do Not Impose Any Obligations* (Norwich, Conn.: L. H. Young, 1830), pp. 3-8, 13.

27. Morse, *A Neglected Period,* pp. 293-95; Diamond, ed., *Guide to U.S. Elections,* p. 401; *Niles' Register* 46 (April 26, 1834): 132; ibid., 46 (May 3, 1834), p. 150; ibid., 48 (May 16, 1835): 186; *Boston Advocate,* March 5 and 28, April 29, 1835.

28. Lipson, *Freemasonry in Connecticut,* pp. 305-6, 325-27; James R. Case, "Freemasonry in Connecticut," pt. 5, "Depression and Recovery, 1816-1845"; *Appendix, Proceedings of the Grand Lodge of . . . Connecticut, 1958* (n.p., 1958), pp. 9, 13.

29. Donald B. Cole, *Jacksonian Democracy in New Hampshire, 1800-1851* (Cambridge, Mass.: Harvard University Press, 1970), pp. 137-39, 174-75; *Boston Advocate,* May 27 and June 11, 1833; Diamond, ed., *Guide to U.S. Elections,* pp. 266, 419.

30. *Proceedings, U.S. Antimasonic Convention, Baltimore, 1831,* p. 85; Blakeslee, "Antimasonic Party," chap. 9, pp. 52-53; Chase, *Emergence,* p. 141; *Boston Advocate,* July 13, November 5 and 7, 1832; *Niles' Register* 43 (December 1, 1832): 213; ibid., 47 (October 4, 1834): 60; ibid., 48 (January 24, 1835), p. 356; Diamond, ed., *Guide to U.S. Elections,* pp. 266, 410.

31. Frederick M. Herrmann, "Anti-Masonry in New Jersey," *New Jersey History* 91 (1973): 149-50, 152-57.

32. Chase, *Emergence,* p. 142; Herrmann, "Anti-Masonry in New Jersey," pp. 152-54, 158-62.

33. Herrman, "Anti-Masonry in New Jersey," pp. 159-60; Duane Lockhard, *The New Jersey Governor: A Study in Political Power,* New Jersey Historical Series 17 (Princeton, N.J.: D. Van Nostrand, 1964), pp. 36-38, 52.

34. McCarthy, "Antimasonic Party," p. 555; Herrmann, "Anti-Masonry in New Jersey," pp. 162-65; Jesse B. Anthony, "The Morgan Excitement," in *History of the Ancient and Honorable Fraternity of Free and Accepted Masons, and Concordant Orders,* ed. Henry L. Stillson (Boston: Fraternity Publishing, 1891), p. 530; Diamond, ed., *Guide to U.S. Elections,* pp. 266, 557, 562.

35. Alec R. Gilpin, *The Territory of Michigan, 1805-1837* (East Lansing: Michigan State University Press, 1970), pp. 63, 75, 84-85, 94-95, 140-41; Formisano, *Birth of Mass Parties,* pp. 22-23, 46, 61-63, 66, 79-80.

36. Formisano, *Birth of Mass Parties,* pp. 61-64; Gilpin, *Territory of Michigan,* p. 94; *Proceedings, U.S. Antimasonic Convention, Philadelphia, 1831,* p. 71; *Biographical Directory of the American Congress, 1774-1971,* 4th ed., s.v. "Biddle, John."

37. Gilpin, *Territory of Michigan,* pp. 139-40, 150; Formisano, *Birth of Mass Parties,* pp. 64-65.

38. Formisano, *Birth of Mass Parties,* pp. 51, 71, 104; Holt, "Anti-Masonic and Know-Nothing Parties," pp. 590-91.

39. Eriksson, "Effects of Anti-Masonry," pp. 33, 76, 83; Frank B. Woodford, *Lewis Cass: The Last Jeffersonian* (1950; reprint ed., New York: Octagon Books, 1973), p. 173; Lou B. Winsor, "Masonry in Michigan," *Michigan History Magazine* 20 (1936): 282, 289-90; Foster Pratt, "Historical Sketch of Early Masonry in Michigan," *Grand Lodge of Michigan Proceedings, 1826-1860* (n.p., n.d.), pp. 36-39.

40. McCarthy, "Antimasonic Party," p. 556; Eriksson, "Effects of Anti-Masonry," p. 76; Diamond, ed., *Guide to U.S. Elections,* p. 266.

41. Arthur Loyd Collins, "The Anti-Masonic Movement in Early Missouri," *Missouri Historical Review* 39 (1944): 45-50.

42. Clement Eaton, *The Freedom-Of-Thought Struggle in the Old South,* 2nd ed. rev. (New York: Harper and Row, 1964), pp. 335-52; the quotation appears on p. 352.

43. Chase, *Emergence,* p. 145; McCarthy, "Antimasonic Party," p. 556; Erik McKinley Eriksson, "Political Anti-Masonry, 1827-1843," *Builder* 12 (1926): 357.

44. H. B. Grant, comp., *Doings of the Grand Lodge of Kentucky . . . 1800-1900* (Louisville: Masonic Home Book and Job Office, 1900), pp. 130-60; J. Winston Coleman, *Masonry in the Bluegrass: Being an Authentic Account of Masonry in Lexington and Fayette County, Kentucky, 1782-1933* (Lexington: Transylvania Press, 1933), pp. 116, 209, 224; Albert W. Bryant, "The Anti-Masonic Movement, Particularly in Lexington," *Proceedings, Lexington Historical Society* 4 (1912): 39-47; Charles Snow Guthrie, *Kentucky Freemasonry, 1788-1978: The Grand Lodge and the Men Who Made It* (Masonic Home, Ky.: Grand Lodge of Kentucky, F. & A.M., 1981), pp. 71-72; *Kentucky Gazette,* January 30, 1829; *Louisville Public Advertiser,* December 31, 1829.


CHAPTER 12

1. Roseboom, *History of Presidential Elections,* p. 112.

2. Brown, *Webster,* pp. 77-79, 147; Irving H. Bartlett, *Daniel Webster* (New York: W. W. Norton, 1978), pp. 103-4, 147-48, Nathans, *Webster and Jacksonian Democracy,* p. 83; Webster to Nathaniel Mason, in Daniel Webster, *The Writings and Speeches of Daniel Webster,* ed. James W. McIntyre, 18 vols. (Boston: Little, Brown, 1903), 16:247-48; Caleb Cushing to Webster, January 16, 1835, Webster Papers; Henry W. Kinsman to Webster, January 18, 1835, ibid.; Edward Everett to Webster, February 1, 1835, ibid.; Stephen White to Webster, February 28, 1835, ibid.

3. Brown, *Webster,* pp. 8-11, 129-31, 194-95; Webster to Jeremiah Mason, March 19, 1830, in *Webster Papers,* ed. Wiltse, 3:36; Webster to Ambrose Spencer, November 16, 1831, in *Writings and Speeches* 16:214-16; Webster to Davis, August 14, 1834, ibid., pp. 242-43; Everett to Stevens, November 2, 1835, Letterbook, Everett Papers.

4. Brown, *Webster,* pp. 92, 112-13; Bartlett, *Webster,* p. 147; Webster to Jeremiah Mason, January 16, 1835, Webster Papers; Webster to Edward Everett, July 2, 1835, ibid.

5. Darling, *Political Changes,* p. 194; Duberman, "Charles Francis Adams," pp. 114-23; Charles Francis Adams, "Political Speculations," No. 7, Miscellany, Adams Papers, MaHS; idem, Diary, entries of May 22, August 24, December 26, 28, and 29, 1835, in ibid.; Samuel Prentiss to Webster, May 18, 1835, Webster Papers.

6. Robert Gray Gunderson, *The Log-Cabin Campaign* (Lexington: University of Kentucky Press, 1957), p. 32; Brown *Webster,* p. 113-14, 119-20, 125; Dorothy Burne Goebel, *William Henry Harrison: A Political Biography* (Indianapolis: Historical Bureau of the Indiana Library and Historical Department, 1926), p. 310; Nathans, *Webster and Jacksonian Democracy,* pp. 95-99; *Niles' Register* 49 (September 19, 1835): 36; *Washington National Intelligencer,* April 2, 1835.

7. Nathans, *Webster and Jacksonian Democracy,* pp. 97-98, Brown, *Webster,* pp. 129, 138-39; Clay to [?], July 14, 1835, in Clay, *Works* 5:394; Weed to Seward, October 11 and December 3, 1835, Seward Papers; Ayres to Harrison, November 11, 1835, and Harrison to Ayres, November 20, 1835, *Niles' Register* 49 (December 12, 1835): 244; *Pennsylvania Reporter and Democratic Herald,* January 8, 1836.

8. Brown, *Webster,* pp. 128, 130-33; Ershkowitz, "Anti-Masonry," p. 10; Denny to William Hiester, October 19, 1835, in "Anti-Masonic Days Recalled," pp. 227-28; Edward Everett to Stevens, November 2, 1835, Everett Papers; Webster to Charles Henry Thomas, March 19, 1835, Webster Papers; Webster to Everett, November 2, 1835, ibid.; Denny to Webster, November 5, 1835, ibid.; Henry D. Sellers et al. to Webster, November 10, 1835, ibid.; J. Wallace et al. to Webster, November 16, 1835, ibid.

9. Bartlett, *Webster,* pp. 147-48; Brown, *Webster,* p. 134; Webster to Antimasons of Allegheny County, November 20, 1835, Webster Papers; Webster to Denny, November 20, 1835, ibid.; Irwin to Webster, November 27, 1835; ibid.; Webster to Irwin, November 30, 1835, ibid.; Webster to Tracy, [late] November 1835, ibid.

10. Goebel, *Harrison,* p. 135; Brown, *Webster,* pp. 141-44, 147; Bartlett, *Webster,* pp. 148-49; *Washington National Intelligencer,* December 18, 21, and 22, 1835; *Pennsylvania Reporter and Democratic Herald,* December 29, 1835; Minor to Webster, December 17, 1835, Webster Papers.

11. Blakeslee, "Antimasonic Party," chap. 10, pp. 51-53; Brown, *Webster,* pp. 142, 145; McNeal, "Antimasonic Party of Lancaster County," pp. 92-93; Charles Francis Adams, Diary, entries of December 26, 28, 1835; *Boston Advocate,* January 1 and August 24, 1836; *Vermont Patriot and State Gazette,* May 23, 1836; *Danville North Star,* May 30, 1836; *Pennsylvania Reporter and Democratic Herald,* May 13, 1836.

12. Goebel, *Harrison,* pp. 313-14; *Boston Advocate,* August 24, 1836; *Gettysburg Anti-Masonic Star and Republican Banner,* May 16, 1836; *Albany Evening Journal,* May 7, 1836; Van Buren to William W. Irwin, May 19, 1836, Van Buren Papers.

13. Roseboom, *History of Presidential Elections,* pp. 112-13; Diamond, ed., *Guide to U.S. Elections,* pp. 266; McCarthy, "Antimasonic Party," p. 536; McNeal, "Antimasonic Party in Lancaster County," p. 94; *Boston Advocate,* August 24, 1836; Burrowes to Samuel Parke, October 25 and 27, 1836, Thomas H. Burrowes, Private Letterbook, 1836-49, Van Pelt Library, University of Pennsylvania; Burrowes to William B. Reed, October 26 and November 13, 1836, ibid.; Burrowes to Jacob Alter, November 10, 1836, ibid.

14. Ershkowitz, "Anti-Masonry," p. 11; Shore, "Anti-Masonic Party," pp. 50-51; Mueller, *Whig Party in Pennsylvania,* pp. 56-57; McNeal, "Antimasonic Party in Lancaster County," pp. 97-98; Blakeslee, "Antimasonic Party," chap. 10, pp. 54, 58-59; *Niles' Register* 53 (September 30, 1837): 68; Burrowes to James Todd, December 9,

1836, Burrowes Letterbook; Burrowes to William B. Reed, December 10, 1836, ibid.; Burrowes to Stevens, December 16, 1836, ibid.

15. Mueller, *Whig Party in Pennsylvania,* pp. 57-58; Geary, *Third Parties in Pennsylvania,* pp. 12-13; Goebel, *Harrison,* p. 329; Blakeslee, "Antimasonic Party," chap. 10, pp. 59-60; *Niles' Register* 55 (December 1, 1838): 221.

16. Darling, *Political Changes in Massachusetts,* p. 233; Goebel, *Harrison,* p. 329; *Washington National Intelligencer,* February 14, 1839.

17. Goebel, *Harrison,* pp. 331-32; *Washington National Intelligencer,* February 14, 1839; Harrison to Denny, December 2, 1838, *Niles' Register* 55 (February 22, 1839): 360-61; William Henry Harrison, "Letter from William Henry Harrison to Harmar Denny of Pittsburgh, Accepting the Nomination to the Office of President of the United States by the Convention of the Anti-Masonic Party held at Philadelphia in the Fall of 1838," *Western Pennsylvania Historical Magazine* 1 (1918): 144-51.

18. Goebel, *Harrison,* pp. 333-35; McCormick, *Second American Party System,* pp. 144-45; Mueller, *Whig Party in Pennsylvania,* pp. 59-61; *Harrisburg Chronicle,* May 25, 1839; *Washington National Intelligencer,* May 30, 1839; *Niles' Register* 57 (September 14, 1839): 46-47.

19. Roseboom, *History of Presidential Elections,* pp. 118-20; Gunderson, *Log-Cabin Campaign,* pp. 59-62; Goebel, *Harrison,* pp. 341-45.

20. Roseboom, *History of Presidential Elections,* pp. 120-21; Gunderson, *Log-Cabin Campaign,* pp. 74-75; McCormick, *Second American Party System,* p. 145; Diamond, ed., *Guide to U.S. Elections,* p. 267.

CHAPTER 13

1. Ershkowitz, "Anti-Masonry," pp. 7, 17-18; Blakeslee, "Antimasonic Party," chap. 7, p. 3; ibid., chap. 8, pp. 2-3; McCormick, *Second American Party System,* pp. 11-12, 15, 337-38.

2. As Bemis wrote in 1956, the strength of the Antimasonic party should be measured by its "weight in the balance of power." See idem, *John Quincy Adams and the Union,* p. 278.

3. Ershkowitz, "Anti-Masonry," p. 16; Cross, *Burned-over District,* p. 116; Michael F. Holt, *Forging A Majority: The Formation of the Republican Party in Pittsburgh, 1848-1860* (New Haven: Yale University Press, 1969), pp. 40-41; idem, "Antimasonic and Know-Nothing Parties," pp. 592, 619-20; Pessen, *Jacksonian America,* rev. ed., p. 269; Gungerson, *Log-Cabin Campaign,* p. 39.

4. Holt, "Antimasonic and Know-Nothing Parties," pp. 592, 619; Shore, "Anti-Masonic Party," p. 1; Voorhis, "Morgan Affair," p. 201; Blakeslee, "Antimasonic Party," chap. 11, p. 3; Lipson, *Freemasonry in Connecticut,* p. 9; Cerza, *Anti-Masonry,* p. 39; Charles G. Finney, *The Character, Claims and Practical Workings of Freemasonry* (Cincinnati: Western Tract and Book Society, 1869), p.v.

5. Wilson Carey McWilliams, *The Idea of Fraternity in America* (Berkeley: University of California Press, 1973), p. 233; Shore, "Anti-Masonic Party," p. 75; Pessen, *Jacksonian America,* rev. ed., p. 264.

6. William Stemper, "A Reflection on Masonic Ethics," *Philalethes* 34 (April 1981): 4.

7. Cerza, *Anti-Masonry,* pp. 103-4; *Masonry in the Light of the Bible* (St. Louis: Concordia Publishing House, 1964), pp. 4, 7, 24-25; B. J. Patrick, "Masonry in Utah," *Transactions, Texas Lodge of Research* 12 (1976-77): 78-85; "A Touch of Antimasonry: It Remains Alive in Missouri," (Missouri) *Freemason* 20 (spring-summer 1974): 36-38.

# Bibliographic Note

Any scholar commencing research on the Antimasonic party quickly faces the unpleasant fact that unpublished manuscript collections are limited both in number and scope. With several notable exceptions, the reason is largely that most of the Antimasonic leaders were of secondary or tertiary importance, men whose time in the political spotlight was extremely brief. Many failed to retain their correspondence, memoirs, and diaries, if any; and if these documents survived, the descendants did not consider the materials worthy of preservation.

Among the exceptions are the Thurlow Weed and William Henry Seward Papers at the Rhees Library, University of Rochester. Beautifully maintained, indexed, and serviced, these collections provided an abundance of information on the careers of two founders of the Antimasonic party who, unlike most of their associates, remained in politics for many years and achieved national fame and prominence. Many valuable insights into Antimasonry, both nationwide and in New York, as well as into the transition to Whiggery, can be gleaned from the Seward-Weed Papers. Also in the Rhees Library are the George W. Patterson Papers, helpful for research on the party in New York. In contrast to the Seward-Weed Papers, those of the 1832 presidential candidate, William Wirt, are scattered, the bulk being at the Maryland Historical Society, Baltimore, and the remainder at the Library of Congress and University of North Carolina. I consulted the first two Wirt collections (also available on microfilm) and found they each contained copies of the most important letters from the other two libraries.

The Massachusetts Historical Society, Boston, is a repository for certain papers useful for research on Antimasonry in the Bay State. Among these are the Adams Family Papers, the George Bancroft Papers, the Edward Everett Papers, the Levi Lincoln Papers, and the Marcus Morton Letterbooks, all available on microfilm. With the exception of the Adams Papers and Morton Letterbooks, the collections are tangential to a study of Antimasonry but are valuable in showing the transition made by Hallett and his wing of the party in Massachusetts to the Democrats. The Vermont Historical Society at Montpelier has several collections helpful for the study of Antimasonry in that state, including the papers of William Slade, John B. Hollenbeck, and Nathan B. Haswell (a Masonic grand master) as well as its Miscellaneous Correspondence and Manuscripts Collection. Copies of Slade's letters, 1817-57, are available at the Billings Library, University of Vermont. Unfortunately, no library, either in or out of state, appears to have Gov. William A. Palmer's papers, which have evidently disappeared.

Other than the Weed-Seward Papers, the most important manuscripts relating to Antimasonry on the state level are located at the Rhode Island Historical Society, Providence, including the papers of Antimasonic governor John Brown Francis, as well as the correspondence of legislators John R. Waterman and Elisha R. Potter. The Daniel Webster Papers at Dartmouth College, Hanover, New Hampshire (now readily available on microfilm), are valuable for information concerning Webster's flirtations with the Antimasons and his quest to receive their presidential nomination in 1836. No search for primary source materials proved more frustrating than that which I made in the remnant of Thaddeus Stevens's papers, which are vital to the history of the Antimasonic party in Pennsylvania. Because most of Stevens's papers were destroyed at the end of his life, few remain relating to the period 1829-1843, and most of these are in the Library of Congress, with a handful at the Lancaster (Pennsylvania) County Historical Society. Of more assistance than the Stevens Papers were those of Thomas H. Burrowes, Pennsylvania's Antimasonic state secretary, at the Van Pelt Library, University of Pennsylvania. Unfortunately, no personal papers of Pennsylvania's Antimasonic governor, Joseph Ritner, appear to be extant.

# Index